ARTHUR GODFREY

ARTHUR GODFREY

The Adventures of an American Broadcaster

by ARTHUR J. SINGER

McFarland & Company, Inc., Publishers

Jefferson, North Carolina, and London

The author extends special thanks to the following:

A&E Television Networks, for quotations from the **BIOGRAPHY**® series program entitled "Arthur Godfrey: Broadcasting's Forgotten Giant."

Cable News Network (CNN), for quotations from a Larry King interview about Arthur Godfrey.

CBS Broadcasting, Inc., for excerpts from the Arthur Godfrey broadcasts. © CBS Inc. All Rights Reserved.

The Jenkins Family Partnership, for lyrics from "This Is All I Ask." Words and music by Gordon Jenkins. Copyright © 1958, 1986 renewed by Jenkins Family Partnership (ASCAP) used by permission. All rights reserved.

The Hal Leonard Corporation, for "Too Fat Polka (She's Too Fat for Me)." Words and music by Ross MacLean and Arthur Richardson. Copyright © 1947 Shapiro, Bernstein & Co., Inc., New York. Copyright renewed. International Copyright Secured. All Rights Reserved. Used by permission.

The Lipton Company for permission to quote the Lipton tea advertisement from Arthur Godfrey's last network radio show on April 30, 1972, and the lyrics to the Lipton song that introduced *Arthur Godfrey's Talent Scouts* each week.

Peer Music, for lyrics from "Der Fuehrer's Face" by Oliver Wallace. Copyright © 1942 by Southern Music Publishing Co., Inc. Copyright renewed. International copyright secured. Used by permission.

The Saturday Evening Post Society, for quotes from "This Is My Story." Reprinted from *The Saturday Evening Post*, copyright © 1955.

Thirteen/WNET New York and the Educational Broadcasting Corporation, for quotations from "The Fifties: Moments to Remember." Courtesy Thirteen/WNET New York.

Front cover: Godfrey at work. (WTOP collection.) *Frontispiece:* Arthur Godfrey—entertainer, pilot and environmentalist who brought national attention to Teterboro via his radio and television programs in the 1950s. (Author's collection.)

Library of Congress Cataloguing-in-Publication Data

Singer, Arthur J., 1939–
    Arthur Godfrey : the adventures of an American broadcaster / by Arthur J. Singer.
        p.   cm.
    Includes bibliographical references and index.   ∞
    ISBN 0-7864-0704-2 (illustrated case binding : 50# alkaline paper)
    1. Godfrey, Arthur, 1903–1983.   2. Radio broadcasters—United States—Biography.   3. Television personalities—United States—Biography.   I. Title.
PN1991.4.G6S57   2000
791.44'028'092—dc21
[B]   99–36993 CIP

British Library Cataloguing-in-Publication data are available

Manufactured in the United States of America

McFarland & Company, Inc., Publishers
    Box 611, Jefferson, North Carolina 28640
        www.mcfarlandpub.com

To Gert Singer, my mother,
who shared with me her love of radio and television

I can still hear the sounds from our kitchen on Monday evenings:
the thud of your iron, the creak of the ironing board,
and Arthur Godfrey's voice drifting out from the radio to my bedroom.

Acknowledgments

THIS PROJECT HAD ITS ROOTS IN A 1988 conversation with Al Ham, who spent many years as producer and arranger at Columbia Records. It was Al who encouraged me to pursue my idea and sent me on to the late Ben Lockwood, former CBS vice president for sales, who immediately began making calls to introduce me to the people who had worked with Arthur Godfrey. From those early conversations with the late Tom Sheehy and others I began to learn the inside story of how Godfrey's programs worked. It was not long before I met Remo Palmier, who on at least three occasions was willing to meet with me for extended periods to discuss his long association with Arthur.

On the television side it was Jack Sameth, then of Thirteen/WNET, who gave me my first real sense of what happened to Godfrey in his later years. John Adams at Thirteen/WNET then alerted me to the storehouse of information that existed in Arthur's estate collection. And it was Joan Zacher and subsequently Ellie Applewhaite, Bill Baker, and Susan Marchand, all of WNET, who allowed me access.

Early on, Robert Schmidt, Arthur's son-in-law, was helpful in giving me a family perspective and insight into Arthur's later years. Much later, I had the opportunity to correspond and talk with Richard Godfrey, who has written his own memoir about his dad and who provided me with missing details about Arthur's life. Along the way, Michael Godfrey allowed me to spend an afternoon reviewing several files containing his father's correspondence.

This book had many iterations. There at the beginning to help me enter the mysterious world of publishing was the late Bill Weete of Random House. Many colleagues in television assisted me in this project, particularly Bill Harris and Charlie Maday of the Arts & Entertainment Networks, John Griffin, Del Jack, and David and Nancy Sutherland.

Many in the museum and library fields provided valuable help along the way, including Ron Simon of the Museum of Television and Radio in New York; Mike Mashon, then of the Library of American Broadcasting at the University of Maryland; and Michael Henry of the same library. Other archival help was received from the CBS News Library (Sam Suratt) and CBS Program Information (John Behrens), and the following libraries: Hawaii State Library, Library of Congress, Emerson College Library, Newton (Mass.) Free Library, Dover (N.H.) Public Library, Hasbrouck Heights (N.J.) Public Library, and Boston Public Library main branch. Also helpful were David Lawrence and Bill Whiting of the *Miami Herald*.

I owe particular thanks to my good friends from the Radio Collectors of America for background information and valuable advice. Organizations like this keep us all aware of the glory of what American radio once was and the potential it still has.

At the Thomas J. Lipton Foundation I received wonderful assistance from Mary Pfeil and members of the Lipton Ambassadors Club, including Anthony G. Montuori and Howard Anderson.

I feel privileged to have had extended conversations and in several cases developed personal friendships with the following people interviewed for the book: Steve Allen, Ed Bond, Pat Boone, Fred B. Cole, Chuck Horner, Peter and Lois Kelley, Larry King, the late Granville Klink, Dorothea Marvin, Hank and Lenore Meyer, Max Morath, Remo Palmier, Carmel Quinn, Doreen Roberts, Andy Rooney, Jack Sameth, Ralph Schoenstein, the late Tom Sheehy, and Dr. Frank Stanton. They were all very generous with their time and, in a number of instances, with their hospitality during visits to their homes.

Other interviewees to be thanked include Dick Hyman, Peter Lassally, Jane Meadows, Ruth Ann Perlmutter and, for use of his comments from our A&E interviews, Julius La Rosa.

Many individuals provided valuable background information, including Fred B. Cole, Richard A. Daynard, Ron Della Chiesa, Arnold Foster, Gail Gans, Richard K. Hayes, Bob Jennings, Herman Klurfield, Art Rose, Dolores Sheehy, Mel Simons, the medical staff of Massachusetts General Hospital, and employees of Arthur Godfrey Field and Teterboro Airport.

A number of people helped me in the technical preparation of materials for the book, especially Darla Bruno; Amanda Sullivan, the world's best researcher; Marjorie Singer, who took time away from her own graduate studies to do research as well; and Michael Singer, whose knowledge of aviation proved invaluable and who was always ready to take my late night calls when computer problems arose and then would calmly walk me through to solutions. I also received valuable publishing advice from Nancy Beck and Barbara Williams.

And lastly, I can never express enough gratitude and thanks to my wife, Donna, who was always there to hear the good and the bad and to offer sage advice as I journeyed through this project, and who never wavered in her enthusiasm though it required many sacrifices along the way.

Table of Contents

Prologue

ARTHUR GODFREY WAS ONCE THE most recognized man in America. His voice was listened to by more people each day during the 1940s and 1950s than anyone in history up to that time. In his heyday, he was on the air for ninety minutes each weekday morning on the CBS Radio Network and for sixty minutes each weekday morning on the CBS Television Network. Each Monday evening, he hosted a top-rated series on radio and television. And to top it off, each Wednesday evening he had a top-ten hour-long variety show. At a time when all of this was done live and when only three networks existed, he was more important to the success of his network than almost anyone beyond the company's president and chairman. At one time, he was bringing in an estimated 12 percent of CBS's annual revenues. He was, as the Associated Press once put it, "as close an approach to a one-man network as radio and television ever produced."

His shows lasted on CBS Television from 1948 through 1959 and on CBS Radio for 27 years from 1945 through 1972.

As a professional, Arthur Godfrey was not easily categorized. He wasn't a newsman. He wasn't an entertainer. Arthur Godfrey was primarily a host and raconteur. His direct, folksy style was extremely low key, evolving from his many years as an AM disc jockey in Washington, D.C. As one television critic later put it, he was "laid back" long before it became fashionable. His ability to seemingly talk one-on-one to each individual in his vast audience made him almost a family member in most American households. His broadcasts were the equivalent of personal conversations, creating such a sense of familiarity that he was known simply as "Arthur." Most of his programs included a stable of announcers, singers, and musicians. There were frequent guests, but rarely show business celebrities. Arthur Godfrey and his "friends" were more like ordinary people with varying degrees of

1

talent. His programs were full of gentle humor, but Godfrey, who was once dubbed "The Peck's Bad Boy of Radio" by comedian Fred Allen and as "The Huck Finn of Television" by others, always approached his work with a "let's raise a little hell" attitude. Scripts were prepared but rarely followed. This style lent a sense of spontaneity to almost every minute of his programs. You were never sure what would happen next.

His approach also made him an extraordinary salesman. Arthur Godfrey personally presented every commercial on every show he did. For many years that meant doing them live. He was considered by many to be the greatest salesman who ever took to a microphone.

Arthur Godfrey was a stimulating, energizing, but extremely difficult man to work for. He was a consummate broadcaster who knew the aesthetic and the technical sides of his craft well. He expected nothing less than excellence from his producers, writers, and engineers.

His career existed side by side with many avocations. He was a fine pilot, an accomplished sailor, a world traveler, a fierce defender of American military power, an early environmentalist, a loyal Republican. He was also a blatant womanizer and a disengaged father and husband. He was always on the go. Physically, he was a wreck, having had both his hips shattered in a near fatal automobile accident. He had lost a lung to cancer. But through it all he maintained a self-effacing style and a gifted sense of humor.

He was all of a piece. And wherever possible and appropriate, he shared his life experiences with his audiences on a daily basis.

On the day after Arthur Godfrey died in March 1983, CBS interviewer Diane Sawyer asked commentator and former Godfrey-writer Andy Rooney what people would remember most about the late broadcasting star. Rooney's response was perceptive and telling. "He won't be [remembered]," he said. "It was his approach to broadcasting, his understanding of its impact and its potential to entertain and enlighten, not his own personality, that was his real contribution."

Rooney's prediction has proven correct. Most Americans alive today don't know the name Arthur Godfrey. Unlike his television contemporaries, Milton Berle, Ed Sullivan, Lucille Ball and Jackie Gleason, whose programs have been repeated for new generations to watch and appreciate, Arthur Godfrey has no place in the public eye or in the public mind. Particularly because most of his programs were done live, but also because they were often scriptless and rambling, his programs were not transportable.

But for that matter, neither was most of network radio and early network television transportable. Each represented an approach to communication and a use of the broadcasting media that varies considerably from practices of today. Each required a different response from the listener or viewer. It was a different time in America. Values were different. Access to information was different. Mobility was different. Social issues were different.

Perhaps it is the fate of broadcasting (and now cablecasting) that because they are so immediate, so tied to technological advances, and so intertwined with present events and mores, their own history has never captured the public's imagination, at least not in the way we trace the past of our politics, our wars, our motion pictures, or our sports teams.

Yet it is all there for the taking—the joy, the accomplishments, the personalities and the legacies—from a time when broadcasting was a young and innovative medium.

Sometime before his last radio network broadcast in 1972, after 27 consecutive years of daily broadcasting, Arthur began to consider an autobiography. "Many times I have been urged to write the story," he said on that final broadcast. "I haven't done it for two reasons. One, I've never thought it really mattered that much. And two, there has been no time. But now... In retrospect the career has been such a fantastic series of illogical, incredible events that I'm beginning to think maybe it *would* be worthwhile."

But he never wrote the book. When he was approached by others to undertake it, he could never get comfortable with the idea. Somehow this man who was considered by many to be the greatest communicator of the century, a man who influenced the course of broadcasting, who had created careers for scores of performers, who had literally put large corporations in business through his commercials for them, could not come to grips with putting his life on paper.

If Arthur Godfrey *had* written his autobiography, he probably would have begun with the same thoughts he presented on that final radio program: "In order to understand this career," he explained, "you have to understand that the last thing I ever had on my mind was stardom.... It never occurred to me that I would be a star, ever, any time. I just wanted to be the man who did the best job of doing whatever he was assigned to do. Whether it was describing a parade or a football game or announcing for a program or whatever it was in the beginning...."

1

The Family Roller Coaster

ON THE EVENING OF HER 75TH birthday, Kathryn Morton Godfrey received a special gift from her son. He dedicated his hour-long television variety show to her. Dressed up like his father and her husband, Arthur Hansbury Godfrey, he opened his top-ranked Wednesday night program by appearing on stage in a racing sulky pulled by a single horse, then spent the hour performing some of her favorite Irish and ragtime songs, and closed the show with one of her most famous march compositions. As she watched from the audience, he introduced her to his millions of viewers. "Take off your hat, I want everybody to see your beautiful hair," he told her. For one of the few times in her life, Kathryn was speechless. She smiled as the audience applauded and the show came to a close.[1]

Only Kathryn could grasp the true significance of that hour. Here was her son Arthur, the most popular broadcasting personality in history, not only recogniz-

ing her love of music and one of her compositions, but showing a genuine affection for his father and proving again that she had been right about her son: he *was* a genius.

Kathryn had always believed that. "You could bring the house down" in vaudeville, she would say. "You're as funny as Will Rogers. And the way you play that banjo—" She had thought all her five children geniuses. As soon as they were out of diapers, recalled two of his sisters, "she had us on some stage or other playing the piano, singing, reciting, or dancing."[2]

One of the things that attracted her husband Arthur Hansbury Godfrey to her was her auburn hair—"Titian-red" he called it. Her hair "hung to the floor" and she wore it wound about her head in thick braids.[3] "She had merry eyes, a ready smile and hands that were never still," recalled her daughters. In addition, she sang, composed music, played piano, and acted in amateur shows. "She could cook beautifully,"

Arthur would later recall, "though she didn't like to keep house."[4] But perhaps her most important quality, the one that influenced her children the most, was her optimism. She believed that with hard work, a person could do anything he or she wanted to do. That spirit not only pervaded the Godfrey household, it also created a sense of hope that would carry the family through desperate times when there was no work, no food, and seemingly no ability to sustain themselves as a family unit. Kathryn might have thought her children were geniuses, but a backward look would suggest that it was she who held the keys to survival and success for each of them.

Kathryn Morton was born into a life of relative luxury in Oswego, New York. Her father, Charles Corroll Morton, owned one of the huge grain elevators on Oswego Harbor on Lake Ontario. Kathryn's mother, Alice Ralston-Parke Morton, was an attentive mother of four and an accomplished party giver. Oswego had become a thriving commercial center, and artists and lecturers came to town regularly. Alice thrived on inviting them to the spacious Morton home, which was filled with paintings and books. Among those who graced her "salons" were Oliver Wendell Holmes and Samuel Clemens, alias Mark Twain, who was very attentive to young Kathryn. When the hour grew late, Kathryn and her younger brother would be sent to bed, but Kathryn would tell how they would stay up and watch and listen to the conversations and performances "through the hot-air register in the floor of the nursery."[5]

It was a life of comfort and culture. "My, but the drawing room was elegant," Kathryn would later tell her children.[6]

Kathryn was given a violin at an early age and she taught herself to play the instrument by ear. As was tradition at the time, her two brothers were given a college

education, while Kathryn and her older sister Alice were groomed for marriage with gentlemen of good families. But when the U.S. instituted a tariff on grains, Charles Morton could no longer find a market for Canadian barley. His business went under and with the sale of their house, the good life in Oswego came to an end. "I never see an auction sign on a lovely old house without thinking of that awful day when we had to sell nearly everything we owned," Kathryn would say.[7] The family moved to New York City where Charles established a new business. Kathryn was sent to a year of finishing school, where she was taught to read music and showed great promise, winning three scholarships to the New York Conservatory of Music for voice, piano, and piano composition. Her compositions were already being published in a music magazine of the day.

But Kathryn's mother was putting her energies into preparing her older sister Alice for marriage and with money an issue now, the Conservatory idea was put aside, scholarships and all. Kathryn remained at home creating craft items for sale to help with the family budget. To satisfy her creative needs, she wrote short stories, several of them good enough to be sold to the *Atlantic Monthly* and *Harper's*. Her closest ties with music were limited to teaching what she knew to a group of young girls in the neighborhood. By now, she was a strikingly beautiful woman.[8] Eventually, brother Sherwood invited her to live in his home in Newark, and it was there that she began a courtship with Arthur Hansbury Godfrey.

On Thanksgiving Day in 1902 the couple was married. She was 23. And though she thought Arthur to be 36, he was actually 45. They honeymooned in Niagara Falls, then took an apartment in the city. Arthur gave Kathryn a piano and three months later, he arranged for her to have an audition at the Metropolitan Opera House. The audition was a success. "She was magnificent!" he would tell the children later. But the next day she took sick and never went back to the audition hall. Six months later, on August 31, 1903, Arthur Morton Godfrey was born. "Look at the shape of his head," she said to the new father. "He'll be a genius."[9]

Unlike Kathryn's early life, Arthur Hansbury Godfrey's was a mystery. Tall, bright-eyed, with a Teddy Roosevelt mustache, Arthur would "expound on everything from politics to how to eat an egg" in his proper British accent. "Dad sometimes spoke of his childhood in England, but we children never met any of his relatives," recalled the younger of Arthur's sisters. When they met, he told Kathryn that he was one of seventeen children of John and Mary Godfrey of Liverpool, England. He said his father, John Godfrey, had once been Viceroy to India and owned both a brewing company and a hotel. How accurate these stories were was always a point of conjecture. In later years Kathryn would explain, "Sometimes he'd tell me a tale nobody in the world would believe, and I'd find out later it was true. Then he'd tell me another I believed, and I'd discover he'd made up every word of it!"[10]

Growing up, the elder Arthur became expert at hunting for hounds. He had brought to this country several hunting prints from England, and they hung in the family's various dining rooms through the years. Hunting, he would say, was "jolly fine sport."[11]

A fine storyteller, he'd give dramatic accounts of how he had run away from Rugby at the age of 12 to become a ship's cabin boy, a story that would later influence his own son's decision at age 15 to run away to join the U.S. Navy. Eight years later, Arthur Hansbury returned home from his adventures—on the very day his own father died. With his large

inheritance, he and seven other young men "chartered a yacht and cruised around the world for six years."[12] As the story went, he and the others were eventually shipwrecked off the coast of Africa and dramatically rescued. Back on land, and broke, he got a position as traveling secretary to a Mr. Burdett-Coutts who managed the philanthropies of a British Baroness. In the late 1880s, when Burdett-Coutts came to New York, the senior Godfrey decided to stay in the U.S., becoming secretary to George M. Pullman, inventor of the Pullman Sleeping Car.

In 1899, he became secretary of the American Hackney Association, a club whose membership was composed of a well-heeled group of young aristocrats including Reginald Vanderbilt, Pierre Lorillard, Jr., and Alfred Vanderbilt I, with whom he became good friends. Over time, the senior Godfrey became highly respected and very well known among the horse set. Traveling regularly in other people's private railroad cars, to Newport, Saratoga, and other fashionable places where his friends gathered, he reported on the events with stories and photographs for the *New York Times*, the *New York Herald*, *Country Life*, and other publications of interest to horsemen. Soon, he was editor of the *Horse Show Blue Book* and editor of *Rider and Driver*. In addition to all this, he was often a judge at horse shows, an adviser to noted breeders, delivered slide lectures for a fee, and was a gifted after-dinner speaker. Life was good to Arthur Hansbury Godfrey, and it was at this high point that he met and married Kathryn and son Arthur was born.

With the birth of Arthur, Kathryn's hopes for a professional career were permanently dashed. Still, the couple was overjoyed, and the Godfreys moved to a small house on 112th Street.

Another son, Bob, was born two years

later, and that same year, 1905, the Godfreys picked up and moved to Hasbrouck
Heights, New Jersey. Located just across
the Hudson from Manhattan and just ten
miles northwest of the city, the village
had, for many years, been a summer retreat for New Yorkers. But now the permanent population was beginning to grow,
and it seemed like the perfect location to
raise their family. A third son and two
daughters soon followed. Arthur was
quickly thrust into the role of big brother,
unaware of the attendant responsibilities.

At first, life for young Arthur was idyl-
lic. The Heights opened up to the vast
swampland of Teterboro, where fish and
crabs were plentiful and muskrats offered
good hunting. Allowed to roam free,
Arthur flourished in the beauty of the
countryside. It had an indelible positive
effect on his interests and values for the
rest of his life.

At the Franklin School, freckle-faced,
chubby-cheeked, auburn-haired Arthur
was "a bright, albeit restless, student." He
did well in math, but poorly in English.
"Why write," he reasoned, heralding his
future talents, "when you can say the same
thing and save the time?"[13] Years later,
broadcasting's master conversationalist
made several attempts at an autobiography, but writing was never his forte.

"His grooming—well, it was just like a
boy who does everything for himself," according to one of his favorite teachers, a
Miss Quigg. "He came and went as he
pleased and … if he went home from
school and wanted something to eat, he
got it for himself. When he got up in the
morning, he got his own breakfast."[14]

From his mother, he learned music.
"When I was a kid, six, seven, eight years
old, my dear mother had taught me to read
at sight on the pianoforte. She used to
brag about that, that she could put any
piece of music in front of me, and conduct
me, and I would read it at sight," Arthur

later recalled.[15] Kathryn also taught him
woodlore, another subject that would be
central in his career and his life. And like
his mother, Arthur had boundless energy
and curiosity. "I wish I had inherited more
of her talent," he would say.[16]

From his father, Arthur learned to love
sailing, conversation, and horsemanship.
But the relationship was very formal and
very disciplined. "Dad was very strict
about our table manner. I sat on his right.
When I did something wrong I got the
back of his hand across my face. I didn't always know why he'd hit me—I'd ask my
mother later—but I knew that if I cried,
he'd hit me again."[17]

In 1913, when Arthur was ten, the
family fortunes waned dramatically. The
country's love affair with horses was ending, replaced by the automobile craze. And
with World War I underway, the market
for his father's articles on horses and
horsemanship had dried up. To make matters worse, professional baseball had over-
taken horse racing and become the national
pastime. Daughters Kathy and Dorothy
Jean recalled:

"The course of Dad's sleigh ride was
erratic. There were times when we had
turkey for Thanksgiving and times when
we had boiled potatoes with gravy made
from a can of soup. Sometimes we had
clothes from Best's Fifth Avenue shop,
sometimes we had to stay home from
school for lack of shoes. Mother and Dad
might dine one night at fashionable
Tuxedo Park with Pierre Lorillard, Sr.,
and be driven home in a French motor-
car. A week later Mother might not
have the five-cent trolley fare to Hackensack."[18]

"A large part of [my] story is one of
grinding poverty, spaced with periods of
comparative prosperity," Arthur would
later tell Peter Martin at the *Saturday
Evening Post*. "I remember going to the
grocer's and saying, 'Mother would like to

know if we could charge a loaf of bread until next week?' and the grocer telling me, 'Sorry, son, but you folks already owe us two hundred dollars. Tell your father to stay away from that chain store and come here, where he's been given credit, when they pay him for one of those stories he writes.'...The humiliation of not being able to get a nickel's worth on trust anywhere became an obsession with me, which is probably why to this day I insist on paying all bills and signing all checks myself."[19]

So Arthur was pressed into family service, delivering milk and groceries, mowing lawns, shoveling snow, cutting firewood after school each day, and working full time summers as a carpenter's helper, and later as a mail clerk in the local bank. On Sundays, after the milk route, he would pump the church organ for 25 cents. "One Sunday," a schoolmate later remembered, "the music died away and everybody thought the organ had quit. When we looked behind the organ, we found out that it was Arthur who really quit. The poor kid was so tired he just fell asleep pumping."[20]

By this time his father's income had shrunk to nothing and mother Kathryn was working nights playing piano at the local silent movie house. That wasn't enough either. The family home was foreclosed early on, and in the ensuing years the Godfreys moved from house to house regularly. "We moved 26 times in Hasbrouck Heights, sometimes by choice, more often by request."[21] They were notorious for non-payment of rent. Things grew worse. The children were farmed out for weeks at a time to neighbors and relatives. At one point, rather than sell her husband's books to pay a note, Kathryn sold her wedding ring and her only sym-

Godfrey's youth was spent in Hasbrouck Heights, New Jersey. He was the oldest of five Godfrey children and by age ten was working summers and before school to keep the family afloat. (Joan Zacher collection.)

bol of the career she would never have—her piano.

Arthur Sr. would go the city each day attempting to find work, but "my father wouldn't work with his hands. He let mother do it; she was the one who kept us alive."[22]

Through it all, Kathryn kept believing that things would get better: if they could just hold on a little longer. But her optimism far exceeded reality. She appeared to be in a perpetual state of denial.

"At one point," according to Michele Maiullo, director of the Hasbrouck Heights Public Library, "the neighbors got together. The kids were getting thin. Everyone had chickens in those days and they each gave an egg and presented them to Mrs. Godfrey, who promptly made an angel food cake and invited all the neighbors over.... To say he grew up in grinding poverty was to make light of the situation."[23]

The crowning blow came in early 1919.

By that winter, Arthur, age 15, was working both before and after school for the Shaefers, who ran the local bakery. The war had ended, but now the influenza epidemic was rampant. When his father contracted the flu, Arthur's mother asked the Shaefer family if Arthur could stay with them. While he was there, the Shaefer's youngest daughter contracted and died of the virus. Then Mr. Shaefer himself as well as his baker came down with the flu. "Suddenly, I was running the business," Arthur recalled. "They hired another baker and I stayed out of school for a while to help carry the shop through."[24]

The Shaefers were eternally grateful, but the principal of Hasbrouck Heights High School wasn't sympathetic. He summarily removed Arthur as captain of the sophomore debating team, Arthur's favorite school activity. Exhausted, disillusioned, Arthur "looked at this self-righteous Joe," cursed him, walked out of the school, and never returned.

He left home and went to New York City to "seek my fortune. I didn't run away from home, because there wasn't any home to run away from. Ours had fallen apart."[25]

2

Runaway

To hear Arthur Godfrey's stories of his two years on the road after he left home is to listen or read in disbelief. The stories rival Charles Dickens' and Horatio Alger's compelling descriptions of the destitution and aimlessness of young men. He was 15 years old. He had no money, no contacts, no knowledge of travel beyond the grandiose stories that his father had told him. Absolutely certain he could remain at home no longer, he unwittingly had set himself on a course where all he could rely on was his physical capacity, his basic manual skills, his curiosity, and his innate intelligence. It was a two-year excursion into a real-life hell.

His travels took him from Manhattan to New Jersey to Pennsylvania to Ohio. The cast of characters included pickpockets, prostitutes, bums, and sexual deviates. Fortunately there were others as well, men older than himself, who helped lead him out of the morass.

Years later, when legions of followers,

critics and rivals alike were constantly amazed at Godfrey's exceptional ability to communicate effectively with people of all walks of life—from presidents to cab drivers, from elderly parents to little children, from matrons to young attractive women—they had only to look back to the wide range of humanity that peopled his life on the road as a teenager and young adult.

Arriving in Manhattan, Arthur Godfrey had the good sense to write a note to his mother saying he was going to seek his fortune, that "he wouldn't return home until he could pay all the bills."[1] His father had the New York police looking for him for weeks without success. There was no contact between Arthur and the family for many months.

He rented a room at the 23rd Street Y.M.C.A. for a dollar and fifteen cents a week, selling newspapers to pay for it. "I bought seven papers for a nickel and sold them for two cents apiece. With other lads who peddled papers, I ate at a hole in the wall, a horrible place where coffee was a penny, a hamburger three cents. The Lord knows what was in those hamburgers."[2] Soon, he found a better job—as an office boy in an architectural office, Jallade and Lindsay, on Liberty Street. The pay was ten dollars a week in the form of a gold certificate.

It was the winter of 1919. World War I had ended in victory the previous November. From the Y he watched the destroyers and troop ships coming into the Hudson River loaded with troops from the war. He'd walk down to the Battery "where I always loved to go and watch the ships because I was nuts to go to sea," and take rides on the Staten Island Ferry. "[I'd] hide in the john so you could go back and forth all day long for a nickel."[3]

On a Saturday in May, after several weeks on the job, with a whole week's pay of $10 in his pocket, he walked down to the Battery. There was a boat tied up that said "25 cents to the Statue of Liberty." Feeling affluent, he bought a ticket. On the boat going to Bedloe's Island he got into a conversation with a young woman. They hit it off, climbed the stairs of the Statue together, and "had a session of half scuffling, half necking and skylarking around until we'd missed five or six boats."[4]

On the way down, Godfrey told her he had just been paid and offered to take her to dinner back on shore. She agreed, then told him she was going to the ladies' room and would meet him at the gangway to get on the boat. " I waited there for about four boats and I [finally] said the hell with her...crossed the gangway, got on the boat, came back to the Battery, and went to the lunch wagon, and [discovered] that my pocket book was gone." In later years he would take great pleasure in adding, "I got rolled at the Statue of Liberty."[5]

Now he had an immediate problem. He hadn't paid his rent at the Y, and was too ashamed of having been played the sucker to go back and face his roommate, who was a traffic cop right downtown. "He would have beaten the hell out of me." His instincts led him further astray: "I couldn't face coming out with the truth of what had happened to my pay and asking for an advance at the architectural office either. I suppose I wasn't thinking very clearly. I was pretty stunned."[6]

Now the long descent began. That night he slept on a park bench with the bums in Battery Park. It had turned very cold. In the morning he went back to the lunch wagon and washed dishes in exchange for breakfast.

Days passed. "The bums showed me how to buy ten cents worth of shoe polish to shine shoes and put them on with your hands until I could afford a brush. I learned how to play jazz on the thing. It was fun. I enjoyed what I was doing."[7]

But nights were different. "In those days they had...we used to call them crap hunters. Degenerate bastards that went around looking for kids like us. They would come up...I learned the technique from the other kids...what you did was tease them. Let them take you to dinner. When it comes to the end of it, tell them you have to go to the men's room and run like hell! One night one of them chased me all across the Brooklyn Bridge. The bastard could run but he couldn't run as fast as I could and I got away from him."[8]

One evening, a woman befriended him in Battery Park. "She wore long shoes and a dress to the floor and she was full of paint." I had no idea that there were such things as prostitutes then.... If you *weren't* a kid like me, you would have known immediately that she had to be a prostitute or she wouldn't be painted like that. Everyone does it now. In those days, only the whores did and the ones who worked in the burlesque theatres."

Arthur was in bad shape. His shoes were worn out. "I stunk because the only place you could wash were those horrible men's rooms where you went downstairs in the Battery. That's where the degenerates were waiting. You'd go down there and wash yourself in a bowl as best you could. I didn't own any underwear. Just this crummy pair of pants, dirty shirt. God, I was a mess."[9]

They pooled their money and she took him to dinner. "Then she took me to the Tribune building where the *New York Tribune* was published down on Platt Road. And we walked down and underneath this building was the first story and it was open to the outside. Only protected from the rain by the ceiling. The newspaper rolls were stacked together. And we'd get down between them, back to back and the heat from our bodies would warm us and the newspaper stuff would keep you insulated. And that's the way we would sleep." [10]

Eventually, Arthur came across a promising advertisement in a newspaper. The U.S. Army was looking for typists at Camp Merritt, New Jersey, a point of disembarkation where they transferred men out of the service and back into civilian life. He had learned to type on his dad's typewriter and in high school, so he went to the camp, took the test, and was hired at $90.00 a month. "And not only could I sleep in the barracks, [I] could eat Army chow and wear Army clothes."[11] He began sending some money home.

Enter Vincent Stahl. While at Camp Merritt, Arthur Godfrey met the young man from Clymer, Pennsylvania, who was about to be mustered out of the Army. Told by Stahl that he could make up to fifteen dollars *a day* working in a coal mine near his home, Arthur headed to Clymer. He began working in a coal mine, "lying on my belly and using a pick in a tunnel that was two feet by two feet."[12] Within days, with coal dust continually filling his

lungs, he found that his breathing had become a problem. The company doctor arranged a transfer to work topside, but after witnessing an accident that cost a man his leg, he fled the site and the town.

He was next lured by talk of lumberjacking, but physically, at 110 pounds, he wasn't up to it. "I couldn't even lift the ax. It was an awful mistake."[13] So was a quick attempt at farming. He hopped a freight and landed in Akron, Ohio.

It was mid–October 1919. Desperate, he remembered the advice of the police chief in Hasbrouck Heights who had once told him that when in trouble, go to the police station. He did, and the Akron chief gave him a cot and some food and the next day helped get him a job as a tire finisher for the Goodyear Tire and Rubber Company.[14] The job lasted till the spring of 1920 when a railroad strike closed the factories and, once again, he found himself out on the street. It was back to work as a dishwasher, a job that he supplemented as a "steerer" for a crap game. "I'd stand on the street with my hat at a rakish angle, and as guys walked by I said, 'Crap game upstairs, buddy. Crap game upstairs.'"[15]

But fortune was about to smile on 16-year-old Arthur Godfrey. When he came to Akron, he had found a roommate named Dan Cullinane. Cullinane, a college graduate, also worked at Goodyear, and he too was laid off by the strike, though he had a few dollars set aside to carry him through. He was older and more knowledgeable than Arthur, and it wasn't long before he was giving Arthur advice. "If you'd scrape your face with a razor and lose those adolescent pimples you'd look halfway good," Arthur recalled him saying. "He jumped me about my profanity too. He even argued that somehow, sometime, I ought to go back to school."[16] And he definitely didn't like the work Arthur had gotten himself into. A practicing Catholic, Cullinane encouraged him to attend mass with him, and when Arthur did, he also arranged for him to meet the church's young priest. Still young, impressionable, and looking for a better life, Arthur quickly decided that he wanted to study for the priesthood. The priest advised him that he'd need more education.

Arthur felt that was impossible, since he had no family and no home. "We didn't have night schools in those days. The priest said, 'You always talk about the Navy and how much you'd love to be at sea. Why don't you join the Navy?' I said, 'I tried, Father, but I'm too young. They won't have me.' 'Where did you go?' 'I went to Akron.' He said, 'Let's go to Cleveland tomorrow, you and I.' I don't know whether he knew this old chief bos'n's mate was over there or not, but he had about two years to go for retirement. Big gold hash marks. Old timer. And I walked in, he said, 'What do you want, punk?' I said, 'I…I want to join the Navy, sir.' 'Get out of here, we don't take kids. This is no kindergarten. How old are you?' I said, 'Nineteen, sir.' He said, 'Nineteen! You don't even have fuzz on your face.' And he looked at the priest, who didn't say a word, he just looked at him and smiled. The old chief said, 'Oh, certainly, Father. Hold up your hand, son.' And I was in."[17]

3

Radio Operator, U.S. Navy

IT WAS ONLY A TWO-YEAR period, but 1918 through 1920 were watershed years for the United States and the rise of American broadcasting.

First came the end of World War I in November of 1918. Home came the troops, and an era of immigration, international isolationism, and regionalism came to a close. In its place was a country teeming with change and apparent individual opportunity.

Private enterprise was on the move. And nowhere was this shift more apparent than in the new field of broadcasting. With the end of the war, the U.S. government came under increasing pressure to relinquish its absolute control over the radio frequencies.

During the war years, all private wireless facilities were given over to the U.S. Navy. But in 1919, Lee DeForest had resumed his informal experimental broadcasts of phonograph music, opera, and announcements, only to be forced off the air

by a government radio inspector who told him, "There is no room in the ether for entertainment." That view was not shared by amateur radio operators who wanted the right to unseal their equipment and get back on the air. The American Radio Relay League, now numbering some 125,000 owners of receiving equipment, fought the Navy's attempts to continue their monopoly.

It was also an unpopular view with some of America's leading electronics companies. In 1919, they showed how serious they were about opening up broadcasting as a non-governmental industry. General Electric, Westinghouse, AT&T, and former American Marconi stockholders founded the Radio Corporation of America. By 1920, the U.S. Government had given in.

Radio was not yet on the mind of 16-year-old Arthur Godfrey as he took the oath on May 11, 1920, and entered the United States Navy. Though soon enough,

15

Seventeen-year-old Arthur Godfrey, U.S. Navy. (Joan Zacher collection.)

he'd be immersed in the new medium—at least from the technical side.

The Navy sent him to Hampton Roads, Virginia, for three weeks of basic training and six weeks of seamanship. He excelled, exhibiting signs of the endless reserve of energy and ability he would later bring to his work in broadcasting when doing three different radio programs a morning—or later, three different live network television shows a week—with no problem at all. During his nine-week stay, he rose to platoon leader with a room to himself, was named coxswain of the race-boat crew, and, on his own, had mastered Morse code by watching the blinker lights that flashed code off and on all night. " I accomplished [all] this by following the simplest rule in the world: I paid attention."[1]

Studying through the night, he'd oversleep regularly. The Navy did not like that and by mid-term, Godfrey was drawing duty each day shoveling coal to power the buildings. But he passed the course, and when the time came to put in for a school, he chose radio school. When tested, he was able to send fifteen words a minute— so good that he was given a counter offer: to immediately become an assistant instructor in code right there at Hampton Roads. He accepted.

Years later, listeners would send him post cards in code that he'd then read on the air.

At Hampton Roads he also completed his religious studies and was baptized a Catholic by a priest on the base. "Anybody would have thought I was doing fine, but the priest said, 'Arthur, you can stay an instructor for the rest of your cruise, [but] it's not getting you anywhere. You don't know anything but code. You need study.'"[2]

Again, the young Godfrey had sought out the advice of an older authority figure, a pattern he would repeat many many times later in life with the likes of presidential adviser Bernard Baruch, several

U.S. presidents, and leaders in broadcasting, the armed services, medicine, and science. Listening and learning from others, no matter what stage of life he was at, would always be one of his strongest traits.

As he had done with Cullinane and the priest in Akron, he now took the Hampton Roads priest's advice, and turning away from the role of instructor, immediately put in for a transfer to the radio school at Great Lakes, Illinois, where he could learn radio theory, his original goal. It was to be a fortuitous move.

At Great Lakes, Arthur Godfrey prospered. His innate intelligence, his curiosity, and his initiative could hardly be contained. He scored the highest grades possible as he learned all about radio theory—electricity, transmitters, and vacuum-tube receivers. By the end of his fourteenth week, he was "a demon" with the wireless key. "I could send as fast as the chiefs," he'd later recall.[3] Once again, he was made an instructor even while completing his course of study. He completed the nine-month course in half the time and was named a petty officer—third class radioman—and got a pay increase to sixty dollars a month.

It was there that he met a young Hawaiian boy from Maui. "He had a steel guitar…and I was fascinated with the thing, and I wanted to learn. 'No, no,' he said. "You learn to play ukulele and you can accompany me. We make a little Hawaiian music.' So he somehow procured a small ukulele…and taught me the chords on it. And I began to play with him…pretty nice Hawaiian songs."[4]

A year passed with Godfrey enjoying his work as an instructor, but by the summer of 1921, he was again feeling at a dead-end. He put in for sea duty.

"I'd been in the Navy two years. I was a radio operator in a naval radio station, and I was wearing a hash mark because I'd re-enlisted…. I thought I was quite a guy.

Prit - Arms!

I was 19—according to my record I was 21—and I was tall and beginning to fill out. I'd won a silver watch in a boxing match and I was cocky, obnoxious and proud of my rating badge and my $60 a month. I was sending $15 home and $15 to the bank; I'm afraid I squandered the other $30 a month."[5]

He was assigned to a destroyer that cruised around Charleston (S.C.) harbor all during the winter of 1922. His affable personality, his forthrightness, and his diligence impressed the skipper, C.P. Cecil, who thought he saw in Godfrey a future Navy officer. With Cecil's help, Arthur began studying on weekends for the U.S. Naval Academy. The following summer, a visiting admiral came aboard his ship and was so impressed with the technical work Godfrey had done in the radio room, that he was made a second-class radioman and received a commendation and an increase in pay to $72 a month.

He took the exams for Annapolis, passed them, and would have sat waiting for his appointment when war broke out between Turkey and Greece. The U.S. was prepared to send a number of destroyers to the area and was looking for radiomen. Godfrey couldn't resist. "I had missed World War I, and I wasn't going to miss this one." He put in his application, was accepted for service aboard the U.S.S. Hatfield, "and off we went to Constantinople."[6]

Arthur Godfrey's first experience with war came in Smyrna, a port city of Turkey, where the American destroyers were detoured en route. The Greeks still controlled the city and fire had broken out in the Armenian sector. He wrote home that the "scene was straight out of Dante's Inferno." The harbor had been a sea of thrashing, screaming humanity as citizens

tried to escape the flames. He wrote that his ship had taken on board as many of the swimming refugees as possible, but that "no one knew how many others had been lost."[7]

"Riding at anchor in the Bosporus," he would later write, "was one of the greatest fleets ever assembled." Ships of every maritime country were present in the area, and thousands of men, including many British, Italian, and French soldiers as well as Russians. Constantinople was a frequent port of call for Godfrey's ship. "Enlisted men were supposed to be off the streets by midnight. But that didn't cramp our style."[8]

Arthur and a group of fellow sailors had formed a musical group called Admiral Bristol's Bobo Six, and on every shore leave they'd take to the beer gardens and other dives and perform for free drinks and applause.[9] An early photograph shows Arthur at the Parthenon in Athens, in white sailor hat and uniform, sitting on some rocks, banjo in hand. "He's gone back to his music!" said his mother on seeing the photo. Determined that he had to have his own banjo, she ordered one "on the installment plan and shipped it off. 'He'll come out of the Navy one of these days,' she observed. 'If he can play the banjo well—who knows? He might go into vaudeville.'"[10]

What his mother and family didn't know was how rough the dives could be. After hours of drinking, singing, boasting, and showboating, there were frequent brawls and Arthur Godfrey was in many of them. One evening in the late forties, he went to see *Mister Roberts*, a Broadway play that featured a scene with Navy enlisted men returning to their ship after shore leave with all kinds of injuries. Arthur spent the next morning on his radio show plugging the play and telling

Opposite: "Port Arms!" wrote Arthur on this photo he sent home to his parents and family in 1920. During his U.S. Navy tour he would become an expert radio signalman. (Joan Zacher collection.)

In Greece, at the Parthenon, during his Mediterranean tour of duty in 1922. Arthur learned to play banjo and ukulele from a fellow serviceman. (Joan Archer collection.)

Later in life, according to his agent Peter Kelley, Godfrey used to tell about a visit he had with a fortuneteller during one of his visits to a port. "She made three predictions: Number One, he would be a famous entertainer; Number Two, he would have a life-threatening accident [which he did]; and Number Three, and the part he liked best, that he would live a long life, but would be shot by a jealous husband at age 90. The fortune teller was two-thirds correct."[12]

The U.S.S. *Hatfield* returned to the U.S. just before Christmas and Arthur, with just five months of service left, returned home to his family "looking tanned and fit in his uniform, and smelling of soap, cigarettes, and chewing gum."[13] His return "was tumultuous…. He couldn't wait to open his bag and give us the presents he'd brought." He regaled them with stories. His sisters fell asleep on Christmas Eve "to the sound of Arthur and Dad and the boys singing carols as Mother played the piano."[14]

It was to be the last time that he saw his father. "We got to be pals that trip. He was proud of me because I had saved my money, and we talked about getting a dairy farm and about how I'd come home and help run it."[15]

about his own experiences. For the rest of his life he sported, as one colleague described it, "a scalp as full of stitches as an official American League baseball." *Life* magazine once reported that "an X-ray would undoubtedly show subcutaneous deposits of broken beer bottle and splintered table leg. In the left side of his mouth he carries a heavy bridgework to replace the bicuspids he lost to faster hands…. Godfrey was very shifty in his time, but in that league nobody could always win."[11]

Back at sea, Godfrey was half-asleep in his bunk one afternoon when a vision of his father appeared to him. Shortly afterward, a radio message came to the ship. It was for Radioman 2nd Class Arthur Godfrey, telling him that his father had died. The time given was precisely the time that afternoon when Arthur had experienced the visit.

On May 16, 1924, Godfrey's four-year tour of duty officially ended. He was 20 years old. With $2000 in savings, he headed home to Hasbrouck Heights with dreams of building a business of some kind. What he found when he arrived, however, was that his newly widowed mother had lost her job at the movie house, and that the gas and electricity had been shut off. He immediately reorganized the household, setting everyone to work.

"'How in hell did the place get like this?' he asked. 'There's no system around here, damn it!' He used to run his fingers through his hair and whistle as he studied the bills. 'How in the world can anybody run up a $200 grocery bill?' he asked his mother.... There were ancient bills for moving expenses, as well as bills for medical supplies, kerosene, coal, and shoes.... Dad's chair had become Arthur's chair, as head of the family."[16]

Soon his $2000 was all but gone. Family friends helped him get work: first as an audit correspondent with the Metropolitan Life Insurance Company, and then as a $100-a-week copywriter for a New Jersey firm writing advertising for a perfume company—a job that probably soured him on copy and copywriters for the rest of his life. He bought himself a used car. Whatever plans he had to move on were refocused on Hasbrouck Heights.

That summer, he met a young schoolteacher, Ruth Stevens. The two hit it off and were soon inseparable. It was his first serious relationship with a woman, and having fallen head over heels, he and Ruth soon announced their engagement. At first, she was welcomed into the family by Mrs. Godfrey. But when Arthur, anxious to get married, suggested to his mother that they move in with the family and that Ruth take over the management of the household, his mother resisted. Instead, she said she would find a job and take the financial pressure off Arthur. In the past, she had made inquiries to several of the newly operating radio stations, hoping to rekindle her singing career. This time, desperate to earn more money, anxious to avoid having another woman in the house and wanting to please her oldest son, she grasped at a straw: a once-a-week job at a Newark station.

When she presented Arthur with what she considered good news, he blew up. "We will never forget the expression on Arthur's face," recalled his sisters. He began roaring about all the false expectations she was always setting up and demanded that they sell the piano, considering it a symbol of her idealism. "Why don't you get it into your head, Mother.... *Nobody's* a genius in this family. *Nobody!*" His mother stood her ground. "How do you *know*?" she responded.

That night, Arthur and his brother Charlie packed and left. "Dear Mother," their note read. "We are going West. Will write when we find a job." Arthur's ledger was open, showing all the bills paid but no money left. "Not a damned cent," he had scrawled across the bottom of the page. [17]

4

On the Road Again

THERE IS A CERTAIN DIVINE IRONY in the fact that Arthur Godfrey's mother saw professional opportunity in broadcasting long before her son did. She saw it for herself—a connection between her singing ability, her knowledge of music, and the rapidly growing medium of radio, which didn't require you to go out to the movie theater or to the vaudeville house for entertainment. But when it came to Arthur, she had always focused on the opportunities for him in vaudeville.

Either way, her talk of making music a career for herself or him or any Godfrey had driven him from home once again. Arthur seemed less concerned about what field he would enter than about making money and getting moving, and he didn't see where vaudeville or radio offered him much of either. He didn't yet see the logical crossover potential for himself: his musical ability, his ability to tell tall tales and charm women, and his salty, slightly off-color humor that attracted men as

well—all characteristics that would make him the biggest name in broadcasting one day. If he saw a connection to radio at all, it would have been based on his skills as a radioman, the technical side of the business.

Yet, every one of the seemingly disconnected life experiences he had during and after his Navy years would play a major part in his future career in radio and television. To begin with, he had learned to live and deal with all kinds of people, from lumberjacks and priests to gangsters and Navy commanders. He was smart and observant and he understood what made people tick. He wasn't afraid of hard work; work energized him. The reason Godfrey later became one of the most effective communicators in America, at one point having been heard by more people than anyone in history until that time, was because of these experiences. He had toured large parts of the country and the world, experienced different cultures, knew what poverty was really like, understood the value of money, was always open to advice and new ideas. He didn't consider himself musically talented, yet whenever he had time off, he'd pick up the banjo and entertain the locals. He was highly gregarious, was not above getting himself in trouble, and was ready at a moment's notice to try something new if it might mean a good time. All of this would serve him well in his career to come. But not yet. Maybe his duty overseas, just when radio had started to have its dramatic impact on Americans, had resulted in his missing all the excitement and being oblivious to its potential for him. Whatever the reason, throughout the 1920s, he poked around the edges of American life, while radio became an integral part of it.

Back on November 21, 1920, when Godfrey was just getting settled at Great Lakes Naval Station, Frank Conrad, a Pittsburgh engineer for Westinghouse Corporation, signed on KDKA, the first commercially licensed broadcast radio station in the U.S. The first program was a report of the Harding-Cox presidential election returns, interspersed with phonograph records and banjo music. The station became an overnight sensation in Pittsburgh, and amateur operators spread the word throughout the Northeast. There were few if any other stations on the air, and the KDKA signal carried far beyond Pennsylvania, especially at night. Out-of-town newspapers throughout the country began carrying the station's program schedule. For Westinghouse and others, an immediate market sprang up for an inexpensive receiving gadget called a "crystal set."

Radio was quickly all the rage. As one chronicler explained it, "Practically the only signals on the air in 1920 were in radiotelegraphic code. To hear news, music, and other entertainment instead of the monotonous drone of code in the ear-

phones was an electrifying experience for any listener, amateur or professional."[1]

"In its first year...KDKA pioneered... many of the types of programs which [became] standard radio fare: orchestra music, church services, public-service announcements, political addresses, sports events, drama, market reports."[2] By the end of the year, 30 licenses for other broadcasting stations like KDKA were issued.

By the spring of 1922, when Arthur Godfrey steamed off to Asia Minor to his own excitement, over 200 broadcast licenses had been issued in the States. Said Herbert Hoover, then U.S. secretary of commerce and the man responsible for administering the Radio Act of 1912: "We have witnessed in the last four or five months one of the most astounding things that has come under my observation of American life. [The Department of Commerce] estimates that today over 600,000 persons possess wireless telephone receiving sets, whereas there were less than 50,000 such sets a year ago."[3]

On August 16, AT&T, then the country's only national telephone system, launched its own radio station in New York City: WEAF. It was given every financial, technical, and managerial resource it needed. Soon, it became the center of the first radio network broadcast when, on January 4, 1923, connected by AT&T telephone lines, the station fed a five-minute saxophone solo by wire for broadcast over WNAC in Boston.[4]

By May 1923, 576 more station licenses were given out around the country. The WEAF network was expanded so that by 1924, the year Godfrey finished his Navy hitch, six stations were broadcasting three hours of network programs per day. That October, a special 22-station hookup carried a speech by President Coolidge from coast to coast.

If Arthur Godfrey was listening to radio at all that fall of 1924, he was doing it on the fly. He and his younger brother Charlie, who stayed with him only briefly, drove to Detroit, Michigan, believing, apparently, that work in the automobile industry would bring them steady money and possibly careers. Arthur got work as a body finisher in an automobile plant. Though he was a tough young man on the outside, ambitious and often driven, his body did not always accommodate him. As it had before in the coal mine, and would countless times in the future, it let him down in Detroit. He contracted pneumonia, lost his job and, in need of cash, sold his one symbol of independence, his car. He found a temporary job as a counterman in a restaurant, then as a desk clerk at a gangster-controlled hotel, and finally as a cemetery lot salesman.

"Selling those cemetery lots brought me the first big money I'd ever made."[5] He found sales to his liking—the challenge, the personal contact, the chance to do something "his way." With no indication that he was given any training or coaching, Arthur Godfrey excelled. He would never forget that experience. Years later, when he would single-handedly bring in 12 percent of all CBS revenues by selling products on the air, he would tell the story of how he did it:

"You'd go from door to door and make inquiries as to [whether] this family [was] Protestant or Catholic," he later explained to Tom Snyder on the NBC *Tomorrow* show in the late 1970s. "If they were Catholic, you say, 'Thank you very much.'.... No use talking to Catholics. They got their own cemetery. So I had to find the Protestants. And then...talk about...'Are you Protestant?'...anything to make them stand and talk to you a minute while you tried to sell 'em on the fact that you're an honest guy and that you really were interested in whether or not they...had invested in a cemetery lot.... 'Do you own a cemetery lot?' 'No.' 'Oh,

gee, you know that's one of the great troubles of the country, the guy comes home in a basket and where you gonna put him?' [*Laughs*] Yeah. And I sold a great many lots. And I went by the cemetery about five years ago in Detroit. Looked at it and the section that I had is completely filled."[6] Arthur earned $10,000 in five months, an astonishing sum in 1926.

But still seeking a career that would engage more of his interests, and still very impressionable, he took some bad advice and invested in a traveling vaudeville troupe. Three months later, after touring from Chicago to Los Angeles, the act went under, along with his entire $10,000. His earlier instincts about vaudeville not being right for him had proven correct.

Yet to Arthur it was just one more adventure. He had incredible resiliency. "I hocked my banjo and rode the freights back to Chicago."[7] He took a job as a cabbie, then as a nightclub entertainer, strumming and serving as master of ceremonies in a club purported to be owned by Al Capone. Three years after leaving the Navy and eight years after running away from home, he was going nowhere again.

Enter an old Navy buddy in a Coast Guard uniform. They reminisced and, apparently seeing that Arthur was truly missing the good old days, he encouraged him to enlist in "this hooligan Navy."[8] Believing he could get a Coast Guard commission with his Navy training, yearning for some security again, Godfrey signed on. He was sent to radio school at New London, Connecticut. And there he met the woman who would become his first wife.

Catherine Collins was working in Hartford for an insurance company. Kay, as she was called, took a liking to Arthur. He saw her regularly. And on March 3, 1928 they were married in her hometown of Somerville, Massachusetts. When he was accepted to a Navy run school in

Washington, D.C., in order to become a first-class radioman, she traveled with him. He studied and worked day and night, completing the course successfully. The next stop was a Coast Guard Depot outside of Baltimore, where Arthur was sent to design radio equipment. Kay followed.

Kay wasn't with him that Saturday night when he and his Coast Guard buddies ventured out of the depot and over to a speakeasy (it was still Prohibition days) where they served "needled beer." Arthur held forth, singing and playing his banjo. It was midnight when the owner set the radio to local station WFBR and an amateur show called *Saturday Night Function*. The announcer appealed for anyone who could sing or play a musical instrument to come down to be on the air. "You're as good as those monkeys," one of his pals exclaimed, pointing to Arthur.[9] They all agreed and with Arthur in tow, off they went to the radio station.

He played his banjo and sang "I'm In Love With You, Honey" and some sea chanteys, and he was asked back for the following week's show. After his third appearance, the station manager asked him to come aboard and do three 15-minute performances a week. They had even found a sponsor—the Triangle Pet Shop that sold birdseed. He was billed as "Red Godfrey, the Warbling Banjoist," and was paid $5 a show. Arthur Godfrey didn't know it yet, but his odyssey had ended. Quite by accident or maybe not so much by accident, he had found his career. A career that would last over 50 years.

5

Red Godfrey,
the Warbling Banjoist

ALMOST EVERYONE IN BROADCAST-
ing has a story to tell about "being there
at the right place at the right time." It was
especially true in the early days of radio
when just about everything was being
made up the day it was done, and young
employees were asked to do lots of new
things. In October of 1929, Arthur Godfrey was not only a full-time Coast
Guardsman, he was moonlighting three
evenings a week at WFBR, playing the
banjo and singing. One evening the announcer who normally introduced Godfrey and his show, and who also read the
commercials on the program, failed to
show up. So Arthur just picked up the
script and did his own announcing. The
president of the station liked what he
heard. "You can talk fifty times better than
you can sing,"[1] he told Arthur and offered
him one of the two commercial announcer
spots on the staff. The pay was $25 a week,

a nice addition to his Coast Guard salary,
especially with a baby on the way at home.
Arthur agreed to the extra job and the
extra money.

It proved to be a challenge. Arthur
would end his day's work at the Depot,
travel to little WFBR, and work from six to
midnight. He introduced the shows, did
all the commercials, sang and strummed
on his uke and banjo, and played records.
That experience was, as he later recalled,
"the most valuable contribution to my
career."[2]

But, not surprisingly, his Coast Guard
work began to suffer. He received a stern
warning from the unit's personnel officer
that he better shape up or he literally
might be "shipped out" to a lesser assignment outside of Baltimore. Godfrey could
see no option. He was committed to the
Guard for three years and was convinced
that the radio work he was now beginning

to enjoy so much would have to come to an end. That is, until he had a talk with the governor of Maryland.

Each week, one of his assignments was introducing Governor Albert Ritchie, who did a weekly broadcast on the station. Ritchie was a fan of Godfrey's work and when he learned of his dilemma and that Baltimore might lose him, he took matters into his own hands. A meeting was arranged for Arthur with Rear Admiral Billard, head of the U.S. Coast Guard in Washington, who, fortunately, was familiar with Godfrey's work for the station. He offered Arthur a choice—promotion to ensign or his release—but then, surprisingly, added his own advice: Arthur should go with broadcasting. Arthur agreed, and with his release, he went back to WFBR as full-time broadcaster.

The next year provided an invaluable crash course in broadcasting. Like most stations of the time, WFBR was a tiny place, in terms of both facilities and people. It consisted of three rooms: a control room, a small room for announcing, and a slightly larger room, big enough to hold a small band. "We had three or four engineers—one was always on duty—and two announcers. We had a chief announcer and a program director. Pretty soon I was given both of the latter jobs blended together. And there was a pianist on call...so that if we wanted to rest the machines that spun the records, Chester would play for fifteen minutes. And we had a combo called the WFBR Trio to play what was called 'luncheon music' and 'dinner music' and occasionally to accompany a soloist.... But most of the time it was just me and

"I was America's first disc jockey," Arthur would often explain. He broke all the rules and led the way for others to do more than announce the music selections on the air. (Joan Zacher collection.)

the engineers. I was program director, the announcer, the receptionist; I was everybody."[3]

The program director's slot was a particular challenge. WFBR was not affiliated with a network. There were endless hours of airtime to fill. Mornings were taken up fairly easily by church services and women who came to the studios to "speak for the Ladies' Aid or the Bible societies or the SPCA."[4] Evenings also featured other speakers, the WFBR Trio, and live performances. "But in the afternoon there were long periods when all we had [listed] was To Be Announced. It was to fill these gaps that I first began fooling around with records. I'd ask the engineer, 'What have we got next?' and he'd say, 'It's a To Be Announced, kid. Get out the records.' I'd get them out and sit at the little turntable with a carbon mike in front of me and only a sheet of glass between me and the engineer, and spin them.

"Two and a half years later, working for NBC in Washington, I became the country's first disk jockey, but at WFBR I just put records on the turntables and announced the titles like anyone else. Oh, I played around a little bit with a touch of humor here and there; for instance, I'd pick up a record and say, 'Because of difficulties beyond our control, the program which was listed, To Be Announced, will not be heard. We offer instead a fifteen-minute musical interlude'."[5]

Godfrey quickly learned "how to conduct auditions and pick talent for the airwaves," just the grounding he needed for what would later be one of his most ambitious and successful undertakings at CBS: *Arthur Godfrey's Talent Scouts* show.[6] And filling airtime was a challenge he'd rise to again twenty years later when, at CBS, he had over a dozen hours of live television and radio to fill each week.

In early 1930, Kay gave birth to a son, Richard. And a Godfrey family reunion followed. An old friend of Kathryn Godfrey's in New Jersey happened to pick up WFBR and heard Godfrey announcing a U.S. Marine Band concert. "It's Arthur," she told his mother. "I'd know his voice anywhere."[7] Kathryn called the station, and for the first time in five years, she and Arthur talked. He sent her train tickets and she traveled by train to Washington where she met Kay and the baby, approving of both. But if she had hopes that Arthur would be settling down to family life as well as a career, her hopes were soon dashed. With his new work consuming him, his life as father as well as husband came to an abrupt end. Kay took the baby and moved to Boston. "It was show busi-

ness and I wasn't interested in show business," she remarked years later.[8]

Indeed it was show business. And big business now. Since Godfrey had joined the Coast Guard in 1927, radio had exploded and the foundation for most of what has become broadcasting and cable today was formed. In November 1926, the first company organized solely and specifically to conduct a broadcast network was formed. Until that time, AT&T, RCA, GE, and Westinghouse had all been working together and competitively in establishing radio, selling telephone-line time, radio sets, and radio equipment. But the business of programming was not being conducted in a businesslike way. David Sarnoff, a Vice President of RCA, was convinced that radio's real future was in programming. Sarnoff, who began as a Marconi radiotelegraph operator, gained fame as the operator who had maintained contact, from Marconi's New York station atop the Wanamaker building, with the survivors of the Titanic disaster. As early as 1916, he had seen the future of broadcasting as a "household utility in the same sense as the piano or phonograph," and that significant money could be made by selling "music boxes."[9] He had been proven correct. But now, as a vice president of RCA, he began looking past the day when everyone had bought a radio set. Radio was too big to allow programming to be done helter-skelter. The result of his efforts was the National Broadcasting Company, operating as a subsidiary of RCA.

On November 15, 1926, NBC, as it was quickly dubbed, began with an inaugural broadcast transmitted by telephone lines to over 25 stations and reached an astonishing five million listeners. Artists included the New York Symphony Orchestra, opera singer Mary Garden in Chicago, and humorist Will Rogers in Independence, Kansas. A year later, coast to coast network operations began and NBC established two networks of its own, with affiliate stations across the country. [10]

There were now over 700 stations operating but only 7 percent were affiliated with the network, NBC. The demands on these stations to produce enough programming every day to fill their schedules were only increasing. Arthur Godfrey was experiencing that first-hand at WFBR in Baltimore. There was real need for another network, a need that was soon met by a new company. In 1928 it emerged as the Columbia Broadcasting System, under the control of the family of cigar manufacturer Sam Paley and, in particular, his young advertising-oriented son, William S. Paley. While David Sarnoff looked down on broadcasting from the corporate top, Paley took up the mantle of the stations themselves, quickly developed more attractive affiliation contracts, and by 1929 had established CBS with 49 radio station affiliates in 42 cities.

Until that time, money to pay for the operations of the local stations was hard to come by. Where ownership was in the hands of newspapers and retail stores who believed that providing such a community service enhanced their primary businesses, there were adequate funds for operations. But for many stations, owned by individuals or companies with little capital, it was tough going. Advertising was primitive: scripted announcements read by announcers with rarely a mention of price or store hours or anything specific. It was all very formal, the assumption being that neither the public nor the government would tolerate more. But William Paley saw advertising as the ultimate engine for the industry, CBS in particular, and the answer to the lack of sufficient programming at the local level. He had first experimented with advertising when he was with the family business, buying airtime on

WCAU in Philadelphia in 1927 for one of their brands, La Palina. "The La Palina Smoker" featured an orchestra, singer, and comedian and had an immediate positive effect on cigar sales.[11]

So Paley made an innovative offer to independent local stations: join as CBS affiliates and receive twenty hours of commercially sponsored programs a week, plus significant amounts of additional programming that was "sustaining." All for $500 per week. Unlike NBC, which gained much of its income through the radio equipment manufacturing of its parent company RCA, CBS and Paley's revenue would come from advertising. The more affiliates he could offer advertisers, the more consumers the advertisers could reach. He set to work to solidify relationships between national advertisers and high-quality national programming for his affiliates.

By 1929, the year when Arthur Godfrey joined WFBR, NBC with its two networks had begun following CBS' road to money, sponsors, and more national programming. Together, the two organizations, NBC and CBS, were changing the face of radio. National programming was growing by leaps and bounds, a fact that impressed a Baltimore newspaper columnist and would soon impact the life of Arthur Godfrey.

But who could imagine at that time that local Baltimore announcer Arthur Godfrey would someday be delivering to William S. Paley not only his most popular programs but more advertising money percentage-wise than anyone else in the history of CBS before or since?

In less than a year, Godfrey had become a Baltimore institution. And at least one prominent person in town thought he was ready for bigger and better things. Arthur had developed a good relationship with Betty Snyder, a columnist for the *Baltimore Sun*, who urged him to move on to a network-affiliated station where he could gain exposure and eventually a network assignment. She arranged an interview for him at WRC in Washington where he auditioned and was offered $50 a week. It was considerably less than what he was now making in Baltimore, but WRC was the NBC network's station in the nation's capital. He decided to take it. It was November, 1930.

6

NBC's Tuxedoed Announcer

WRC IN WASHINGTON, D.C., WAS a flagship station of the prospering NBC network. There were only four stations operating in the city in 1930, but with its NBC network affiliation (and ownership) WRC was far and away the most popular. The NBC network was providing Washingtonians an increasing array of high-caliber entertainment shows. Each weekday evening, the network offered up the runaway hit show *Amos 'n Andy* (which was listened to by 53.4 percent of American households).[1] Each Thursday, there was the hour-long *Fleischmann Yeast Hour* with singing sensation Rudy Vallee. And the network was beginning to make preparations for a new comedy-variety series, featuring the famous vaudeville and burlesque star, Eddie Cantor, the first headline entertainer from those fields to begin a weekly comedy-variety hour when it premiered nine months later. NBC's national announcers, like Graham McNamee and Milton

Cross, were already familiar voices in homes everywhere.

The crash of the stock market the previous year had only added to WRC's importance. As the federal government grappled with the economic fallout of the collapse, Washington, D.C., was becoming the center of attention for most Americans as they sought answers and relief from growing business and personal woes. And though NBC was still several years away from providing regular newscasts from the Capitol, it was beginning to use WRC's resources to provide speeches from elected officials and reports from magazine and newspaper columnists stationed in town.

Compared to WFBR, WRC was a powerhouse. It boasted a large staff of announcers and engineers and large studios strategically located in the Press Building. Godfrey's early assignments at WRC, which carried programming of both NBC's Red and Blue Network services, were all at the local level—weather reports, news bulletins, introducing local programming, and reading commercial messages. Everything was scripted. His only connection to the network was during station breaks, "punching locals." "When the NBC chimes went bong, bong, bong, I was one of those who intoned sweetly '[This is] WRC in Washington.'"[2]

"Announcers were radio's jacks-of-all-trades," wrote Leonard Maltin in his book *The Great American Broadcast*, "expected to be able to handle everything from calling the plays at a football game to accurately pronouncing the names of foreign-born composers on a classical music program."[3] As radio developed, announcers became the glue that linked the programs one to another. Announcers were the primary providers of information to the listener: they told us who was about to speak or sing, what time it was, what programs were coming up later in the day or evening. They also were key to the business of radio—they read the commercial messages that paid the bills. Announcing quickly became a respectable and highly admired occupation. There was no formal training outside of the stations or networks themselves, but it did help to have a distinctive voice. Thus, the work often attracted singers and actors. More often than not, successful applicants had college degrees.

Announcers dressed for the occasion. If it was a cultural program, they would often wear tuxedoes. In every case, they would *stand* at the microphone, script in hand, speaking as if they were in front of a vast crowd.

Arthur Godfrey worked under the station's chief announcer, Herluf Provenson, a man who emphasized good diction and sophisticated, dramatic reading of announcements and station identifications. Provenson was not alone. At the network headquarters in New York was a woman named Vida Ravenscroft Sutton, who served as speech specialist. She was constantly coaching the network announcers who, in turn, set the standard for the locals. "The NBC Announcer's Audition—full of tongue-twisting phrases and formidable names of Russian composers—became the stuff of legend in the radio business. If you could pass that test, you could do anything on the air."[4] According to long-time NBC announcer Andre Baruch, one of the phrases used in the test went "the seething sea ceased to see, then thus sufficeth thus."[5]

The American Academy of Arts and Letters gave a medal each year called the Diction Award, and it was highly coveted. Godfrey followed along, doing his best to imitate the formal stylizing of the leading announcers of the day—Cross, Alwyn Bach, even CBS's David Ross. "It must have been awful," he would later recall, "a broad A here, a New England twang there, and a Southern drawl in the middle."[6]

Like the other announcers, he promoted himself in every way possible. Even before he was doing any national shows for WRC he "had little cards printed that read ARTHUR GODFREY, ANNOUNCER, NATIONAL BROACASTING COMPANY. I never failed to give you one of those cards either. We had to audition for every extra show we got and, of course, when one of us was chosen by a sponsor to announce a new program, all the rest of us hated his guts."[7]

"Every once in a while some misguided soul would write us a fan letter saying 'You are my favorite announcer. Please send me a photo of yourself.' We would carelessly leave such letters on the station manager's desk where he would be sure to find them. We would go over to Harris & Ewing and pose for 'portrait studies'—you know the kind: pipe in hand and shirt open at the throat. And would listen to the big announcers and dream of the day we could do a show like that."[8]

Working hard, by mid–1931 he had not only been nominated for the Diction Award, with Miss Sutton coming to Washington to personally coach him ("Her efforts were in vain, I just couldn't stop droppin' my Gs"), he was also given regular network announcing assignments, usually during the daytime and late in the evening when audiences were smaller. His national announcing assignments included military band concerts for which he introduced and read background information about each selection, the *National Farm and Home Hour*, and introducing political analysts who were appearing more and more frequently on the networks.

"Before a program of that sort, all of us characters would gargle…then come out and bite our nails until it was time for us to go on and speak a piece. On the air we'd say, with overwhelming charm: 'From our Washington studios in the nation's capital, the National Broadcasting Company takes great pleasure in presenting Mr. Zilch. Mr. Zilch!' I did that many a time and I am sure that I personally was the biggest stuffed shirt and the silliest ass ever heard on anybody's radio."[9]

But they were not all Mr. Zilches. Soon Godfrey was meeting and welcoming to the WRC studios U. S. senators and congressmen, the vice president of the United States, the chief justice, cabinet members and bureau chiefs. " I soon learned how to chat with men like that and make them feel at home, so that they were more at ease during broadcasts."[10] But Arthur was even more industrious. Vying with other announcers with college degrees, he put in extra time reading up on his guest and the subject before they arrived. If the opportunity presented itself, he would discuss it with the guest. For Arthur Godfrey, the greatest thing he learned from these meetings was poise. "Since I was but a year removed from being a rough and ready enlisted man, an official of any rank scared the hell out of me." He found that engaging them not only flattered and interested them, but it made a lot of good friends for him. "I studied these men carefully, tried to find out what made them tick…I learned how to argue with a man intelligently without incurring his wrath…. One big lesson I learned from them was—the bigger the man, the less stuffed is his shirt"[11]

Unlike most announcers, he had a close relationship with all of the engineers at the station. His Navy and Coast Guard training gave him a leg up when it came to the technical side and he was highly popular with the technical men, often helping them haul amplifiers and other equipment to remote broadcast locations.

To supplement his announcer's salary, Godfrey earned fees from local sponsors for singing their theme songs during announcements. He also took on other assignments, including a local children's show called *Aunt Sue and Polly*. He poured his money into a new hobby—aviation— and invested in a flying school at the Congressional Airport, where he spent most of his free time. He was thriving, enjoying every minute of it, though it often meant signing the station on at seven A.M., and signing it off at midnight.

7

The Fortuitous Accident

Riggs Road, stretching north-east from Washington, D.C., through Langley Park, Maryland, is a busy road these days. Heavily traveled, it provides a link to the Beltway and the other main roads that handle traffic north of the city. But back in 1931, Riggs Road was basically a country road, running past woods, streams, and country clubs. One use of the highway was to gain access to University Boulevard, which arced west to the old Congressional Airport. Once the busiest of a dozen or so small airports that ringed Washington, it sat on 160 acres and was home to one runway, a training school, a hop-flight service (for $1.50 per passenger), an agency for the sale of airplanes, a public restaurant, two tourist camps, and a fruit and vegetable stand. Dozens of student and amateur pilots used the airport, including Arthur Godfrey.

At some point Godfrey discovered gliders, bought his own, and started teaching others how to fly them. The income was modest. The opportunity to fly was no doubt what drew him to it.

On September 26, 1931, shortly before noon, he left WRC and headed northeast out Riggs Road to fly his glider. It was a clear, sunny day, with just enough wind to make it perfect flying weather. "I had done the late shift the night before," he recalled, "and had slept until eleven or so, had breakfasted and felt like a million dollars. The boys at the airport had called me saying, 'Come on out. It's a beautiful day and the wind is just right for gliding.'"[1]

About eight miles from the airport, on a fairly straight stretch, with Arthur Godfrey barreling along at about fifty miles an hour, a truck approached from the other direction at about the same speed, and suddenly lost its left front wheel. The truck driver lost control and his truck veered into the opposite lane just as Arthur's car approached. It was a head-on collision.

"It happened so quickly I didn't even

34

have time to touch the brake. I just sat there holding the wheel in both hands— listening to the glass crashing and tinkling all around. I was told later that the two men in the truck cab sailed over my car into the bushes and luckily only scratched their faces. I remember seeing the motor come in through the instrument panel and come to rest sizzling and smoking on the seat beside me. I felt no pain and I remember saying some silly thing like 'Holy catfish!' Then I looked down at my left hand. Blood was spouting out of an ugly gash, across the back of it and up my forearm around the elbow. I thought, 'Boy, I'd better get that to a doctor,' reached around with my right hand to open the left-hand door and felt the first blinding, blazing flash of pain. Apparently the door flew open just as I lost consciousness."[2]

When the ambulance attendants arrived they found Arthur's slightly chubby frame intact. But internally, he was a wreck. "Both knees [were broken], both hips, twenty-seven fractures in the pelvis," he would later recount, sounding like any grown-up reciting The Twelve Days of Christmas. "Four ribs," he continued, "there was a severed tendon, compound fractures, fracture of the skull; I was a mess." In addition, there was a "spontaneous pneumothorax"—a big hole in the lung—which collapsed it, causing a comparative vacuum on the right side and thus pulling his heart out of position over to the right side of his chest. "Both kneecaps were completely smashed."[3]

His body had served him well for 28 years, taking him from Hasbrouck Heights to the Black Sea. Now it was unclear how much he could ever rely on it again.

He didn't regain consciousness for a week. When he did, he thought he had surely died. "The room was piled high with flowers—from radio listeners, God bless 'em. I hadn't dreamed so many people knew my name."[4]

He would be in the hospital for four months. For many weeks, he lay in a straitjacket of bandages and casts, from his armpits to his knees. His left arm was in traction. He couldn't raise his head and at first thought he had lost his legs. "Oh no," reassured an attending nurse, grabbing his toes. But he couldn't feel a thing.[5]

Fresh flowers came daily and get-well cards by the hundreds, many from nighttime listeners across the United States. "And me just a punk radio announcer on the Washington outlet of NBC. I never have gotten over [that]. Moreover, it gave me, for the first time, some notion of the enormous power of radio."[6]

Daily bulletins were issued in all five of the Washington papers, and there were feature stories from time to time. "I never got so much space again until twenty-five years later when I let [staff member] Julius la Rosa go."[7]

"I'll never know how they put that pelvis back together," Godfrey wrote in the Saturday Evening Post. "They molded, pushed, pulled and worked at it for hours."[8] Afterwards, the surgeon told him he had enormous vitality. That vitality would also make all the difference in his fight with cancer, 28 years later.

But the rest of the prognosis was grim: the best hope the doctors could give him was life in a wheelchair. One regular visitor was the NBC vice president in charge of the Washington office, Scoop Russell, who helped ease the shock: NBC would pay the entire bill and keep him on salary until he was well enough to work.

Days and weeks went by slowly. Kay had long since moved to Boston and remarried, taking with her the son he hardly knew. Staff members from WRC, flying buddies, and reporters came by. (There were probably a number of young women friends too.) Later, when he was able, he would read the newspapers and magazines.

And there were physical therapy sessions where Godfrey concentrated all his brain power and energy on proving the doctors wrong—he would walk again.

Still, there were endless hours to fill. Radio became his constant companion and from early morning to late at night, he kept his set on.

The choices were few. During the day, he could tune in to WRC, his own station, or the CBS affiliate in town or the independent stations. Weekdays there were homemakers' shows (Edna Wallace Hopper on beauty, Mrs. Julian Heath on cooking); talk shows on bridge, etiquette, and poetry; and "light daytime music" (marimba bands, Glenn & Glenn with songs and patter, the *Vermont Lumber Jacks* quartet). Not much for a red-blooded former sailor and coastguardsman to chew on.

Things improved by evenings, however. NBC had premiered *Lowell Thomas and the News* at 6:45 P.M. each weekday. CBS had H. V. Kaltenborn reporting three times a week at 8:30 P.M. There was *Amos 'n Andy* at 7:00 each evening, *Rudy Vallee* each Thursday for an hour; the *A&P Gypsies* on Mondays at 8:30 P.M.; *RKO Theater*, Fridays at 10:30 P.M.; *Sherlock Holmes*, Mondays at 10:00 P.M., one of only five "thriller dramas"; the *Lucky Strike Dance Orchestra* at 10:00 P.M. three times a week; and a number of musical variety and concert music shows. And there were the distant stations he might pull in in the evening, though they all signed off by midnight.

Weekends on CBS and NBC's Red and Blue networks were filled with live classical music (the New York Philharmonic with Arturo Toscanini, the RCA Victor Concert Orchestra, the Atwater Kent Hour, the Salt Lake Tabernacle Choir), more musical variety hours, and a few religious talk programs.[9]

At first, he lay there mimicking the network announcers, "They were good and they were famous and they were all making big money. They differed from me in another way too: They had talent. All I had that I could lay my hands on was a God-given voice that wasn't too unpleasant to listen to, just so-so diction and a deck hand's vocabulary [which] kindlier folks [referred to as] picturesque speech."

Decades later, he would parrot the formal delivery of the name announcers of the day: "People like the late Graham McNamee, 'Good eeevening ladies and gentlemen of the radio audience! This is Graham McNamee speaking.' Or Milton Cross: 'Yahw announcer is Milton J. Cross.' Bless their sweet hearts; they were always talkin' down."[10] He studied "their inflections and intonations, mastered their little tricks with words; imitated their affectations—the broad a's and rolled r's...and generally drove my nurses nuts."

But the more he listened, the more he was struck by one overwhelming constant in all of the broadcasts he heard: a distance, a formality that set the people at the microphone apart from the listener on the other end. It was true. When Norman Brokenshire opened with, "How do you do, ladies and gentlemen, how *do* you do?" he was talking as if listeners were gathered in one place—a hall, a park plaza—when in reality they were in their separate living rooms. The announcers, be they network or local like himself, were stuffy, overly precise, and off the mark.

"And that's how I learned the secret... of my success in broadcasting. For one thing, I learned what not to do."[11]

He confirmed his observations when visitors came to his hospital room. They would join him in listening to Rudy Vallee or the Mills Brothers or singer Ruth Etting. But curiously, he noticed, as soon as the announcer came on to give a commercial, they would begin talking to him and the other visitors. From that he reasoned that the only time people listened to commercials was when they were alone with the radio. "I decided that we who did the broadcasting had the wrong idea entirely. We had no audience! There were no "ladies and gentlemen out there per se! There was no vast audience! Those who were paying attention were alone in a room—and they were absolutely unmoved by some unctuous gent looking down his nose and reading a blurb written by someone who was doubtless a huge success at writing ads for the eye, but who didn't know the first thing about writing for the ear!"[12]

Underscoring the point even further, Godfrey would later quip, "A boy and a girl together should have something better to do than listen to the radio."[13]

Having gotten to know the advertising men and their clients around the radio station, he knew how much return they had come to expect—about the same as to a direct mail or local newspaper campaign. "I decided that I could do better than that."[14]

He thought back on his experiences as a house-to-house salesman, dealing one-on-one with his prospect. He saw radio now in the same way. "I would knock on some woman's door and when she opened it bellow, 'Good morning, ladies and gentlemen. This is Arthur Godfrey speaking.' She'd slam it in my face and phone for the cops."

He promised himself that he "must not do anything like that on the radio. I must remember that for my purposes there is only one person listening to any one set. I must talk to him or her just as I would standing on the front porch with my hat in my hand. Some won't like me at all and they'll slam the door. But others will."[15]

He also decided that just as he had believed in the products he sold door-to-

door, he had to know about and believe in the products he was asked to pitch on the air. "I resolved that when I got back on the air nobody could ever pay me enough money to make a statement on the radio I didn't believe in."

"If you're lucky," he went on, " you'll have one person alone who will give you his attention or her attention provided what you have to say makes sense and there's a rapport established between you…. So the microphone became to me a person, and I talked to the mike as a friend."[16] "Personalized broadcasting" was what he later called it. One-on-one conversation is what we call it today. According to *Time* magazine in its cover story on him in 1950, "It was a revolutionary discovery."

He also had ideas about how to make WRC's programs more interesting and he shared those ideas with Scoop Russell during his weekly visits. Russell was all for having him give them a try.

But Godfrey didn't get to apply his new theories until he limped out of the hospital on crutches after four months and returned to his job at WRC. Physically, his recovery would take much longer. It would be two years until he could bend his knees, 22 years until his right leg was " unlocked" by a revolutionary hip operation. But he never lost the limp. "I wound up a pretty bad cripple for the rest of my days."[17]

Yet in another way, the accident would prove to be more fortuitous than almost any other event in his life. And for the radio industry as well.

Back at the microphone, he dropped his usual introduction to the evening's feature program and began with a quiet, friendly "Good evening." Radio announcing would never be the same.

8

The Godfrey Way

THERE IS SOMETHING ALMOST mystical about being alone in front of a live microphone in a small radio studio. First, there is the silence. Here in this brightly lit room, surrounded by soundproof glass and soundproof walls and soundproof ceilings, with the heavy door closed tight, it is what one would imagine space flight to be like. Or those finite moments when one has dived into a pool and is gliding through deep water.

There is the machinery: The audio board that sits facing you, filled with colored punch buttons and switches, and the lighted viewmeters mounted behind it. In days past, the dull silver turntables to your left. In later years, the cassette tape machines or CD players to your right. Today, the computer and monitor, holding access to all the pre-recorded messages as well as the music. The microphone, extended toward you, alive and ready to carry your every breath, your every word, from this place to another. The headphones, resting

on the console countertop. The speakers on the wall so you can hear what is going out over the air. And the clock, the omnipotent clock, with its sweep second hand, strategically placed so that you are always aware of it and the deadlines it imposes. All of these tools—silent, ready, and waiting for your next move.

Then, there is the well-worn swivel chair you sit on, a constant reminder of all of the others who have occupied it before you. And the little notes everywhere—"No smoking." "Night man be sure to pull AM records." "Logs to be filled out hourly." "Smile."—written by others days, weeks, months, possibly years before.

And finally, there is the smell of the place. That good electronic smell that reassures you that a good engineer has seen to it that all the equipment is working.

It is not surprising that many broadcasters love to fly their own planes. There is the same sense of isolation, of oneness with equipment and oneself. There is a sense of power, and at the same time, a sense of dependence on all of those dials and buttons and the wires behind them. Yet you clearly are at the center of things and the world seems to be rotating around this place.

Radio studios tend to be small, with only enough room for the control board area, you, a second chair for a guest, a telephone that lights instead of rings. It is not a place to be unless you have business there.

But what you are most aware of in that closed studio environment is time. It is as relevant as the air you breathe. It is the currency of radio. And it is always passing. Either you have so much time until you go on or so much time until you finish your shift. Everything revolves around the time. Your brain, your voice, your words are critical, but time is the real master. It is a finite commodity, and that is why so much of radio is predetermined, scripted, written beforehand. Only then can a producer be sure that what he or she wants to have said—*all* of what he or she wants to have said—can be said in the allotted amount of time. That is why radio networks and stations have news writers; there is only so much time for the newscast. And that is why commercials are written to a specified length; the advertiser has paid for either 10 seconds, 20 seconds, 30 or 60 seconds. And why there are copywriters and traffic coordinators who plan out the schedule and produce the almighty "logs" or schedules. Time is precious.

It has always been that way in radio. The broadcast day is defined by hours, not programs. A station goes on the air at a certain time, goes off the air at a certain time, changes hosts or formats at certain times.

Access to the airwaves is the prize—to the DJ with a love for music, to the journalist with a thirst for reporting, to the advertiser who seeks access to audiences to sell his or her wares. But access is parceled out in time—a four-hour air shift for the announcer, a 30-second spot for the advertiser.

Time is the only thing that commercial radio has to sell. And time is also the ultimate program arbiter. Everyone has a program or an interview or a record or a report to air. Everyone wants a show. But there are only so many hours to divide up, no matter how compelling the case.

The confinement that time imposes on an announcer is striking. Time is his constant companion. An air shift of four hours or more creates an isolated world of its own. You do not see your listener. But that in itself creates the tremendous desire to reach out to that listener. And that desire to reach out was what Arthur Godfrey brought back to WRC in January 1932 after a four-month absence.

He dove into his work at a frantic pace, working from sign on to sign off, taking any assignment offered.

He sounded different on the air. He was still adhering to the rules of time and script, but he had dropped the formal way of speaking, first by speaking directly, later by adding colloquialisms like "ain't," "gosh," and "gee whiz." Management, tied inexorably to the traditional formal announcing style, was quick to spot the difference and it didn't like what it heard. Expecting Arthur's voice to "boom out, full of the spurious oomph that announcers liked to affect, [they] first thought he was still sick and should rest for a while longer. The chief announcer put an arm around him and said sadly, 'Old man, you just haven't got it any more.'"[1] He was asked to correct his style. But Godfrey was stubborn, undaunted, and he kept to his new one-listener-at-a-time approach.

"I guess I was a considerable pain in the neck to everyone. I hobbled around on crutches and got in everybody's way."[2]

Between on-air shifts, he began to experiment with mixing material from different recordings on different turntables. Recording tape had not yet been invented, so it required jumping from one source to another in "real time," live on the air. There were records of sound effects—musical fanfares, applause, laughter—and he carefully marked the records themselves at the precise spots where they began and ended. Then he would go on the air and create the illusion of full orchestras or studio audiences when in reality he was still alone in the control room. "I could ask a question of an artist, [start] the record at a pre-marked place, have her answer me, and then, with a sound effects record, have an audience giggle at our little joke."[3]

He experimented for advertisers as well, and was soon enhancing their scripts with sound effects behind the on-air reader. Listeners were fascinated, often unsure of who was in the studio. He'd answer phone calls on the air (long before technology allowed the caller to be heard on air) and if the caller was complaining about his ruse, he'd say, "What's the matter old boy: you don't care for this program? Tsk! Tsk! Tell you what you do: see that little knob on your radio that turns the dial? O.K. grab it 'twixt thumb and forefinger. Now turn it! So long, pal."[4]

On the *Aunt Sue* show, he began selling the sponsor's product differently: "You tell mommy Uncle Arthur said to get some Schneider's Dan-Dee Bread right away. If she gets any other bread, don't you eat it!" On his network announcing chores, he also began to act on instinct.

Allowed to write his own material for the military band concerts, he " began to make up stories about the composers…. Many's the time that I acquainted the listeners with the little-known 'fact,' for instance, that Ludwig Van Beethoven wrote

his *Sonata Pathetique* whilst cruising down the Rhine in an old birch bark canoe presented to him by a descendant of Pocahontas." Listeners did not dispute him. "We were all convinced that nobody ever listened to any of those programs except the engineers in the control room."[5]

As announcer for the popular but fully scripted and formal national *Farm and Home Hour*, heard daily on the NBC Blue Network, he signed the show off with "This is the National Harm and Fome Hour," followed by the NBC chimes in the wrong order. The next day he was taken off the show. The chief announcer strongly suggested he switch to the engineering side of the operation. But WRC's audiences loved it. As sponsors continued to sign on, the chief announcer and program manager had no other choice than to spend the entire year putting up with Arthur's new approach.[6] In later years, Godfrey would note the most important thing his WRC battles had taught him about commercial broadcast management: "They don't care what you say on air as long as it sells."[7]

For every commercial he was hired to do he made an extra $5 or $10, and was now able to earn a respectable $75 or $80 in an average week.

In early 1933, Scoop Russell approached Arthur with a new opportunity—a way for him to sell goods and his approach to radio in a new format, and bail out the local management as well. Rival CBS had changed its Washington station affiliation from WMAL to WJSV. NBC saw this as an opportunity to unbundle all its Blue Network programming from WRC. It leased WMAL, creating two Washington outlets for itself. Godfrey was "elected" to start up a morning record show on WMAL, the new affiliate. He would host it, give the time and weather, sell the spots and read the copy—seven days a week. He was skeptical. "Why me?" he asked Russell. "Because you seem to be the only announcer around here who can talk, fool with dials and spin records all at the same time." When he asked Russell when he was going to sleep, Russell replied, "Take your girl friends home early and get to bed at a decent hour. The program department will select the records for you. You just play them—you can sleep while the records are on."[8]

Godfrey was furious. Early morning men "swept the floor, answered the phone [and] served as [their] own engineers."[9] Radio research was almost non-existent at the time. But as *Collier's* magazine later put it, "Most industry people held the prevalent belief that nobody was tuned in anyway." He saw it as a demotion and considered his NBC career at an end. But with no other job on the horizon, he took it on.

The show premiered on March 4, 1933, the same day as Franklin Delano Roosevelt's inauguration for his first term. Later, when he and FDR had an opportunity to meet, Godfrey told him about the coincidence. After that, "whenever I was privileged to speak with him for a moment he'd remind me of it and say, 'Glad to see you're still in office too!'"[10]

On air, Godfrey undertook his new routine: playing phonograph records, using sound effects, announcing the time, and reading bits of promotional information. There was no commercial copy to read on the new station because there were no sponsors. By the fifth morning, "suffocated by boredom," as a later publicity story put it, he "simply took matters into his own hands." And, as he would become famous for doing years later on the CBS network, shared his frustrations with his audience:

"It's now seven o'clock and the first record I see on the schedule is the Overture to Orpheus, and ain't that a terrible way to start the day?" When the record was finished, I said, "Phew—what a noisy mess! If anybody's still listening to this station, he's nuts! I suppose you want to

know what time it is? O.K. it's four and a half minutes past seven—get it? Seven-o-four-and-a-half. Set your watch, because I ain't gonna tell you again. What do you think this is? Western Union or something?"

Then I'd put on the next record, after which I'd say, "Better set your watch again—it's eight minutes past seven now. The weatherman says in the paper it's gonna be clear and cold today. Well, he's right because it sure is cold out there—but it ain't clear: It was snowing up a storm when I came in fifteen minutes ago. Look out the window—see for yourself." After a bit I'd say, "Well, its ten minutes past seven, let's see what this next record is they got scheduled. Oh NO! Not selections from Aida. That's the goofy program director we've got. The stuffy old coot. He picks out these records at four or five o'clock yesterday afternoon for this morning's broadcast. I'll guarantee you, he's not listening to them. He's sound asleep. Nobody with any sense would listen to this stuff at this hour of the day."

I'd put the record on and it would get to a particularly noisy part and I'd lift the needle, pick up the record and smash it over the open microphone into a thousand pieces. There would be stunned silence, while the transmitter engineer in the control room started at me aghast, and I'd say softly [into the microphone], "I bet you won't have to listen to that one again, I betcha."[11]

Nothing like this had ever been heard before on Washington radio—and probably not anywhere else either. While Arthur was doing his daily shenanigans, the other stations and their announcers were adhering to good diction, scripts, and the usual formality. Yet all of this was designed not so much to entertain his audiences, but to get him off the morning shift.

When Kenneth Berkeley, the program manager, finally called him in, it was only to tell him to keep up the good work. "I'm told it's very entertaining," he said. "Keep right on the way you're doing." One day, desperate to end his 7 to 9:30 A.M. assignment, he gave Scoop Russell a 'razzberry' over the air, adding that he [the boss] certainly wouldn't be up that early to hear it. "But if he is," added Arthur defiantly, "I won't be here tomorrow morning."[12] That too was to no avail. Scoop told him to continue and Godfrey dutifully kept getting up at 6 A.M. each day for his shift. Within three months, the show had caught on.

At this point, WMAL's first station manager was appointed; the job was given to an announcer Arthur had helped train. Believing he had been passed over, Godfrey complained to Scoop Russell, who gave him some of the most important advice he would ever receive in his career: "Arthur, the world is full of people who are always cutting their own throats on the barbed wire by trying too hard to reach the grass on the other side of the fence. You're no executive, but you've got the makings of a terrific radio personality. If you keep going like you're doing, someday you can own twenty stations like WMAL if you want to and hire that many managers. Stay in front of that microphone, boy— that's where you belong!"

After that, Godfrey never tried to get off the show again. "From that time on, every move I made was an effort to improve the program."[13] With advice from Vince Callahan, the sales and promotion manager, the show was renamed *The WMAL Breakfast Club*. The idea was to have listeners become members. Membership certificates called "Licenses to Listen" were offered and within a year they had issued more than 60,000. Many listeners hung the "authorizations" over their radios.[14] That was all the data Callahan needed to begin selling commercial announcements at $2.50 each. By year-end *The WMAL Breakfast Club* had 88 sponsors and was bringing in $180,000 a year.

On the other hand, Godfrey was earning only $42.50 a week for that part of his work and only $90 overall from other WMAL and WRC and NBC assignments.

The station was not about to pay him more than the manager was making, no matter how much he was bringing in. Unhappy with his income, but committed to his work, he continued.

By now, Godfrey was back in stride physically, flying again and even fronting a band known as Red Godfrey's Melodians that played the Washington clubs. He burned the proverbial candle at both ends: on dates almost every night and into the morning hours, then rushing in at the last minute to start the radio shows. His occasional hangovers were obvious at times, even to his listeners, who had begun to recognize every nuance in that distinctive voice. Packing everything in as he had always done, he would hardly ever prepare for a shift. Yet, he never ran out of things to say or do once on the air and the more audience and sponsors he brought in, the more it assured him that rehearsals of any kind were totally unnecessary. Twenty, forty years later, he would still be arriving "unprepared" yet raring to go and hardly ever without enough words and thoughts to carry off a listenable performance.

Arthur Godfrey had now become a particular favorite of the thousands of single women who worked for the federal government. As he visualized that one person he was talking to each morning, he now pictured someone young and female. Early on, he was handed copy for a lingerie commercial. "Filmy, clingy, alluring silk underpanties in devastating pink and black," he read. Finished, he added, "Whew! Is my face red!" WMAL management waited for the inevitable complaint call from the sponsor. Instead, there was a stampede of ladies to the local department store demanding the items. Again, it only convinced management that he should stay on the morning shift.

But on January 2, 1934, his NBC days came to an end. It all began on a positive note. Ben Bernie, who led one of the top bands of the twenties and early thirties, had a popular weekly show on NBC at the time. Whenever he came to Washington to do a remote broadcast, he asked for Arthur to be his emcee, and January 2nd was to be one of the nights. Godfrey rose at 6:00 A.M., did his morning show, stayed at the station till 1:30 P.M., then left for the Willard Hotel to rehearse with Bernie. Three hours later, he was at the Press Building at WRC as Uncle Arthur on the *Aunt Sue and Polly* show, then rushed back to WMAL for a five-minute program, then, at eight o'clock, he was at the Willard again to announce the Ben Bernie show, then back to WMAL to announce *The Poet Prince* show, and he finally returned to the Willard to announce Bernie's repeat show for the West Coast. "By the time I left the Willard, I was dragging. When I reached my apartment I got my boss [Kenneth Berkeley] on the phone. 'I'm bushed,' I said. 'Get yourself another boy for the morning program. I'm going to sleep.' 'All right,' said the manager, who promptly went back to sleep himself and forgot the entire conversation." Having left word with the apartment desk not to be disturbed, Godfrey slept late, took off for Congressional Airport to do some flying in his glider, and, in typical fashion, showed up thirty seconds before air time for the *Aunt Sue and Polly* show. After the show, Berkeley hauled him in. "I don't like your attitude. Where have you been?" Arthur reminded him of his late night phone call, explaining that he would not be in and why. The manager wasn't satisfied.

"I blew." Arthur talked about how many hours he had worked the day before, how he hadn't even been paid to do the Ben Bernie stints, how much money he was making for the stations, and—just as he had done at Hasbrouck Heights High School—he quit.[15]

9

A Call from Walter Winchell

IMPULSIVENESS WAS NOT ONE OF Godfrey's most helpful attributes. Throughout his life, he was often quick to anger or quick to repent. He could be giving and caring one minute and totally disregard you the next. Impulsiveness cost him dearly. Once, at the height of his career, he fired his music director on the spot, only to call him back minutes later to apologize. It was too late. The man took his leave. At more positive times, if he heard someone sing whom he liked, he'd immediately offer the individual a spot on one of his shows. Most cast members were hired that way. Those were his positive impulses. But when Arthur walked out on WMAL and NBC it was clearly the negative forces at work. And within hours, after walking the streets of Washington, he was genuinely sorry he had quit. He was convinced he would never get a job like this again. "I'll be thirty-one next August, and here I am all washed up." Next day, he apologized to the manager, Kenneth

Berkeley. His apology was accepted but his job was not offered back to him. Rightly or wrongly, Berkeley had had it with Arthur Godfrey. And Scoop Russell, in deference to his local manager, backed him up. Though Russell did promise to pay him till he found another job, Godfrey was finished at NBC.

"I really did think I was all washed up with the radio business. I was so thoroughly steeped in the doctrine of the invincibility of the National Broadcasting Company that I thought any other facilities were just [a] waste [of time]." [1] That included CBS. He had received some money from the insurance company after his accident and had invested part of it to start a flying school. "To hell with broadcasting," he thought. "I'd rather fly anyway. I won't eat very well, but it will be fun." But only a few days later he received a call from Harry Butcher, CBS' top man in Washington who oversaw the CBS-owned and -operated station in the capital, WJSV.

Godfrey had met Harry Butcher at a cocktail party some time earlier. He remembered that that evening Butcher was in the company of a Major Dwight D. Eisenhower. Arthur was flying high with NBC at the time and he hadn't paid Butcher much attention.

There have been many Harry Butchers, as well as Scoop Russells, throughout the history of local broadcasting—astute men and women who are consummate managers with good business heads and who also have a sixth sense as to what their audiences want. They turn out to be terrific talent scouts, who can see beyond youth and early mistakes and recognize potential in all kinds of men and women. They are willing to give young entertainers and performers and news people their first and sometimes their second or third chances to prove themselves. The Harry Butchers are the people behind the stars, the visionaries who encourage them to excel, while knowing all along that in time they will probably lose these young people to yet another manager who operates on a bigger stage. Butcher had been trying to produce a viable program opposite Godfrey, even trying an organ program with Bob Trout, who fortunately went on to a different career in CBS News. Butcher had found himself listening to Godfrey regularly, and now he had a chance to bring him to CBS.

He and Arthur met at the airfield. "What's the matter with you?" Butcher asked. He looked around at the sorry little aircraft. "This isn't for you. You should be *on* the air, not *in it!* Come on and work for CBS on WJSV." Butcher offered him a morning show. Godfrey expressed interest, but having learned a good lesson at WMAL about how talent can be used by management, he added, "But on a commission basis. I want a guaranteed salary and a commission. I'm tired of making money for somebody else and reaping

peanuts for myself. I want a guarantee of at least fifty dollars a week, and a dollar per spot participation."[2] Butcher agreed. It was the first of many negotiations that Godfrey would win over his thirty-eight years with CBS. He might have been overly impressed with his own good looks and popularity, but when it came to sales ability, he knew he was the best in the business. Arthur Godfrey grew rich by holding out for what he believed was only his fair share.

During the two weeks leading up to his premiere on WSJV, 80 percent of his WMAL sponsors quit that station and signed on with Godfrey at his new address. No one at WMAL could have predicted such a turn of events. WMAL was down, but it wasn't out. Berkeley countered by hiring Don Douglas, a well-known NBC talent from New York to take over *The Breakfast Club*. Godfrey, still caught in the glow of the NBC aura, and not accustomed to big league competition, was genuinely concerned. Then he came up with an idea. Douglas was scheduled to premiere in Arthur's old seat on a Saturday morning. Godfrey proposed to Harry Butcher that he, Arthur, would go on the air Friday at midnight and stay on all night. "Maybe the listeners will tune me in early Saturday to see if I'm still alive after the all-night deal, and forget all about this joker." "O.K." responded Butcher. "It will be a good for at least a line in *Variety*."[3] They would have the airwaves all to themselves. And that went for listeners too—if there were any.

The logistics weren't easy; the Washington studios were closed, unavailable at that hour, and Arthur would have to broadcast from the transmitter shack in a swamp near Alexandria, Virginia. Butcher offered him a telephone, a mike, and one engineer. Friday at midnight, with telephone, turntable, and a stack of records, Godfrey took to the air in what was the first all-night call-in show in radio history, saying, "This is Arthur Godfrey. I'm going to play some records, and I'm going to be on all night with you. We're doing a test to see [from] how far [away] we can get listeners."[4] Throughout the eight hours, he gave out the phone number and invited requests. When calls came in, he'd put the phone up to the microphone for listeners to hear the caller's comments as well as his own. One woman from New York called three times, propositioning Arthur along the way.

As morning neared, he complained about the swamp and the lack of coffee. "What happened next is one of the all time believe-it-or-nots of radio," he later recalled. "Before dawn there must have 3000 or 4000 automobiles out there with coffee, sandwiches, and cake. It was hard to believe so many people were up at that hour. The U.S. Park Police and the Virginia police were yanked out of bed to direct traffic. And by the time the night was ended, I had talked on the phone to at least one person in each of the 48 states, plus a dozen from Canada, a couple in Panama, and one or two in South America. People even called by radio phone from ships at sea, and telegrams and radiograms—and later mail came in from all over the world."[5]

But one call made all the difference. At 4:30 A.M., the phone rang. "Hello, Arthur. This is Walter Winchell."

Walter Winchell, a nationally syndicated newspaper columnist, had a rat-a-tat style and a particular skill at linking important news and entertainment news that was an early precursor of the kinds of celebrity journalism that became the rage in the 1990s. Winchell had a huge national audience for his daily column. And he was always on the look out for new talent to tell his readers about.

Winchell congratulated Godfrey on his feat and explained that he was hosting a party in New York and among those present—and listening to the show along with the other guests—was Ben Bernie, the bandleader. Bernie had told Winchell and the other guests that he knew this Arthur Godfrey; that he worked with Arthur when he did his remote broadcasts from Washington. Winchell asked Godfrey to play some Bernie selections. Arthur complied, mixing in imitations of Bernie, as well.

A few days later, Winchell wrote about Arthur in his national column. "Godfrey is stuck down there across the Potomac from the Capitol. But he is big time. His quips are sly—and his fly-talk is terrifically Broadway or Big Town. Some shrewd radio showman should bag him for New York to make our midnight programs breezier.... I haven't picked a flop yet."[6]

Within days, Godfrey's mail brought him 32 contracts and business proposals, including a $3,200 certified check from a Manhattan night club. Overwhelmed, he went to New York to ask Winchell for advice. Winchell had been listening to him every night for several weeks and writing about him almost daily. "He was lying in bed being shaved by a barber," Godfrey recalled. "'Boy,' I thought, 'this is living!'" Winchell advised him to take the night-club offer. They discussed the pros and cons. "I can't get up in front of people," he told Winchell. "I'm a radio man, not a night club performer."[7] So he accepted an offer from CBS, for network appearances from New York at $100 a week. It was a seven-year contract, though he hardly ever got any work out of it.

There were two exceptions, however, both during those first few months: the first was a network show called *Manhattan Parade*, which he later referred to as "Manhattan Pee-rade," broadcast Tuesday and Thursday afternoons. Godfrey would do the morning show he had just begun on WJSV, then hop a flight to New York City, do the show, and return that evening to

It was influential syndicated columnist Walter Winchell who first brought Arthur Godfrey to national attention after he picked up Arthur's all-night inaugural broadcast for WJSV. Arthur would call it "the luckiest day of my life." (Library of American Broadcasting, University of Maryland.)

Washington. But when, in passing, he casually mentioned a product advertised on NBC, he was fired. In March, he began doing commercials on network programs sponsored by Chesterfield Cigarettes because the sponsor felt that the "tobacco belt" sound of his voice would appeal to listeners.[8] A dozen years later, Arthur was to become inseparably associated with Chesterfields. But not in 1934; the company didn't like what it heard and he was dropped.

Tail between his legs, a humbled Arthur Godfrey now turned his full-time efforts to the new WSJV show. "I had gotten to thinking like a smart-aleck Broadway showman, and people don't want Broadway every day. But little by little, I regained the humility I had lost. I got back to sunsets, fishing, horses. My interest in people returned."[9] The show improved, clients were pleased, and fans began to increase.

Sometime later, Winchell helped him again. By then, Godfrey was back on top in Washington. They had caught up in New York and in the process of conversation, Arthur told Winchell what he was earning. Winchell was appalled. "Listen kid," he said. "In this business you've got to make it while you're hot, 'cause you'll be cold a long, long time! Don't let those guys give you that 'can't afford it' line. Nuts! You must be bringing in at least a quarter of a million bucks a year to that station for time they couldn't give away if you weren't there. They're paying you a lousy four thousand for it, and you ought to be getting at least that much a month." Winchell told him, "Sometimes you have to get nasty with people and swing a club!" When Godfrey asked him what his club might be, Winchell told him it was his audience, that Arthur had to show Butcher and CBS what they'd lose if he wasn't there. So Godfrey stopped showing up on certain days and on those days the sponsors wouldn't pay. When Butcher called him, he wouldn't take his phone calls. Finally Butcher gave in, offering him one hundred dollars a week. Godfrey refused, telling him he didn't want a salary any more. What he wanted was 20 percent of the gross take on the show. "And I will dictate the price to the clients." Butcher protested. But Arthur won out.[10]

He was now an "independent artist." And it wasn't very long before the gross income to the Washington station from his programs was over a half-million dollars per year, unheard of in local radio at the time.

10

Washington Days

IT WASN'T NEW YORK, BUT IN 1934 Washington, D.C., was hardly the boondocks. With Roosevelt's inauguration in March, the city quickly became the nerve center in the battle to overcome what was now officially recognized as a deep economic depression. As FDR announced program after program to correct the economy, it seemed everyone who was anyone was making a trip to the nation's capital either to serve, testify, or protest the new government's activist policies.

Like WRC and WMAL, WJSV was more than a local radio station. Owned and operated by CBS, it was its Washington headquarters as well, the network's pickup point for news out of the city. That year, CBS launched three daily newscasts that included not only reports from CBS' headquarters in New York City, but also from the capital. As radio news grew, so did WJSV, eventually serving as home for Elmo Davis, George Fielding Eliot, John

Charles Daly, Eric Sevareid and other key names in the new field of radio journalism. WJSV occupied the entire 8th floor of the Earle Theatre Building at 13th and E streets in downtown Washington. It included four studios, including one large floating studio, completely soundproof, that was used by the network. WJSV boasted a major mobile unit—a complete production studio on wheels—that was used all over the city for network and local programs. There was a house band.

The year 1934 was a banner one for the Columbia Broadcasting System (which was the way Bill Paley wanted CBS referred to wherever possible). Network radio was thriving in the midst of a national depression and reaching 20 million households. Over 65 percent of all U.S. households now owned a radio set. Though still second to NBC, the network now featured many of the top-rated shows, including *Burns & Allen*, *The Joe Penner Program*, *The Bing Crosby Program* featuring the

The WJSV radio staff assembled in the reception room of the Earle Building Studios in Washington for this 1937 Christmas photo, including Engineer Granville Klink, Jr. (top row, second from left); CBS VP and owner operator of WJSV Harry Butcher (top row, fourth from left); Arthur Godfrey (next row down, third from right); switchboard operator Marie McGrain (bottom row, third from left); and Arthur's closest colleague during his Washington days, Arch McDonald, the voice of the Washington Senators, as Santa Claus. (WTOP collection.)

Mills Brothers, vocalists Mildred Bailey, Morton Downey, Kate Smith, and two of the three women's serials on in the evening, *Just Plain Bill* and *Myrt and Marge*.

Godfrey called his new morning series *The Sun Dial Show*. It ran from 7:00 to 9:30 A.M. six days a week. In many ways, he ran the *Sun Dial* in the same way he had *The Breakfast Club*. He still did time checks, only now chimes introduced the frequent updates. He still played phonograph records, but now that he could pick

the selections, there was a heavy emphasis on novelty tunes. He still did all the commercials, arrived only minutes before air time (if then), and ad-libbed the entire program. But there were several new elements.

For one thing, the show was less structured, allowing Godfrey to read letters from listeners and comment on his life away from the microphone. He now could grouse about anything he felt like. He interspersed the music with announcements of upcoming events in the city and the suburbs, talking in a folksy way about who was running the event and why it was worth your getting out to it.

Then there was Mug Richardson. Margaret "Mug" Richardson had been Miss North Carolina of 1934. On her way to Atlantic City to compete in the Miss America Pageant that year, she stopped off in Washington. Somehow she and Arthur met. He was taken by her beauty and by her accent. He invited her up to the show. "They had a ball with me because of my thick southern accent," she recalled in later years. "They just kept asking me to read advertisements for them."[1] Mug didn't win the Miss America contest, but shortly afterward she was invited by Godfrey to become his "right-hand person" at a salary of $35 a week. She accepted and they began a 17-year association.

"Mug was all the staff I had," Godfrey noted in 1953.[2] Mug would answer his phone calls (there were lots of them), handle publicity, pick the records, go with him when he gave speeches, and collect news articles, letters, and other ideas she thought he might want to use on his programs. She'd sit beside him on the air each morning with her file of materials. He used what he wanted. But she was more than a Girl Friday. She quickly became his strategist. He began to record every show he did, and he and Mug would stay up for hours reviewing his performance. Mug would balance out Godfrey's desire to perfect his work with reality, that what he did best was just be Arthur. He showered her with gifts and if they were romantically involved, it was never common knowledge. He relied heavily on her taste and she was comfortable criticizing him when he needed it. As one staffer put it: "She ultimately became the person in charge of Arthur Godfrey." "She was my loyal devoted friend and severest critic and a constant source of encouragement," Godfrey

would recall in 1955.[3] It was probably no accident that when she left his side in 1951, he began to have his troubles with staff and the press.

But perhaps the most significant new element in the WJSV shows was Godfrey's attitude toward the sponsors: the only ones whose business he'd accept were those offering quality that he could see, touch, and feel.

"I realized that in order to have any influence that amounted to anything, I had to possess integrity; you had to believe what I had to say. There was only one way that I could make you believe what I had to say and that was to live the way you would want me to live if you wanted to believe me. Everything I did was done with that in mind, that it must be on the level, strictly; nobody could buy me for anything. And that was established by actually getting rid of clients who bought participations in a show when I found out that what they wanted me to say about their product wasn't true." He'd drop them. Few advertisers were ready for that. Some offered big money if he'd reconsider, but he rarely did.

"I knew that I didn't have any talent; I knew that if I was to have any longevity at all, I had to be somebody upon whom you would depend. Somebody who, whether you liked what I did or not, you had to believe what I told you because you knew it was true, and that's the way we established it, in Washington first and then New York later, the truth.... That when you listened to Godfrey, gosh darn it, what he said about a product was right; he believed it or he wouldn't tell you."[4]

"I remember one time I had a store in Washington that sold $40 suits for $7.50. And I [was reading off the script] and said, 'Wait a minute, wait a minute, $40 suits for—What's the matter with these things? $7.50?' I said to the audience, 'Let me look into this; don't, don't go near there today;

wait 'til I find out. Something wrong here. Maybe had a fire, I don't know, let me find out.' I had…Mug…go down to Seventh Street and [buy] one of these things and [she] brought it up to the office and sure enough it was a four-dollar suit. So I just kept in my office…. About ten o'clock here comes the store owner with three or four lawyers, gonna sue. And I took 'em into my office and I said, 'Here's one of your suits, we bought it this morning. You want to sue?' He shrugged his shoulders and walked out. Things like that got around town. People knew that I would not take anything I didn't believe in."[5] But that didn't mean he fawned over the sponsors he kept. He continued to razz them.

One of his favorite targets was Zlotnick the Furrier, who had a stuffed polar bear out in front of his shop in downtown Washington. "Every day the script ended with 'Zlotnick the Furrier, 12th and G Northwest, at the sign of the big white bear.' And one day I passed the store, and I saw that bear…It was a horrible, filthy lookin' thing. And when I came to that sentence 'at the sign of the big white' I said 'White? Did you folks ever take a good look at that bear? It's *filthy!* Sammy Zlotnick, you should be ashamed of yourself. The Board of Health should get you for this. Come on! Clean it up!' Well of course, everybody went down town to take a look at the filthy bear. And he was the happiest man in the world. When people came in to his [Zlotnik's] store and asked him why he didn't sue, he'd say 'For what? You came in, didn't you?'"[6]

Zlotnick's sales skyrocketed and to the furrier, Arthur could do no wrong. Once, according to a *Washington Daily News* account, Godfrey told his early morning audience that Zlotnick had a particular fur coat on sale "for a few hundred 'potatoes.'" A few hours later a listener arrived at the furrier with just that—two hundred potatoes—and Zlotnick made good on the

Godfrey offer.[7] The attendant newspaper publicity increased business even more.

"These were little tricks like that that I used to do to try to find ways to make you my listener…remember the name of the product and where you got it." [8]

Godfrey's creative energies could not be contained by the morning show alone. In 1935, he bought a 50 percent interest in a nightclub called Club Michele. He was the maestro and had his own orchestra, called Arthur Godfrey and all the Little Godfreys, a phrase he later applied to his cast on the CBS network shows. A local program was built around the orchestra and called *Godfrey's Gazette.* It ran Thursday nights at 9:00 opposite Rudy Vallee, who was then the most popular singer in the country on radio and on records. The Vallee show, which started in 1929, was one of NBC's most popular offerings, reaching an average of 38 percent of American homes each week. Arthur's *Gazette* held its own against Vallee, and Washington became the only city in the country where the NBC show did not hold sway.

"My sponsor…was Joe Cherner, an automobile dealer who sold 'Chernerized' second hand cars. Our sock act was a [young woman] I'd hired to represent 'the used car special of the week.' I called her Miss Used Car Special. When [she] walked on and I'd ask, 'Who are you?' she'd say, in Mae West tones, 'I'm a 1934 Ford V-8 De-Luxe 2-door sedan.' She made that simple bit of information so sexy it could have been illegal.

"'Pretty classy chassis you've got there,' I'd say. 'Have you ever been Chernerized?'

"'Have I ever been Chernerized!' she would exclaim. 'You should have seen what that handsome mechanic did to me this morning! I've had my valves ground and my carburetor tuned and my body has been polished until it glows.'"[9]

Offensive and politically incorrect by

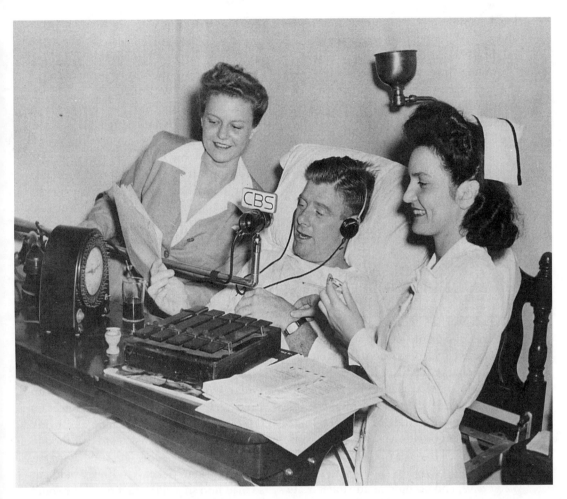

A hospital stay in October 1944 didn't hold Arthur back from his daily broadcasts on WABC New York and WJSV Washington. With the help of his assistant, Mug Richardson, he set up shop and broadcast right from his bed. Remotes like this were almost always Arthur's idea. (Joan Zacher collection.)

today's standards, at the time it was acceptable and effective. Rudy Vallee didn't have a chance.

There were also local and network assignments for Godfrey, hosting shows like *The Christmas Cheer Club*, that switched around town to cover popular dance bands as they performed at the city's various hotels and restaurants and the Loew's Capitol Theater. He was also in demand to emcee conferences and banquets, many of them broadcast by WJSV.

Often, the *Sun Dial* show would go on

location, with Godfrey broadcasting from the Tidal Basin during the height of the cherry blossom season or from other locales around the city. In 1944, when Godfrey had his appendix removed, he even broadcast from his hospital bed.

He still had energy left over to originate a one-hour *Moon Dial* show, from 11:00 to midnight every weeknight, for National Beer. "All of these shows were done live. I not only put the station on in the morning, I put it to bed at night, and in between times I did theater appearances, local commercial programs, and night clubs."[10] All for separate compensation, he might have added.

Among those who knew Godfrey well in those years was a young broadcast technician with the unlikely name of Granville Klink. Klink had been hired by CBS in July of 1937. Godfrey was in his heyday then, but something new had been added: the Associated Columbia Broadcast Technicians. CBS technicians had unionized and the days when an on-air talent like Godfrey could spin his own records were over. Klink's very first assignment was to "sign on the station at 6 A.M. and spin Arthur's records," which he did continually for the remainder of Arthur's years in Washington.

Klink was an accomplished engineer who was in demand not only at WJSV but at CBS as well. He went on to be the engineer-in-charge of all of FDR's Fireside Chats. He traveled the country with the president, along with CBS correspondents. He handled thousands of CBS news and entertainment broadcasts emanating from Washington. He was assigned to such CBS network radio shows as *Gene Autry* and *We The People*, and accompanied singer Kate Smith on her tours of the Army Camps during World War II. It was Klink who was at Godfrey's side for his famous broadcast of FDR's funeral procession. And it was Klink who later set up CBS's microwave system for Godfrey's famous live radio broadcasts and early telecasts from his Leesburg farm.

Granville Klink worked for CBS in Washington for sixty years. He greatly admired Arthur, writing a memoir about him that chronicled the almost frantic pace Arthur kept:

"Arthur lived in Vienna, Virginia. And he had worn a well-worn path from the farm to the front entrance of the Earle Building.... Virginia State Troopers had stopped him so many times on his early morning dash up Virginia Route #7, that those who recognized his car just stood back and watched him speed by. I think Arthur's occasional kidding of them on the air had a lot do with that.

"He usually arrived on E Street about 10 to 15 minutes before 6 A.M. airtime, jumped out of his car and up the elevator to the 8th floor. There was always an elevator [operator] waiting for him. ... He left the engine running in his car for the waiting...garage attendant who would then drive it [away] for parking.

"The staff announcer and I were primed and ready to go on the air as soon as he walked through the studio soundlock. He'd just walk in, maybe get a mike check, and just begin. This was natural talent on the hoof!"[11]

Occasionally Godfrey would be late for sign-on, having been stopped by a newly assigned State Trooper who was not familiar with his early morning dash up Route 7. On those days, the announcer on duty would sign the station on and Klink would start playing his records off the top of the pile. After being late and having received a traffic ticket, Godfrey would get so mad he'd smash the first record he could get his hands on. "You had to get used to those things. It would shake you up a little bit, but we knew he was going to be a little unique in some of his ways. So, we got used to that. It was very entertaining, I think."[12]

"After [Arthur] got started, he would often kid around with Marie McGrain, the early morning WJSV switchboard operator. Her board was just outside the soundlock and Arthur could watch her from the studio. If the switchboard showed no signs of activity, he would take the radio audience into his confidence and tell them that Marie was lonely way out there at the switchboard, so please give her a call and cheer her up. In a short time, the switchboard would light up like a Christmas tree."[13]

Klink particularly admired Godfrey's technical expertise. "He was very meticulous about how he sounded on local and network originations and expected the technician in the studio control room to pay particular attention to audio balance, microphone set up and mixing on all of his programs." Many years later, on a *Moon Dial* show for which Godfrey had pre-recorded his own voice material from New York, he personally typed out and sent detailed instructions and a well-defined script for the Washington engineer, who was to add the music at the time of airing:

ARCH McDONALD'S MOON DIAL
11:15–11:45 P.M.
Thursday, Jan 4th, 1945.

Transcribed by Arthur Godfrey

NOTE TO KLINK: Not knowing whether or not you've done one of these things of mine, I'm going to great lengths to explain exactly what's what. If a lot of it is all too, too obvious and unnecessary please fo'give me, suh! I'd rather give you too much dope than leave you out on a limb. Right? Right!!

All my music is 78 RPM, except the theme music. Start my transcription and the theme simultaneously at 11:15:00 on the nose—and these timings given below should work out perfectly—I hope! Be sure to open my switch and start all records exactly on the second given—WHETHER OR NOT I'M STILL TALKING OR MUSIC IS STILL PLAYING—on acct of sometimes I deliberately talk over a record to help preserve the informality of the show and to help hide the fact that this is a transcription. INCIDENTALLY, I myself give the necessary transcription credits, so it won't be necessary for any other announcements. Here we go!

What followed was a rundown of the entire show by minutes and seconds.

"Arthur Godfrey was a very kind hearted person," Klink recalled in his memoir. "When one of our WJSV telephone operators was in the hospital during the early days of television, he called one morning and asked me to buy a television set, install it in her hospital room and charge it to his account. Hospital rooms in those days had no television sets or radios. At Christmas time, he always gave those who worked directly with him, war bonds, a wallet, etc. When I worked with him on special shows, he would give me an additional $25. That was big money in those days."[14]

Godfrey seemed to be doing everything right. And, unlike the NBC management, Butcher and the WJSV management were smart enough to stay out of his way.

In 1953, Godfrey reminisced about those good years in the late 1930s. "I wasn't rich, but I was well off. I bought my first farm in 1935 and I was happily breeding horses and feeding cattle and learning farming the hard way – by paying through the nose. I had a thirty-two-foot ACF cruiser in which, for nearly seven years, I stalked the striped bass, bluefish, and sea trout in the Potomac Bay…. Bob Ashburn and I had a little flying school going down at Hybla Valley, just south of Alexandria, Virginia…. Life was busy and full, and my programs were the tales of my adventures. I talked of flying incessantly, promoting the schools and the air lines and the aviation branches of the armed services."[15]

11

Radio's Fly Boy

THE RE-ENTRY OF HALLEY'S COMET into the earth's atmosphere in the late 1980s could not begin to generate the public reaction of wonder, anticipation, and fear that it had back in 1910 when it made its first twentieth century appearance. Those were simpler times, and a natural phenomenon such as the comet, with all of the questions it raised about the mysteries of outer space, consumed the free time of many Americans that year. It also caused a fair degree of hysteria. "Many, many people thought it was the end of the world," Godfrey later recalled. "People sold everything they had....This was the end of everything."[1] None of the excitement was lost on the Godfrey family.

On a fall evening after sunset, 7-year-old Arthur and his parents gathered on the front lawn with some neighbors to watch the comet. The Godfrey house in Hasbrouck Heights was on a little hilltop, offering a commanding view of the sky. But it was a sound, not a sight, that riveted the attention of these young families that night.

"All of a sudden a roar started up," Godfrey recalled. "It got increasingly loud. Terrible roar. Strange to all of us. And it seemed like it was overpowering, taking over all of us. And of course, those who were frightened that the end of the world was here were influenced by that roar too, and they knew that was it. This was the end. And some of them fell to beating their breasts, and beating on the ground, and begging for forgiveness and so forth, and it scared the hell out of me.... I wasn't frightened of the noise or the comet, I was scared of these people going nuts. I didn't know what was going on.

"And just then I happened to look up, and an airplane went by, treetop level. I can see him today, with his cap on backwards, the goggles, the shirt fluttering in the apparent wind, sitting way out there in front, and he was doing a good 35, 38 miles an hour, you know. And went across.

My mother fainted. My father let go of me to grab his wife, and they never saw the airplane till it was out of sight, because it was, as I say, at treetop level. And I never forgot that. I thought that was the most beautiful sight I had ever seen in my life. And I vowed that one day I'd learn to fly one of those things."[2]

Arthur Godfrey's name does not appear in most books on aviation history. Yet his contributions to the industry are legendary. Over the course of his life, he logged over 14,000 hours in planes of every variety. He was authorized to fly virtually any aircraft owned by the U.S. Air Force and the U.S. Navy. At the time of his death, he had flown virtually two-thirds of all the aircraft models manufactured in the U.S. during his lifetime. He was involved in numerous international aviation adventures worthy of books and films in their own right. He flew with legends like Eddie Rickenbacker, Dick Merrill, Tony LeVier, and Tex Johnston, all of whom would vouch for his skill as an aviator. While his accomplishments in the air are not nearly as noteworthy as those of the Wright brothers, or of Charles Lindbergh, he made, through broadcasting, a significant contribution of his own.

"Few Americans, including professional airmen, have championed aviation with the conviction and keen perception as the genial redhead," wrote *Flying* magazine in 1958. "On radio and television, in newspapers and magazines, and in countless speeches, this deeply patriotic American has led an unrelenting crusade to bring about a basic public understanding of airpower."[3]

His efforts once led Senator George A. Smathers to tell Congress that "Arthur Godfrey is one of the best-informed men, either in or out of the government, on the matter of this nation's air power."[4] They prompted Air Force General Curtis LeMay to comment: "Arthur Godfrey's constant devotion to adequate American airpower, civilian and military, has done much to help our people realize the need for overall air superiority."[5] And it led Eastern Airlines president Eddie Rickenbacker to present him with a retired Eastern DC-3 as a gift of thanks.

Ten years after his first glimpse of an airplane, Godfrey managed to barter his way to a ride in one. It was while he was working as an instructor at the Navy's primary radio school in Hampton Roads, Virginia. He went over to the air station one afternoon to get acquainted with some of the pilots. The crew of an F-5L flying boat was having trouble with their radios. When Godfrey fixed the problem, they invited him aboard for a ride. The friendship continued, Arthur trading odd jobs for rides. The captain let him take the controls once or twice.

After returning from his tour of duty at sea, Godfrey managed to hop an occasional flight with old-time barnstormers. But it wasn't until 1929, after he had started his radio career in Baltimore, that he could afford to learn to fly in earnest. His first lesson was in an OX-5 Travel Air biplane, and cost $35. That was a week's wages back then, so the lessons were few and far between. But the more he flew, the more he wanted to fly.

When he arrived at NBC in Washington, Godfrey finally had the money to pursue his avocation in earnest. His instructors were hard-working men who made a living in aviation the old-fashioned way. George Brinkerhoff operated the nation's oldest airport at College Park, Maryland, for decades. And Bob Ashburn, soon to become Godfrey's flying school partner, worked as an airline mechanic at night so he could keep Beacon Field running by day. He taught Arthur all about single-engine flying, and about seaplanes. Together, they flew hundreds of hours.

His greatest thrill behind the controls of an aircraft occurred the first time he reached 2,000 feet in a glider, powered only by the columns of rising air he had managed to find and take advantage of. "That thrill in '31 exceeds all others, including my first solo and the time last spring when I flew an Air Force F-101 Voodoo in excess of 1,100 miles an hour," Godfrey told *Flying* in 1958.[6]

It was his passion for gliders that placed him on the road to Congressional Airport on that fateful day in 1931, in the path of the truck that would shatter his bones, but not his spirit. He refused to let his injuries keep him out of the air. To the contrary, after many months of hospitalization, he was behind the controls of an airplane again long before he could walk or drive. When he finally received $5,000 from the insurance company for injuries sustained in his accident, he paid his lawyers $1,500, bought three airplanes with the rest, and started a flying school with Ashburn and some friends. "We were fat in airplanes— an Aeronca C-3, a Taylor Cub and half interest in an OX-5 Challenger," he recalled. "But man, were we thin on students!"[7]

So Godfrey, ever the salesman and now speaking in the innovative style he had perfected during his hospital days, began telling his radio listeners about flying. "In those days, everyone who flew was [considered] a nut.... I started talking about it on my early morning shows: how beautiful it was to fly; the experiences you had when you were in the air...." He once told his listeners about the late summer sunrises "and what an experience it would be if they'd come down and let me fly them in my airplane from just before sunup, so they could see the sun rise twice in the same day. Well, I made a big mistake.... Something like 2,500 people came out to that airfield to get that ride. And I had to call up every son of a gun I knew within 50 miles that owned an airplane to come over and help me fly these people to make it good. Which we did."[8]

He would dream up schemes to increase business at his flying school, like staying aloft for 12 hours one freezing winter day, hand pumping fuel from an extra tank. Whoever could guess closest to the exact hour, minute, and second that he would land—without any power and out of gas—would win a private flying course. He talked up the event on *The Sun Dial Show* and hundreds turned out to watch.

"The airplane had no heat in it. No sides in the cockpit. And the temperature was a good 25 degrees above zero, just below freezing. And after I'd got in the air, about an hour, that coffee which we had been tanking up on began to make itself known. And I was in this, encased in these embalming clothes, you know. It was a pretty sight, when I landed."[9]

Ernie Pyle, the aviation editor on the *Washington Daily News*, was there, waiting with a photographer. The winner guessed his landing time within two minutes. But in spite of the publicity, the endurance flight attracted few paying students, and the flying school went under.

As the small airports around Washington struggled to survive during the 1930s, Godfrey continued to talk about them on his show. And although he never realized any financial gain from his promotional stunts, he continued to take people flying. "I love to take people up," he said, "especially for their first ride. I love to show 'em how safe airplanes really are!"[10] In later years, he heard from more than one senior airline captain that he, Arthur, had given them their first airplane rides back in those Washington days. That alone no doubt made it all worth it.

The nation had been thrilled by Lindbergh's solo crossing of the Atlantic in 1927 and the prospects of what air travel might bring. But in the years that fol-

Andrews Air Force Base aviation show, circa 1939. During the 1930s Arthur used his Washington, D.C., radio popularity to encourage interest in and support for aviation. (Library of American Broadcasting, University of Maryland.)

lowed, few ventured out to try it themselves. "Air travel was by no means fully accepted in the early 1930s," wrote Eastern Airlines President and General Manager Eddie Rickenbacker in his autobiography. "The New York–Washington run was the only one that came near paying for itself. Planes flew empty or with only one or two passengers. Our employees were not selling their product.

"In a way I could not blame them…. Salesmen, who were supposed to be walking into the offices of local businessmen and selling them on air travel, were receiving as little as $60 a month; only a few made $100. And they were men who were expected to

exude confidence in air travel and to impress the public with its advantages."[11]

Enter Arthur Godfrey. Throughout the 1930s, as he traveled between Washington and New York on CBS assignments, he often flew on Eastern, and was often the sole passenger. As a result, he managed to log time flying tri-motor Fords and Stinsons, Curtiss Condors, and the first Douglas DC-2s and DC-3s with America's pioneer airline captains, legends like Dick Merrill.

"Memory can be tricky," Godfrey wrote in the introduction to Merrill's biography, "but I tend to recall that my first flight with Dick Merrill was when he invited me to sit in the right hand seat of an Eastern Airlines Curtiss Condor on a flight from Washington, D.C., to Miami. With my hands and feet ligtly on the controls, he let me 'feel' him through the takeoff and then I flew the bird most of the way....

"We flew over the Everglades above a layer of broken cumulus under a bright full moon whose reflection we could see, thru the cloud-breaks, racing along with us over the awesome wilderness. Thunderstorms spouting bolts of cloud-to-ground lightning lined both sides of the airway. To each of them we gave a wide berth, having nothing beyond the simplest of instruments in those days. With passengers aboard, we strove to avoid all the rough air we could."[12] Godfrey flew frequently with Merrill on these flights to Miami, and spent most of his time in the cockpit. Then he'd get back on radio and give his audiences all the details.

"More and more," he told *Flying* mag-azine in 1958, "I realized how necessary to the welfare of the nation is a healthy, growing air transport system. That realization was a challenge to me as a knowledgeable citizen to do all in my power to advance [the] public grasp of the fact."[13] As early as 1933, he and Rickenbacker took to the air in one of Eastern's new DC-2's and made the first public broadcast from a commercial airliner, describing the sights of the city to the radio audience below. In 1937, when bad weather caused extensive flooding in parts of the country, WJSV sent Godfrey to Louisville and Memphis to report on high water conditions there. At no extra cost, Godfrey did his own piloting. For Washingtonians in the 1930s, his radio accounts of flying influenced many to give it a try, a pattern that Godfrey would later accomplish through his network broadcasts as well. And the on-the-air-talk became one more reason to tune to WJSV and CBS each day.

12

The Washington–New York Shuttle

IN 1937, GODFREY RECEIVED another call from the CBS Network and, by now almost obsessed to make it in New York, he signed on for 26 weeks for a new series called the *Professor Quiz* show. The pay was excellent—$750 per show. But as with *Manhattan Parade* a few years earlier, there was an imposed format that wasn't Arthur Godfrey as much as Arthur Godfrey playing the role of a master of ceremonies. At the end of the season, he asked out of the contract.

Before leaving New York, however, he took all the money the series had brought him and hired his first publicist, Bob Taplinger. The goal was to get his name known among the advertising men and their clients who controlled the shows that aired on the networks. These were still the days when the sponsors and their agencies created the shows and, most importantly for Godfrey, hired the talent. Over the next several months, he and Taplinger wined and dined time salesmen and ac-

count executives, and Godfrey began to gain a name for himself, in part as a potential talent, in part as a big spender. The result was another network show for the fall of 1938.

Singin' Sam, the Barbasol Man, a popular musical variety series created by Harry Frankel, had premiered on CBS in 1930 for Barbasol Shaving Cream. When Frankel died in 1938, the sponsor wanted to keep the show going. And Godfrey, with his guitar, ukulele, patter, and unique voice, seemed a logical successor. Unlike *Professor Quiz,* the show would be done out of Washington.

"We would rehearse from noon to three or four o'clock in the afternoon with his accompanist, Johnny Salb on Hammond Organ and Piano," recalled Granville Klink. "Sometimes, Arthur would fill in with his banjo or play a little piano himself."[1] The first network feed was 7:15 P.M. to the Eastern time zone with another live performance to the West Coast time zone at midnight. Again Godfrey was willing to work round the clock to get on the network. But though the *Singin' Sam* show lasted another six years, Godfrey, for unknown reasons, lasted only one.

So once again it was back to concentrating on the *Sun Dial* show—and a young woman named Mary Bourke. Mary ran the NBC music library at WRC and sometimes doubled as night receptionist. She didn't quite share Godfrey's intense love of broadcasting, but they did share a passion for horses and horseback riding and a love of the outdoors. Godfrey's first wife, Catherine, hadn't filed for divorce until 1937. After the settlement, Arthur and Mary were married and took up residence on his farm in Virginia.

On Thursday, September 21, 1939, the wire recording machines at WJSV were spinning furiously. Management had decided that it might be a good idea to record their entire broadcast day for archival purposes. And so they did, sign-on to sign-off, beginning with Arthur's *Sun Dial* show at 6:30 A.M. and then on through the daytime soap operas like *The Romance of Helen Trent*, a speech by President Roosevelt at 2 P.M., a Washington Senators' baseball game at 4 P.M., *Amos 'n Andy* at 6 P.M. and the rest of the network evening schedule.

"It's six thirty and a hawlf...good morning one and all...this is Sun Dial, WJSV Washington, D.C., and any music you here is re-cor-deed....If I'm not mistook, took with a mistake, this is the Autumnal Equinox, isn't it? Today? I'se think it is. This is the first day of Fall officially, isn't it? I do believe it is. Right, I sorta had a hunch. And we have a full moon comin' up here, a full moon. Let's see...when will it be full? [pause] It will be full on...the twenty-eighth. Oh well, that's one week from today. That's right, it's one week from today. Yes. Well anyways it's a very lovely morning. Six-thirty and a hawlf. And the man says generally fair and cooler today he says. It was fifty-seven and hawlf degrees

on the farm on this morning....etc. [chimes] *It's six thirty-one, twenty-nine minutes of, ah, seven o'clock."*

There's silence, then a record comes on. It's a ballad, "Never in a Million Years," featuring an orchestra and then a vocal. Chimes and another time check. An announcement for the Amateur Boxing Carnival. Another time check. Arthur talks in great detail about a WJSV staff member's boat that is for sale. Another time check. Another record, this time an overly sweet version of "Listen to the Mocking Bird," complete with bird imitations.

What comes through is how quiet and calm the broadcast is. It's soothing and light. Here is this deep rich voice quietly chatting with you as if he were right in your kitchen, sitting at the table sipping coffee and dispensing information for your day and music as well—mainly novelty songs—with Arthur often humming the tune between his bits of business long after it's been played.

He delivers commercials for Pepsi Cola ("You like Pepsi Cola, Mother? The price is only six for a quarter...get that? Only *six for a quarter!*"), a new movie (*The Women*) and a backache aid (Minute Rub). And then the chimes and the time again.[2]

Though Godfrey would go on to coast-to-coast broadcasts, add a cast of singers and musicians on his shows, and have the top American companies as his sponsors, his basic approach to daily shows would stay the same over the next 33 years. The nasal twang, the one side of a two-way conversation with the listener or viewer at home, the rewording of everything from scripts and commercial text to his very own statements, long pauses while he sifted through papers, references to the farm, stories about people you knew or wanted to know or thought you knew because Arthur had talked about them before, good upbeat music, and a slow, calculated but positive let's-have-some-fun, raise-a-little-hell, read-some-letters, talk-about-some-unimportant-things-too approach that drew you in and held your attention long past the time you might have planned to spend listening.

When America entered World War II, Washington was changed forever. No longer the sleepy little city that revolved around an eight-hour government workday, the city became the temporary home of thousands of additional government workers and members of the Armed Forces who kept it humming day and night. Godfrey remained a constant for new listeners and old each morning, a reassurance in worrisome times that although the world was in hell of a spin, another day had actually dawned and there was some continuity and humor to it all.

Godfrey loved novelty songs. And during the war his favorite was "Der Führer's Face." The performer was Spike Jones along with his orchestra. Jones was a comic and a staple on records during the 1940s. His orchestra often began on a serious note, as in his famous "Cocktails for Two" number, and then upped the tempo, adding strange voices and sound effects and completely destroying the intent of the composer. "Der Führer's Face" was a bit different. It was Jones' contribution to the war effort. The lyrics, supposedly being sung in English by a small band of ebullient German soldiers, went like this:

When the Führer says we is the Master Race,
We Heil! (razzberry sound effect) Heil! (again)
Right in the Führer's Face,
Not to love the Führer is a great disgrace,
So we Heil! (razzberry) Heil! (razzberry)
Right in the Führer's Face.[3]

"I used to play that every morning," Godfrey loved to recall. "And Mrs. Roosevelt, bless her heart, used to go in every day, every morning and have breakfast with one of the White House staff. And he would call me up and say, 'Now, Mrs. Roosevelt's coming over here any minute. Don't you dare put "Der Führer's Face" on. Play a nice Viennese waltz while we have breakfast, will you?'" [4]

Arthur Godfrey was 38 when the war broke out, and he had every reason to be pleased that he was well past draft age. He was earning close to $100,000 a year, the equivalent of $1.1 million in 1998 dollars, though U.S. tax rates at the time took more than 80 percent away from him. He had a 120-acre estate in Virginia. Six nights a week it was to bed about nine and up at 4:30 A.M. to make the studio by airtime. Each weekend, he could sail his 19-foot lightning class sailboat on the Potomac or fly one of his three planes. There was a family now: his son Richard from his first marriage, now a teenager, who had come to live with Mary and Arthur, and baby Michael.

But Godfrey was too much an old Navy man to not want to be part of the military again. He didn't know much about military aircraft, but he knew they'd play an important part in the war. And he wanted in on it. When he applied for a commission in the Naval Reserve, however, he was summarily turned down because of his bad hips. Arthur was not about to give up. Among his friends was U.S. Navy Lt. Commander Leland P. Lovette, who, according to Godfrey, brought the matter up with President Roosevelt one day at a conference on naval affairs at the White House:

"'You mean Arthur Godfrey,' the President said, 'the man we hear on the radio in the mornings?'

"'Yes, Mr. President,' Lovette answered.

"'Can he walk?' F.D.R. asked.

"'Yes, sir.'

"'Then, of course, give him his commission,' the President said, with the well-known Roosevelt twinkle in his eye. 'I'm the Commander-in-Chief, and I can't get out of this chair.'"[5]

So Arthur was granted a physical waiver on the condition that he would be assigned to intelligence work. He would also be given his commission in the Naval Reserve. He accepted, surmising that once in, it wouldn't be too hard to get transferred to line duty. But his medical record followed him, and every time he applied for sea duty, he was turned down. And that went for naval aviation as well.

He wound up doing for the Navy one of the things he was best at in civilian life: public relations. In addition, he unofficially spent time with the Reserve units in Washington teaching seamanship, navigation, and small-boat handling. During this period he joined the Coast Guard Reserve, and was probably the only naval officer who ever did so without first resigning his Naval commission. The Coast Guard needed experienced small-boat skippers to teach civilians to do submarine patrol duty in their pleasure craft, and Godfrey was interested in the job, but overqualified. So he enlisted as a chief boatswain's mate, and got as close as he was going to get to sea duty. Of course, his listeners knew all about these expeditions; he never failed to keep them apprised on the morning show.

Godfrey had become a local institution by just being himself—one of the most difficult things to do on radio or television. The microphones, the lights, the fear of not looking good, of making a mistake, consume most people who try to do on-air work. There are countless stories of statesmen and giants of business and industry who have been totally unable to speak once the ON THE AIR sign went on. A whole catalog of bloopers and faux pas has been put out on records or rebroadcast through the years. Hilarious as they are, most are due to nervousness, the attempt to be someone other than oneself, the total

inability to relax in front of a microphone. What comes off as normal conversation most often requires hard work and years of experience. To then be able to add humor that is meaningful to most of your audience is a rare talent indeed.

Godfrey knew as much. He had never stopped thinking about a network show. But now he began to reason that although he still craved a chance to go national, maybe his approach to the network had been wrong. He narrowed his request to the CBS brass: how about his doing a local morning show in New York, a show just like the *Sun Dial* show? The answer continued to be the same: "Your stuff is all right for Washington, but it won't go in New York. That cornball material about the farm and those local cracks are not for the big time." [6]

Until 1941. That year CBS hired a new morning man to work at its local New York City station, WABC, and his on-air act was surprisingly like Arthur's. It turned out that the man had worked for a time at WJSV and had picked up all of Godfrey's mannerisms and expressions. "He had all the gags I'd been using. He even had a License to Listen, like the one I'd invented…. He even had my tone of voice." [7]

Dismayed, Godfrey decided to knock on NBC's door. He told a friend to "Tell them that all I want is to be on the air opposite this CBS thief so I can knock his ears off." NBC jumped at the chance to get him on their local New York City station, offering him $65,000 plus a commission for the first year. Then, remembering what Walter Winchell had told him about using "the club" when he had to, Godfrey went back to Washington and presented NBC's offer to Harry Butcher. Butcher asked for time. Arthur told Butcher he needed an answer before Monday. On Sunday morning, Arthur met a CBS delegation headed by CBS executive vice president and chairman William Paley's right-hand man, Ed Klauber. Klauber told him CBS was prepared to make him an offer similar to NBC's. They would put Godfrey on in New York City instead of the man they had just hired. "I am only prepared to listen," Godfrey responded, "to a better offer." "Suppose we double the money NBC's going to give you," Klauber responded. Recognizing he was now in the driver's seat, Godfrey made a radical counter offer: he wanted no guarantee of any kind, nor did he need to be paid at all, *if* CBS would give him a minimum of one year without any interference. "After that time, I'm to be on the air from six o'clock until seven forty-five every morning. I want 20 percent of the gross take of the show, rates per advertiser to be decided upon by me and your station manager Art Hayes. I want to do the show from Washington, and as soon as I can get enough clients interested in both places, I want to make it a two-station network." The brass agreed to all of his terms. [8]

The ethics of the matter were never a problem for Godfrey. Though the NBC people were furious to discover that they had been used, he never questioned his right to do what he had done. Years later he would say, "The networks do that kind of thing to each other every day. If you want to get anywhere in this game, you have to learn how to play it." [9]

And so Godfrey finally had his wish— he was to be heard in New York City each morning, six days a week, from 6:00 to 7:45 A.M. on WABC, the CBS-owned and -operated station there. The show was fed from Washington. Then from 7:45 to 9:15 A.M. he would do his regular *Sun Dial* stint.

After a slow start the New York show caught on. Somehow, he also found time to become a vocalist for the Decca record label, singing sea chanteys and other offbeat songs, accompanying himself on the guitar. He'd play the recordings on his own shows, then criticize his own performances. With the war in progress, he began his own public service effort: in conjunction with the American Red Cross, he formed the GAPSALS (Give-a-Pint-Save-a-Life-Society) in New York. Broadcasting live from the Manhattan Blood Center, he focused attention on the need and how easy it was to donate, and the results were indeed impressive: over 5,000 pints of blood were given in the first three drives. Equally as important, the New York columnists picked up the announcements each time, adding more publicity to the need for blood. By the end of 1942, thanks to their new morning man, WABC was turning a profit for the first time.

Though he now had two different morning shows in two different cities with two different sets of sponsors, Godfrey gave most of his attention to the WABC effort, spending increasing amounts of time in New York. He filled his nights in the city with conferences and dinner meetings, widening his network of contacts with advertisers and others wherever possible. Yet every morning he was up by 5 A.M. for his two radio shows. His energy level never flagged.

By 1943, his old friend Lt. Commander Lovette had been assigned to command the cruiser Guam. Godfrey wanted to go along as a navigator, and it looked as though he'd get the job, but at the last minute he was turned down, again because of his disabilities. Although he understood the importance of physical fitness in the military, especially during wartime, he was nevertheless frustrated with his situation, and got himself accredited as a Navy war correspondent.

In November of 1944, Arthur made his first television show, "a demonstration of the technique of taking a pint of blood from a donor's arm (my own). At that time there were less than 100 television sets in New York, but the resultant publicity was good for the blood drive."[10] A few weeks later, with his correspondent credentials in his pocket and several gallons of whole blood from his GAPSALS "under my arm, I hitched rides in Navy and Air Force planes and delivered the precious fluid to the hospitals in Saipan on Thanksgiving Day."[11]

Arthur Godfrey arrived in Saipan on the eve of the first B-29 raid on Tokyo. "Those scores of big planes taking off for Japan fired my enthusiasm," he later recalled. "I itched to be at the controls, and I determined then and there that I was going to learn to fly multiengined aircraft." But his visit also filled him with "a violent loathing" for the apathy that he felt existed on the home front.[12] Oh, what he could do for the war effort if he could add a *national* audience to his Washington and New York listenership!

By 1945, between the two radio series, Godfrey was bringing in several million dollars annually to the CBS treasury and a gross income of $150,000 a year for himself. He had become a New York celebrity and was given increasing amounts of press attention. In a long feature article on Arthur in the Sunday *New York Times*, reporter Fred Spooner described "Their Man Godfrey, of the Rain-Barrel Voice" to New Yorkers. It sounded very much like the fellow Washingtonians had known for years:

He is a likable guy, who at 40 years of age resembles a postgraduate fullback…. [He] is the living contradiction of radio's success formula for product salesmanship. He insults his clients amiably, pokes genial fun at their products, audibly deplores the commercial announcements (and the copy writers who prepare them) when he thinks them dull, and sometimes, if he refuses outright to read such matter, is liable to tear it into fragments in front of the microphone. These sponsors pay into the figuratively outstretched hands of WABC and WTOP [WJSV's new call letters] a total of around half a million dollars for the privilege of having their products (or themselves) heckled into fame and sales records by this Huckleberry Finn of the Potomac…. His style? He's a verbal perambulator, never using one word where five will suffice. His timing is slow with leisurely pauses: his voice conversational. He sounds exactly as the average male is feeling at that time of day. And he'll be a natural for television…. Nobody questions his sincerity. He won't compromise. He does what he wants to, utters what homilies he chooses on and off his program. His show is monitored but not censored and the station officials idolize him. They forgive even his occasional mild Rabelaisianism with the shrugged excuse, "That's what makes Godfrey *Godfrey*." He himself says about this attitude of theirs: "I guess they feel about me like that proverbial mother felt about her precocious child. They wouldn't take a million for me, but they certainly wouldn't give a plugged nickel for another one like me."[13]

13

Arthur Godfrey Time:
Finally the Network

AMBITIOUS HE WAS. AND DRIVEN by many forces. Among them, an honest desire to fulfill himself and become all that he could be; a belief that the American people could be educated on all kinds of significant subjects by a messenger like Arthur Godfrey; and an absolute passion to share whatever he had with a larger audience, be it his love of flying, sailing, horseback riding, reading, or discovering new talent.

There were at least three even more compelling forces. First, he liked making money—lots of it; not to squander or flaunt it as much as to allow him the life he loved to live: the farm, planes, the independence. Second, he was a man in a hurry who didn't suffer fools gladly. And third, he believed more in himself and his ability and instincts than in most anyone else's.

Add to this an insatiable curiosity, a constant need to try new things and incredible energy, and one begins to understand what a human dynamo and emerging presence Arthur Godfrey was becoming.

So it was not unusual that early on Godfrey was appealing to his boss at WABC, Arthur Hull Hayes, to let him have a national audience for his morning radio shows. At first the pleas were set aside. He needed to build the WABC show first. But by 1945, Hayes had become a Godfrey convert. With CBS chairman William Paley away on active duty overseas as a colonel in the Army, Hayes appealed to Frank Stanton. Stanton, Paley's second in command on the management side, also took up the fight and pushed the proposal with the program leadership at CBS.

The problem began to narrow. It was not so much that they didn't want to give

Godfrey a try, but that the CBS network schedule of soap operas was already sold out with advertising from early morning to late afternoon. Godfrey countered that housewives listened to many of those shows because there was nothing else on. They craved escape, he argued, and his programs provided escape as well, the only difference being that his stories about farming, fishing, hunting, flying and sailing weren't fiction. It had worked stunningly in New York City and Washington, D.C. "Why wouldn't that sort of fare appeal to the rest of the country?" he asked. "Think of all the blood donors we could get if we were doing this show on the network!"[1]

When the CBS people pointed to company policy that did not allow playing of phonograph records on the network, he said fine, let me have a small orchestra and some vocalists. "They won't be as effective in attracting initial audiences as the big names available on records, but I've always maintained that if a performer can't get along without big name guest stars, he's got no business being on the air himself."[2]

Godfrey was relentless. What about moving the *School of the Air*, he asked, referring to one of CBS's most cherished experiments. Aired daily from 9:15 to 10:00 A.M., for classroom use, *School of the Air* was highly praised by educators, and long offered as an example of public service by the company. But no one could prove its actual use. And it certainly didn't bring in any money.

As he had back in 1941 when he negotiated for his morning show to be carried in New York, Godfrey offered to work for nothing until the sponsors came in, then to receive a percentage of the gross, etc. "I don't get paid until I sell something."[3] Finally, as they had with his WABC campaign, management gave in. They suggested an experiment: When *School of the Air* went off for the summer, Arthur could

occupy that 45 minute morning time slot until fall. It was a questionable time of year for him to try out his show, and with only 13 weeks to prove himself, it was even more risky. But Godfrey took them up on it. "One thing is for sure: the rating can't go any place but up!"[4]

In short order, a contractor for CBS named Lou Shoobe was assembling a cast of performers for *Arthur Godfrey Time*—an orchestra leader, an orchestra, male and female vocalists to sing the hit songs of the day, and maybe a quartet which could do more traditional material like gospel and barbershop. Godfrey was pinning his future at CBS on these hirings, so he insisted on staying close to the process, making the final choices. What he wanted was not only a versatile group of musicians and performers, but also a flexible group who could fit into his unrehearsed, make-it-up-as-you-go-along style. The task also needed to be done quickly: *School of the Air* was ending in a few weeks.

Archie Bleyer conducted the musical auditions. A CBS house staff conductor who had had a popular band back in the thirties, Bleyer established himself as one of the foremost writers of stock arrangements. He was to be the orchestra leader.

Remo Palmier was one of the first on board. A well-known and highly talented steel and electric guitarist, Remo had been named to *Esquire* magazine's All-Star Jazz Band two years running. He had played with Red Norvell's Sextet and Coleman Hawkins as well. "I went to the audition, never having heard of Arthur Godfrey. And it was just a very unusual experience.... Lou had called me and I said, 'I never did radio shows. ... You have to sight-read and play it perfect.' ... And he said, 'No you don't. He's gonna be calling out things right in the middle of the show, and wanting you to play them, you know, spontaneously.' And that's how the shows [later] worked.... [Arthur] would call for these old numbers, like things that went back to the early 1900's. And I should know some of them…. He'd say, does anybody know 'Mary Lou?' And I'd say 'I do.' And he's looking at this 19-year-old and he says, 'You do? Let me see you play it.' So I'd play it."[5] At the tryout he displayed some of that knowledge and was hired on. In time, he would become Arthur's guitar instructor and stay with him for the complete 27 years that *Arthur Godfrey Time* ran on CBS.

In all, the band members hired were as an impressive group of accomplished musicians: Clarinetist Johnny Mince had played with the Ray Noble and Tommy Dorsey bands and, as part of the Glenn Miller Orchestra, was a soloist in the reed section experiment that lead to the famous Miller Sound.[6] Bassist Gene Traxler had also played with Tommy Dorsey. There were also trombonist Sy Schaffer (and later Lou McGarity who had been with the Ben Bernie and Benny Goodman bands), Hank Sylvern (and later Lee Erwin) on organ, and Ludwig Von Flato on piano. Erwin and Von Flato had impressive classical music backgrounds. Joe Marshall soon joined them as drummer.

Bleyer completed the audition process, but turned down the job as leader. "He just threw up his hands," noted Palmier. "He wanted everything in order."[7] And this was not going to be a formal show by any means. Hank Sylvern was chosen orchestra conductor. A year later, Sylvern would suffer a heart attack and Bleyer would return to take on the role of leader.

The vocalist auditions were carried out by listening to recordings of some 400 singers. Arthur chose 25-year-old Patti Clayton, who had been singing with the Ray Bloch and Percy Faith orchestras, and 28-year-old Marshall Young; the Jubilaires, an all-black quartet who sang spirituals; and two groups that didn't last very long: The Four Clubmen, who sang more contemporary music, and Bobby Tucker's Symphonettes. As for the Jubilaires, their hiring raised many an eyebrow. "Nobody would hire black groups at that time," explained Palmier. "Arthur just said 'I like the way they sound and I'm gonna have them on my show.'"[8]

While the planning was going on, the unexpected happened. On April 12, President Roosevelt died of a cerebral hemorrhage in Warm Springs, Georgia. As author Ray Poindexter noted, "Roosevelt had been the first real radio president, the first to utilize the potential power to the fullest extent. He made three hundred broadcasts while in office. Radio's tribute to him from the announcement of his death until he was buried was inclusive…. Programming was drastically changed. Omitted were commercials, comedy shows, soap operas, violent dramas, and lively music."[9]

Because of Godfrey's roots in Washington and his 11-year association with FDR, CBS gave him the key assignment of describing the funeral procession to the nation. He knew its importance, but apparently didn't recognize how emotional it would be as well.

As the procession passed in front of him on Pennsylvania Avenue, he described the scene in the same slow cadence as the drums below:

"The drums are wrapped in black crepe and are muffled, as you can hear. And the pace of the musicians is so slow. And behind them, these are Navy boys. And now, just coming past the Treasury, I can see the horses drawing the caisson and most generally folks havin' as tough a time as I am trying to see it." But before he could finish, his voice gave in to his innermost feelings: "And behind…behind it…is the car bearing the man on whose shoulders fall the terrific burdens and responsibilities that were handled so well by the man to whose body we are paying our last respects now. God Bless Him—President Truman!

[*crying*] We return you now to our studios!"[10]

"I was asked," he later recalled, "as I often had been in those days to do little pieces of public events. And this description I did has become famous. And everybody thinks it's great. I myself was so ashamed that I had broken down in it that I vowed I would never again do any public events—that I was not a reporter. I couldn't be objective. I had to get emotionally involved and that was no good in our business. And so, it changed the whole career. It broke me up because I knew the late president very well."[11]

But people all over America who heard that description felt very close to Arthur Godfrey that day. And they remembered his words and his voice in the months that followed.

Back in New York, the CBS publicity department launched a huge promotional effort announcing the premiere of *Arthur Godfrey Time*, scheduled for Monday, April 30. They sent photos of Godfrey and the cast, and the press releases pushed Arthur's unorthodox style to millions who had yet to hear him in this format. Syndicated columnists out of New York who knew him well also spread the word about the new half-hour network series.

Within days of the launching, the series was among the most talked-about shows on radio. CBS had taken a gamble and allowed Godfrey the opportunity to do what he did locally: operate without a script. It was the first time a network had allowed that much freedom to any performer. Jack Benny and other stars of the day worked with scripts that were often previewed and edited by the networks. In this case, to its credit, the network took the risk, banking on Arthur's past success with listeners.

"When I was 17 years old," recalls entertainer Max Morath, "I went to work in the CBS radio station in Colorado as an announcer. It was right at the time that the Godfrey show first went on. We weren't carrying the show, but we'd sit and listen to him on headphones.... He was just talking. And he didn't have a script. He was, of course, very articulate. But nevertheless, you knew that he was just talking to his people. And it was *so refreshing!* And then he would do the commercials. And you *believed* him. I mean I was in the business. I thought I was a sophisticated radio announcer and I knew that [commercial stuff] was all malarkey. Not with Godfrey.

"It's hard for people today to realize what a mammoth step that was. But at that time I remember keeping the logs on the local radio station. You had to log for the FCC *everything* that went on the air! Down to *the second!* And you had to have a script for everything. Now of course in local radio you could get by, but still, we didn't do much ad-libbing in the local station. And to have a man with Godfrey's power...I mean that voice, just *winging* it, was remarkable."[12]

Local CBS affiliates were soon taking out tongue-in-cheek newspaper ads like this disclaimer from WDWS in Urbana, Illinois:

ATTENTION RADIO LISTENERS! In all fairness to you, we feel it necessary to state that we do not accept any responsibility for anything that occurs on ARTHUR GODFREY TIME. We cannot explain just how this verbally uninhibited character happens to be on the loose but he is, and there's nothing we can do about it!

The opinions expressed by ARTHUR GODFREY do no reflect the views of this station.

There is some very good music on the ARTHUR GODFREY show, so should you be tuned in to WDWS at 2:00 P.M. Monday throughout Friday, don't change stations—you'll like the music and a sensible program will follow. Please remember: this ad-libbing ARTHUR GODFREY was not our idea! If you can stand it, O.K.—tune your radio in to WDWS at

2:00 P.M. Monday through Friday. But don't blame us if it blows up![13]

WBIG's version said, "The musical portion of the program makes for good listening, and we believe you'll agree. It's just too bad Godfrey has to clutter it up."[14]

After the premiere, letters poured in and Godfrey would read them on the air. One from Jersey City read, "When you sing, my canary jumps out of his cage and throws himself at the cat." When one of the Symphonettes appeared in the studio with a headdress, Godfrey asked, "What is that thing?" Told it was the latest thing in turbans, he retorted, "It's wunnerful—wunnerful—but it looks like a hotel bath towel to me." [15]

The openings of *Arthur Godfrey Time* weren't much different from the local morning shows he continued to do. He'd just start talking.

"And now it's *Arthur Godfrey Time*," he began in January 1946 (orchestra joins in with the theme, which at that time was "Chasing Shadows"), "says I with misgivings….Uh, the show is on the air. Is there an opening? I suppose not. Oh *there* it is… 'This is Arthur Godfrey,' it says here, and all the little ones."[16]

On a typical show, he'd relate to the day. "Today is tax return day," he'd say, following it with a long pause. "The day we have to pay up to the government. I don't know what I'm gonna do. I still have a couple of bags of peanuts left. Unsold. … Ray Noble had the best idea for paying his tax. Did you hear him last Sunday night? He wanted to open up a charge account with the government. … They *better* let us open up a charge account if they want to get any money.[17]

The band came together quickly, playing well, if not inspired, under Sylvern. But his lead singer, Patti Clayton, showed early signs that she wouldn't be fitting in to the Arthur Godfrey style. Presented on

air with a cake from CBS, he asked her to lead them in song. Taken aback, she muttered something about not being prepared. "What do you mean you can't do it?" Arthur asked her over the air. "Oh just sing 'Happy Birthday.'"

Later in the show he read a postcard from a listener with a request for a song. "You guys know that?" he asked the Jubilaires. No, they didn't. The listener had asked for a second song. The band didn't know that one either. Arthur brushed over it, telling the listener, "Next time ask for something we know."[18] But knowing how spontaneous he wanted the show to be, he was undoubtedly making mental notes about who would be staying on the team.

He was being billed as the "Huckleberry Finn of Radio and the Grouch Killer." Without sponsors to kid, Godfrey made fun of the CBS brass, coworkers, and radio in general. Syndicated columnists were impressed and spread the word nationally. In his column of June 19, Jack Gaver of United Press proposed that Godfrey should be paying CBS for all the fun he was having on his broadcasts. One afternoon, he dropped in on the show for the repeat West Coast broadcast and found Arthur at the piano in a jam session, just minutes before air time. "The impromptu concert continued almost until Godfrey had to broadcast. Then he retired to the seclusion of what normally would be a sponsor's booth. The rest of his cohorts work in the studio, but he sits alone in the booth next to the control room and switches the singers and musicians in and out as he wills…. Godfrey behaved himself in pretty good fashion for about 20 or 30 minutes, and then, on the spur of the moment, he left his sanctuary and dashed into the studio to help out the small band. First he played the piano—it was a true jam session with no particular tune—then he swung over onto the bench in front of

An early *Arthur Godfrey Time* CBS Network broadcast, circa 1945. Joining Arthur, left to right, are members of the original cast, including band members, the Jubilaires, and vocalists Marshall Young and Patti Clayton. The cast would change, but the show would remain on the air every weekday for 27 years. (Joan Zacher collection.)

the celeste. After a couple of shots of that he warmed the stool in front of an electric organ for a few bars and then changed places with the operator of the nova-chord."[19]

Columnists were impressed with his endurance as well. In a *New York World Telegram* radio column titled "Unpredictable Godfrey: He defies all manner of customs to sell his sponsor's products," Edmund Leamy wrote: "The man's a glutton for work; and no one, not even himself, knows what he's going to do when he goes on the air. Every morning he appears before the WABC mike at 6:30. He is heard over WTOP Washington from 7 until 9:15. At 9:15 while station announcements are being made, he rides in a special express elevator from the third to the 24th floor of

the CBS building here to another studio. He gets there just in time for his new nation-wide hook up show...which runs till 9:45. And as if that were not enough, he does a repeat of this show for the [West] coast at 3:30 p.m.—when everything is the same as in the earlier performance except Godfrey himself. Godfrey never repeats."[20]

By early June, just one month into the summer experiment, the CBS Affiliates Advisory Board voted in favor of switching the *School of the Air* program to an after-school spot the following fall to make room for *Arthur Godfrey Time* on a permanent basis. On June 27, CBS announced that the switch would indeed happen. Their rationalization for moving *School of the Air* was awkward at best: more young listeners would be available at 5

P.M., since many schools were without equipment to broadcast the show during school time. Within a short time, the series was removed completely. But there was really no need to rationalize why Godfrey's show was being continued: it was a smash hit.

Arthur Godfrey ad-libs provided welcome fodder for the syndicated columnists. In his September 7 column, Earl Wilson picked up on two of them: "Introducing one of his singers, [Godfrey] said, 'He won an audition at the Metropolitan—and has already sold two policies.' To one lady listener he dedicated a new song, titled, 'I'll Send You a Kitten Dear, You Could Use a New Puss.'"[21]

And the national press clamored aboard as well. In its September 3 edition, *Newsweek* noted in its Radio section that Arthur Godfrey, "redheaded and freckle-faced frog-throated and grammar-mauling," had developed a national audience but no sponsors. "Nevertheless, still enthralled and hopeful, CBS this week gave him an additional fifteen minutes daily."[22]

Reassured by the sales success of Godfrey's continuing local shows (80 different sponsors paying $80 a spot in New York and $30 a spot in Washington), CBS carried the new network show for more than a year without a sponsor. Then on June 2, 1946, Godfrey's old sponsor, Chesterfield cigarettes, which had hired and then dropped him unceremoniously back in the 1930s, bought a 15-minute slot for $3,000 a week. Arthur began smoking the product and finally, the old Godfrey testimonial magic, which was still working so successfully with his morning shows on WABC and WTOP, began to work for Chesterfield and *Arthur Godfrey Time*. That November *Parade* magazine ran an article and an old photo of Godfrey, showing him with a pack of Camels. "To the astonishment of Chesterfield, CBS and Parade, Godfrey got more than 4,000 reader-listener letters asking 'how come?' As usual Godfrey explained on the air." And from then on ad agencies were at the door to sign on for other sponsors.[23]

CBS had invested in him and once more Godfrey had come through. *Arthur Godfrey Time* would remain on the air five days a week for 27 years. But this was only the beginning. His belief in his own ability, even to the extent of working without pay, his doggedness, and his ability to break through the ether and get inside the listener's mind would continue to pay off for him and for the network.

14

Talent Scouts: Prime Time Godfrey

AFTER SOME SEVENTY-SEVEN YEARS of experimenting, there isn't much in the way of format that hasn't been tried on radio. Recorded music, news, sports broadcasts, call-in talk shows make up the bulk of American radio programming today, with a fair sprinkling of religious stations rounding out the list. A station usually settles on one format as its dominant one, and that is what the sales department runs with. If the format works and enough commercial advertising is sold, then the program manager spends his or her time gathering ratings information and "fine-tuning" the sound to achieve even better quarter-hour listener totals. Program managers hire and fire announcers and disc jockeys and newspeople based on "the numbers." If enough "time" isn't sold to commercial advertisers, then management either turns to the program manager to choose another format or changes program managers.

Back in the mid–1920s, however, the radio program manager held a higher place in the station hierarchy. After all, anything might work as a format—recordings, live music, storytelling, vaudeville acts, news, talk, cooking shows—and the program manager was given carte blanche to develop new formats and try out new personalities. Taking its cue from vaudeville, radio looked on schedules as a series of 15- or 30-minute acts that stretched out over the day and evening to become a total entertainment service. The idea of an all-news station or an all-music station would never have been considered as progressive—radio was synonymous with variety.

The downside was that there were endless hours to fill. Godfrey learned that firsthand during his brief fling as program manager in Baltimore. As more stations developed in each market, the pressure to keep coming up with new concepts, new acts, new voices, kept many a radio program manager on the job well past an eight-hour day.

Not that the burden was entirely on the program manager. As radio took hold, there was an endless stream of vaudevillians, burlesque show comedians, and musicians, pounding on the door, feverish to have a tryout and possibly a new career in this blossoming medium. Many had considerable talent and years of experience. Others, of course, had nothing of the sort and were rank amateurs.

Somewhere early on, an industrious program manager recognized that there might be a way of handling this endless stream of amateurs queued up outside the station each morning. Why not put on a program that acknowledged that these were amateurs—an amateur show—and even give the listeners a role by having them vote for their favorites? Costs would be minimal and it would bring in even more listeners. And most important, it would help the program manager fill up one more hour or so each day.

Soon the air was filled with the voices of wobbly sopranos, altos, and baritones, struggling piano players, neighborhood bands, college-age impressionists and the like, each vying for cash or coupons for food and basking in the glory of three minutes in front of that miraculous silver microphone.

There were no audience rating services in the twenties. But it's clear that the idea caught on. Hardly a station was on the air by 1928 that didn't have its own community amateur hour. Some were done in the studio, others on location. Saturday morning listeners often heard local talent shows broadcast from movie theaters. WFBR in Baltimore was no exception, and it was its late-night amateur hour program that had provided Arthur Godfrey with his ticket to fame.

The need to fill time at the local level was a major factor in the ultimate success of the national networks. What a relief for a local program manager to know that eight or more hours a day would be the responsibility of some far-off program manager at CBS or NBC! The idea of the amateur hour was not lost on those network programming people either. In 1935, an individual by the name of Major Edward Bowes had come to the NBC network with a program called *The Original Amateur Hour*. Each week, the Major Bowes booking staff would sift through thousands of letters and leads to invite to the New York studios the best amateurs available. Many had to compete in regional and local competitions to reach that point. It was the same acts local audiences had become so familiar with, including kazoo players and one-man bands. But at least it was the *best* amateur kazoo players and one-man bands. Listeners were encouraged to send in postcards after each program, voting for their favorites, and the finalists were awarded scholarships. After one year, Major Bowes' *Original Amateur Hour* moved to CBS, where it became a Sunday night institution throughout the 1930s and into the 1940s.

Shortly after the success of Godfrey's new morning network show for CBS Radio in 1945, the powers at CBS set out to find a nighttime vehicle for their rapidly rising star. CBS president Frank Stanton asked WCBS' station manager Art Hayes and others at the network to work on the project and within a few months, thanks to a CBS producer named Irving Mansfield, who had worked with some of radio's biggest starts, including Eddie Cantor and Fred Allen, they came up with one. Actually, Mansfield had developed the idea for a well-known vaudevillian and celebrity event toastmaster named George Jessel. When Jessel turned down the offer, the idea of using it as the vehicle for Godfrey took shape.

The *Original Amateur Hour* had run out of steam in the early forties, but what Mansfield's proposal called for was a variation on the concept. Rather than amateurs, Godfrey would preside over a showcase for up-and-coming professionals. And rather than have these somewhat awkward young people talk directly with him as they had with Major Bowes, why not have a friend or relative or colleague "discover" them and introduce them to Arthur. That would allow Godfrey to banter a bit, showcasing further his schmoozing ability, and give the show a talent-scout quality. The brass presented the idea to Godfrey and he was quick to approve of it. Lipton Tea Company, which had recently signed on as a morning sponsor of the Godfrey show, became the sole sponsor, and on Tuesday evening, July 3, 1946, the first *Arthur Godfrey's Talent Scouts* show was broadcast on the CBS Radio Network as a summer replacement. It was an instant hit.

Early shows included four talent scouts and their performers. Singers of all kinds appeared, from opera to pop music. Musicians and comedians as well. Among those who appeared on the early shows: singer Vic Damone, musician Jose Melis, comedians Wally Cox and Lenny Bruce, and singers Tony Bennett and Rosemary Clooney. Each musical performer was given a special orchestration, prepared by orchestra conductor Archie Bleyer. The orchestra was made up of top CBS staff musicians. This was hardly an amateur hour.

To pick the winner, an "applause meter" was instituted. At the end of the four performances, each would return for a brief reprieve and those in the studio audience would applaud as little or as much as they thought that talent deserved. When applause for the fourth talent had peaked, Arthur would quickly give his best reading of the results: "And the winner is —!"

If there was time, though there rarely was, the winner(s) would rush over to his desk and he'd congratulate them. "And then," as Phyllis McGuire of the McGuire Sisters clearly remembers, "the prize was that you could perform with Arthur Tuesday, Wednesday, Thursday, and Friday on the morning shows. ... And we thought that was just fabulous!"[1]

The show was an instant hit. Within a month, the Sunday *New York Times* would report that the show was reminiscent of Major Bowes, but gone were the "breathless amateurs...[and] tinny piano... replaced by orchestra support [and] a nicely polished production." Irving Mansfield "has not skimped on the details and he is fortunate in the choice of Arthur Godfrey as the easy-going master of ceremonies. Mr. Godfrey has been looking for a twilight assignment for some time but his ventures so far have resulted only in the merciless suggestion that he return with haste to his diurnal chatter. In this case, though he has learned to speed things up a bit, and subversive though it may seem, he sounds much better with a script than without."[2]

In September, *Time* would chime in. *Talent Scouts* had proved to be the top summer replacement and the show would be continuing Tuesdays at 10 P.M. opposite Bob Hope. Godfrey had told the writer that if he could hold his own against Hope, he would probably drop his early morning local shows. "This getting up at five o'clock is something for the birds."[3] Especially, he might have added, the morning after the *Talent Scouts* shows.

If ever there was a perfect marriage between product and pitch person, it was Lipton's and Arthur Godfrey. The company certainly had high hopes when they signed up to sponsor the entire *Talent Scout* broadcast each week, but they could never have imagined how successful it would be.

One reason was that right from the top of the show, when Announcer George Bryant would begin, *"Lipton Tea and Lipton Soup Present, Arthur Godfrey and His Talent Scouts!"* Lipton's and Arthur were presented as an inseparable team.

Peggy Marshall and the Holidays would follow, singing the opening jingle to the tune of "Sing a Song of Sixpence":

Here comes Arthur Godfrey, your talent scout MC,
Brought to you by Lipton's, brisk Lipton's tea.
You know it's Lipton's tea if its B-R-I-S-K,
You know it's Arthur Godfrey, when you hear them play....[4]

The band would come in with Carmen Lombardo's "Seems Like Old Times," the same theme song now used on the morning shows, reinforcing for Lipton's the connection with all-things Godfrey.

Even as each aspiring performer came on, Arthur would introduce him or her by saying, "And now the Lipton's spotlight falls on —." There was no doubt who the sponsor was.

Godfrey would make a pot of tea and considering it was just some leaves and hot water, it was a marvel to see him work at it to hold your attention:

It's a very simple matter to make one if you have the tea bags and the hot water nearby. I think I'll try one [pause]. I always try to get the tag out of it if I can... Doesn't add much to the taste. [pause] Notice the finger. When handling tea you must always keep one finger in the air. I don't know why. [pause] I pour the boiling water on it... and let it sit there and stew...and it's amazing what comes out of there! Amazing! You see how droopy I am now (laughter). Just wait till I have a shot of that tea—That Lipton Tea... Hey while we we're waiting for it to 'stew' did you hear about the lady who hid $200,000 worth of diamonds in her bathroom?...Did yuh?...[He pursues the story then stops, pauses.] Hey, I think we must have a member of the Board of Directors of the Lipton Company down here tonight. He's not enjoying this very much. [chuckles] We betta get back to the commercial for a minute, huh?[5]

Lipton officials were always looking over Godfrey's shoulder. Ed Bond, who went on to become head of Young & Rubicam, one of the country's largest advertising agencies of the day, first heard Arthur on Washington radio when he was assigned to the Pentagon after World War II. Later, he joined Young and Rubicam in New York as an account manager and worked more than eight years on the Lipton's account.

"He [Arthur] had a reputation among agencies of being totally impossible to work with. The advertising director of Lipton's, William Brook Smith, was very straight. There couldn't have been anyone more different from Arthur than Smith. He would work along with our creative department preparing commercials as if Arthur would really use them. He'd take them to meetings with Arthur and say, 'We have to get along.' And Arthur would say, 'Bull, I won't read *that!*' Arthur actually threw him out of the studio.

"The chairman of Lipton was Bill Smallwood. Smallwood and Arthur became friends. But Smallwood told Smith, 'Anytime anything happens that will have a material affect on Lipton's I charge you to tell me!' So Smith would watch the show and [invariably] five minutes after it ended, he'd be on the phone to me complaining bitterly about the ad-libbing. 'Why couldn't he read it right?'"[6]

If coffee had been the preferred drink of America before the war, when the GI's of World War II returned they only added to the popularity, continuing their coffee-drinking habits in civilian life. "It's hard to imagine a product more difficult to sell in this country than tea!" explained Bond. "The biggest competition was Tetley, White Rose, Salada. Arthur single-handedly put Lipton in the position of Number One. Virtually every dollar Lipton spent was on *Arthur Godfrey's Talent Scouts.*

It's not much of an exaggeration to say he did the whole thing himself."[7]

Howard Anderson was Product Manager on tea for Lipton's. His responsibility was to OK all the product references in the materials. "On the whole he did a very, very good job. He made fun of it. But he got results. We introduced the Flow Thru Tea Bag. It was an innovation in the industry. Arthur played a big part in communicating that."[8]

And doing it the Godfrey way. He would hold the commercial copy up in the air for the audience to see, then throw it on the floor and ad lib, "as much as anything to irritate the agency":

I have here a piece of script from the client. Hey Arch—better give me some soft music. This is a poyem…

> *In olden days each housewife had a pot…*
> [very long pause, audience laughs]
> *Of soup…upon the stove…*
> [reads the rest of the poem]

I'll translate it. Lipton Noodle Soup and Lipton Tomato Vegetable Soup is the doggondest soup you ever had in your life. Ever see it in the box? Here I'll put them up here…This is the Chicken Noodle soup. [pause] *A chicken once sat in a nest near the pot.* [pause] *It has a decided chickeny flavor. In fact a delightful flavor. In fact, I think there's some chicken in it.* [pause] *One moment. I will have a look.* [opens package] [long pause] *No chicken been in here!* [pause] *But it's full of noodles…. And this is the other one…Lipton Tomato Vegetable Soup.*[9]

Smith would be on the phone to Bond, screaming, "He's done it again!" But irritated or not, Lipton embraced Godfrey. "He'd come to the offices in Hoboken," remembers Anderson. "And he attended sales meetings." Bond remembers the opening of a new plant in Virginia where Godfrey came and spoke at the dedication. He became family within the company. Unlike most agency people, Bond got along fine with Godfrey. "I'm convinced he was very sincere. For example, when my mother died he sent me a handwritten note." But Bond would sometimes see the other side of the star. "Something would rankle him eventually. He was top dog and he'd let it show…. People always asked me if I liked him. I would always say, 'For an hour.'"

For many years, Bond would go to the Monday night show, "just to be there and represent the client. I got to know Andy Rooney and Chuck Horner, the writers. Jack Carney, the producer, was a real nice guy. Arthur loved the musicians. They were the only people he really felt warm with."[10]

His impact on sales was amazing. Another former Lipton executive, Tony Montuori, remembers that when the company introduced another new product, Lipton Onion Soup. "Sales were going nowhere. But there was one store in California that was always out of stock. Seems there was a man living around there who came up with the idea of adding the onion soup mix to sour cream and making a dip out of it. The recipe was sent to headquarters, then on to Godfrey. One Monday night Arthur talked about it, 'Listen to this stupid idea,' he said, then gave the recipe. 'Hell,' he said, 'give it a try.'[11] By Thursday you couldn't buy sour cream or Lipton's Onion Soup mix anywhere!"

Talent Scouts would last on radio for ten years, all for Lipton's. Within two years, *Talent Scouts* would also be Arthur Godfrey's ticket to television.

15

Settling In

By now, Godfrey was staying in New York from Sunday night through Friday morning. He had a one-bedroom penthouse in the Lexington Hotel, just a short walk from the 48th Street studios. Weekends were spent, as always, in rural Leesburg, Virginia. Each Friday after his morning show, he'd drive out to Teterboro Airport in New Jersey, board one of his small planes, and fly to Leesburg's "cow pasture" airstrip. He would be home at Beacon Hill by mid-afternoon.

Short as they were, those weekends reinvigorated Arthur. It put him close to the land. It brought him home to family—Mary, Michael, now 8, and Patricia, age 6. And equally important, they were his refuge from fame.

Loudon County, Virginia, lies just to the west of Fairfax County and is a gateway into the Blue Ridge Mountains, the Shenandoah, and the Alleghenys beyond. It is rolling countryside, woods and mead-

ows, bordered on the northeast by the Potomac and Maryland and on the northwest by the Shenandoah and West Virginia. It is steeped in history. At its center, just 35 miles northwest of Washington, sits Leesburg, the seat of government, and a staging ground for the British during the French and Indian War and the Colonials during the Revolution. During the War of 1812, the U.S. Constitution, the Declaration of Independence and other vital documents were carried here for safe keeping. President James Madison resided nearby at Oak Hill, where he wrote the Monroe Doctrine in 1823. During the Civil War, Leesburg was a strategic point for troop movements, and at Ball's Bluff, in 1861, Rebel troops pushed the Yankees back across the Potomac. But it was the land around Leesburg, not history, that drew the Godfreys there.

In 1946, during a visit to friends in the area, Mary came across Beacon Hill, a 326-acre estate that was up for sale. The property included a ten-room English Tudor mansion that had been built in 1912. Nestled in Catoctin Ridge, it bordered on Morven Park, a 1,200-acre estate of a former Virginia governor. The land was mostly pasture and cropland. Sensing this was exactly what they had been seeking for a permanent home, Mary telephoned Arthur at his New York office and they made the decision to buy it on the spot.

The house included six bedrooms, five bathrooms, and two half-baths, plus servant's quarters. Godfrey once mused that the original owner "must have been obsessed with a fear of fire. The walls, the floors are all solid concrete. If it had been an earlier time, I would have reckoned he was fearful of an attack from Indians."[1] There were several window air conditioners, and breathless views.

Mary and Arthur added a large living room with a fireplace to complete the interior. An outdoor swimming pool and skeet range soon followed, to be joined later by additional buildings (a skating rink, an indoor riding hall), and much additional land. "Godfrey was really friendly," recalls Francis Peacock, whose great grandfather first bought land in the area well over 100 years before the Godfreys arrived. "But we owned a small woodlot on the edge of the property. And he wanted it." Over time, Godfrey upped the price, and Peacock's family finally sold.[2] So did others, until eventually Godfrey had more than 2,000 acres with ponds and hills and 10 outbuildings, the oldest dating from the late 1700s.

Over time, they added more than 400 head of cattle—Brahmas, white-faced Herefords, and a few longhorns—and over two dozen horses, half of which were prize Arabians. There was a dressage horse and several quarterhorses as well. They also had a herd of bison. A number of acres were set aside for a deer park and other game reserves to keep the animals secure from trigger-happy hunters. The land was densely populated with birds and rabbits. He built new stables and a completely modern all-electric barn. The second floor of the new stables was living quarters for Godfrey's trainer, and often doubled as extra guest rooms. Arthur personally supervised construction of the stables. Cattle were fed inside the barn and also from the tremendous feed pens built alongside it. "Life on the Godfrey farm for the animals is like living at the Waldorf," chirped a fan magazine. "Nothing is too good for them, they have the highest paid guy in the entertainment business waiting on 'em!"[3]

It was a working farm, with well-tended crops, and it turned a profit as well. Mary oversaw the complex operations all week, but on weekends Arthur was the driving force. Up at 8:00 every morning, he'd make his rounds, checking new colts or cattle, tramping the land to check grazing stock and "scrupulously investigating his barns, silos, and hen houses."[4] Riding the tractor or riding his horses, Godfrey was on the go all the time. There were ponies and dogs for Pat and Mike, and Mike and Arthur would regularly step out with a target rifle to rid the hills of woodchuck before they dug holes that could break the legs of prize horses.

By the late forties, Godfrey had even convinced CBS to allow him to do his Friday morning radio shows from Virginia. The reason had nothing to do with the broadcasts. He just wanted more time at home. And whatever Godfrey wanted, Godfrey got. At an enormous cost, CBS approved construction of a transmitter on the farm that sent the signal to New York via microwave so that his early morning WABC show for New York City locals, his WTOP show for the Washington audience, and his 10 A.M. CBS Network radio show could all air as normal. Only while

On the farm in Virginia. The farm was Arthur's respite from public life. (Joan Zacher collection.)

he was in Virginia, just up from sleeping, everything and everyone else, from the records he played on the DJ shows to the cast that joined him at 10 A.M., was in New York.

It was Granville Klink, Godfrey's first engineer at WJSV, who oversaw the wiring for the studios at the farm. Klink had become an expert in such matters, having worked on the FDR Fireside chats and with CBS newsman Ed Murrow when they would haul equipment to the Capitol so

that Murrow could record the opening
session of Congress. The Godfrey den in
the main house was converted to a studio.
"We had all the equipment there. Everything was in place all the time. He had his
turntables and the whole bit."[5]

Granville Klink recalled, "I used to go
down there for breakfast every once in a
while before the show and talk with him.
Sometimes in the summertime he would
oversleep and we would have to go in and
wake him up. And that was quite a job because he was like an angry bear sometimes
when you woke him out of a dead sleep!
But he came around all right."[6]

Godfrey escaped from his fans and admirers, but his family didn't escape so easily. Over the years, CBS sales reps, cast
members, friends and staff, were regularly
invited by Godfrey to accompany him
home. "We'd all drive out to Teterboro,"
recalled former CBS sales vice president,
Ben Lockridge, "board the plane with
Arthur in the pilot seat, and be off for a
weekend in the country."[7]

Once the television shows began, more
and more tourists would drive out to
Loudon to find his home. Americans considered him one of the family, so why not
make a visit? "You know," explained Peter
Kelley, Godfrey's agent, "He used to have
people come to his farm and walk in to his
kitchen and sit there and wait for him to
come downstairs. He finally had to put
guards up at his gate to keep people out
because they all thought that they were his
friends."[8]

His work on the two early morning
local shows continued to be gold for him
and for CBS. By 1947, by one account, he
had 58 clients; by another, 88 with a good-
sized waiting list," so many that *Newsweek*, in a three-page feature, reported that
"he can't always abide by the policy re-
quiring one record between commercials.
So he hums, or whistles, or maybe just
laughs into the mike and picks up more

copy."[9] Mug often saved the day. She was
still picking the music and was at his side
throughout both broadcasts, feeding him
stories, letters, and commercial copy to
read. Asked why he continued to do the
local shows, he honestly declared it was
the money.

Early in 1946, Godfrey had used his
"spare time" to try his hand in theater. He
joined the cast of a Broadway–bound review called *Three to Make Ready*. The
show featured popular singer and dancer
Ray Bolger, who is best known for his role
as the Scarecrow in MGM's *The Wizard of
Oz*. As shows often did in those days, the
new musical review tried out in Boston.
The tryout did well, with one notable exception: Godfrey. He was missing cues and
forgetting his lines. Committed to doing
both of his local radio shows each day plus
his new weekday network morning show,
the addition of the new play at night had
stretched his luck too far. He collapsed
during rehearsal, was hospitalized briefly
for exhaustion, and dropped out of the
show before it opened on Broadway.

By 1948, the *Arthur Godfrey Time* format had been adjusted to perfection. The
cast had been altered; Janette Davis and
Bill Lawrence were the new singers, the
Mariners were the new vocal group,
Archie Bleyer had taken over the reigns as
orchestra conductor, and the band had
been enlarged. Tony Marvin was now the
announcer. There was a new theme song,
"Seems Like Old Times," written by Carmen Lombardo, the brother of perenni-
ally popular band leader Guy Lombardo.
And there was now a small studio audience ever day which could react to Godfrey's comments along with the band and
the cast and the listeners at home. That
created even more depth to the show and
reinforced the excitement that it was all
happening live. Instinctively, Godfrey
found ways to interact with the audience
in the studio without sacrificing his

Throughout the late 1940s, the indefatigable Godfrey continued to broadcast two local early morning radio shows for New Yorkers and Washingtonians before opening the mikes for his nationally broadcast CBS radio network shows at 10 A.M. each day.

relationship with the listener at home. "It's cold outside, isn't it?" he'd say, and the audience would murmur agreement. "Bet you folks in Miami aren't sufferin' very much over that." With most of the studio audience consisting of tourists, there was a good deal of talk about what was going on in the city. The listener at home wanted to be there where all the action was. Godfrey had begun to take ukulele lessons and had added that as a regular feature of the shows as well.

All of these adjustments enhanced his daily performances. There was more room for improvisation now that Arthur could talk with the audience as well as the listener at home. He seemed looser, more buoyant. The audience applause made the musical selections more immediate. Under Bleyer's steady hand, the orchestration for just about every song was a gem. And on the instrumentals, there was time for each of the all-star musicians to shine. And then there were the *Talent Scouts* winners each week to add some additional variety. Enough letters now flowed in to Godfrey's offices every day to provide plenty of laughs and topics for conversation.

All the quarter-hour time slots were sold out. In the beginning, the show had been carried by some CBS affiliates and not by others and had been scheduled all over the map. Now it was carried by all affiliates at 11 A.M. each weekday morning.

ANNOUNCER: "It's Arthur Godfrey Time!"
ORCHESTRA: In full with "Seems Like Old Times" with trombonist Sy Schaffer. Arthur joins in with his improvised whistle.
ANNOUNCER: "Yes, it's Arthur Godfrey time with all the Little Godfreys: Janette Davis, Bill Lawrence, the Mariners, and Archie Bleyer and the Orchestra. [*pause*] Now we give you the man himself, 'Arrrthur' Godfrey!"
[*applause*]
ARTHUR: Thank you Tony! Hello everybody.
Arthur goes on to talk about the gale that's blown in overnight from Chicago: "The roof of the Lexington Hotel where I live was wiggling all night.[*pause*] And it's a typical March day here—windy, rainy and.....pyew." [*audience chuckles*]
A woman has sent him a monthly calendar "which has nothin' to do with the weather but is called the Pessimist's Calendar and goes like this." [*paper shuffling*] "To further some malignant plan, the gloomy year begins in JAN. Misfortune spins her spider web for your entanglement in FEB. You know what

income taxes are. Remember one is do in MAR." etc.
[*audience chuckles*]
"I think that's very cute." And she says, "I am ah partial to baritones, Arthur, and naturally I'm partial to you." [*Arthur chuckles*] "A baritone? Ah gee whiz, so many baritones work so hard to make a living. You mustn't call me a baritone...I am a *barrel-tone*. Thank you Mrs. _____. And just for that I will render a selection...render meaning to rip apart. Listen":
[*Orchestra begins, Arthur joins in on 'Necessity.'*][10]

Arthur Godfrey Time would continue with basically the same format until 1960. Combining all these elements, the show, after only three years, had become an American classic.

If his broadcasting and sales income were not high enough, Godfrey found himself becoming a recording star as well. Since the early forties, he had recorded novelty and sentimental songs for Bluebird, Decca, and now Columbia Records, CBS's own record subsidiary, which, along with rival RCA Victor, was considered the premier label of the day.

As America broke loose from the seriousness of the war years, novelty songs were in vogue. Godfrey recorded such classics of the day as "I'm Looking Over a Four-Leaf Clover" and "I'm a Lonely Little Petunia in an Onion Patch (And All I Do Is Cry All Day)," as well as standards like "Lazy Bones." In the fall of 1947, he recorded a tune called "Too Fat Polka." The lyrics were anything but sophisticated:

> I don't want her, you can have her
> She's too fat for me
> She's too fat for me
> She's too fat for me.
> I don't want her, you can have her
> She's too fat for me.
> She's too fat, much too fat,
> She's too fat for me.[11]

Godfrey sang the song on his radio shows and with that exposure, the record took off, selling a million copies in less than seven weeks. Years later he would recall: "We spent four hours in the studio one day making that record. And when we walked out, I said to Archie Bleyer, the bandleader, 'Never in my life did I waste so much time over junk. Gosh, it's awful.' It sold three and a half million copies. Which was the damnedest commentary on the taste of the American public back then."[12]

Over the next four years, he had six top 20 hits. In addition, he recorded frequently for Columbia's children's record division, Playtime, with favorites like "I've Been Working on the Railroad" and "Oh, Susannah." Now his voice was heard across the radio dial, on CBS affiliates in every city and town as well as hundreds of other radio stations where disc jockeys played his latest recordings. And if you needed more, a trip to the record store gave you instant access to Godfrey on your home phonograph. Columbia estimated that during a single month, as many as seventy-seven million different people played a Godfrey record or tuned in his programs.[13]

With all of this success, it was finally time for Godfrey to give up his early morning local radio shows in Washington and New York which had continued every weekday throughout his early network days. In 1948, he closed them out, after fourteen years with WTOP/WJSV and seven years with WCBS.

16

Television: CBS and Godfrey Take the Plunge

THOUGH TELEVISION, LIKE RADIO, can trace its conceptual roots back to the late 1800s, it wasn't until 1923 that any serious technical progress was made toward capturing movement as well as sound as it happened. And then it wasn't until 1935 that AT&T, RCA, and several independent inventors could say they had solved most of the problems of creating, transmitting, and receiving a reasonably good picture. Only then did RCA and its subsidiary NBC move ahead on experimenting with production and programming for the new medium. As a manufacturer of electronic equipment, RCA had great interest in seeing television grow; CBS, a stand-alone company, had no such manufacturing intent. RCA's David Sarnoff believed that television would become as big as radio, if not bigger, as a home entertainment medium. CBS's William Paley, on the other hand, was highly skep-

tical of television. He thought television would be used in theaters as a form of motion pictures because people were too social to want to stay home to watch. As a result, NBC was more aggressive than its rival in developing production expertise and programming for the new medium, airing its first show in 1936. By 1939, however, both NBC and CBS had launched a limited schedule of daily telecasts over their experimental stations. That same year, Allen B. Dumont began marketing the first home television receivers, and television was showcased at the New York World's Fair.

But television faced several more hurdles. One factor was slow action by the Federal Communications Commission, which oversaw the airwaves. The FCC delayed authorizing full *commercial* operation until May 1941. And then, before manufacturers could tool up for mass production and before stations could be built and put into operation, the U.S. entered World War II. Within five months, all production of sets was halted. And with most young men in uniform, only six pioneer stations continued to operate during the war years.

When the war ended, NBC and CBS increased their activity with their local New York experimental stations, but CBS had come to believe that the black-and-white phase for television was unnecessary. It now advocated initial adoption of a full color system and asked the Federal Communications Commission for a ruling. All the while, RCA pushed ahead with its perfected black-and-white system while it worked on a compatible color system, offering its first RCA television sets for sale in September 1946. During the same period, its subsidiary, NBC, had secured channels in each of the major markets. Finally, in March 1947, the FCC acted. It deemed the CBS color system not ready for commercial use and reaffirmed its earlier monochrome standards. That was the signal for television manufacturers like RCA and broadcasters like NBC to move ahead to bring television to the mass market. NBC was ready. CBS was not. NBC only needed to expand its schedule as television receiver sales took off. CBS found itself not only without the proper outlets, but also without the talent to fill the screen.

In 1947, in a dramatic move that caught NBC by surprise, William Paley began signing up NBC's biggest radio stars—Jack Benny, Edgar Bergen, Amos 'n Andy, and Red Skelton. Whether his intent was that these radio personalities would give him his entrée into television is disputed, yet that is exactly what happened. In the meantime, now that television had suddenly arrived, CBS moved quickly to develop a television variety show (Ed Sullivan's *Toast of The Town*) and a dramatic

show (Worthington Minor's *Studio One*) to offer up in the fall of 1948.

The year 1948 was a watershed one for television in America. In 1946, 5,000 sets had been produced for sale; in 1947, 160,000. Most Americans who did watch television in 1948 watched in bars and taverns. But in 1948, the number of sets produced jumped dramatically to 944,000, bringing the total number of American homes with television to well over one million. It is difficult to know whether the number of set sales fueled the networks' immediate investment in new, high-quality (and costly for the time) television series, or whether the new television series fueled the sales of television sets. It's safe to say it was a synthesis—each fueled the other.

To compare the prime-time schedules of 1947-48 and 1948-49 is to look at the first as a barren landscape, and the second as the real beginning of prime-time network television. During the 1947 season, there was no Sunday or Saturday night prime-time programming on any network except for various special presentations on NBC Sundays. During the week, NBC offered only six hours of shows, most notably the *Gillette Cavalcade of Sports* (mainly boxing) on Monday and Friday nights, and the *Kraft Television Theatre* on Wednesdays. Dumont offered about the same, most notably *Charade Quiz* on Thursdays and a Western movie on Tuesdays. CBS and ABC offered no weeknight shows at all.

But just one season later, 1948-49, there was prime-time programming on each of the four networks all week long. And the premieres that year were to establish television as its own medium: a place to watch, a place to work, and a place to advertise. Such long-running series as *Hollywood Screen Test*, *Town Meeting of the Air*, wrestling, basketball, and *Break the Bank* premiered on ABC. Dumont resurrected the *Original Amateur Hour*, this time with Ted Mack, who had been assistant to Major Bowes on the old radio series, as host. In addition, Dumont offered boxing, football, wrestling, and a number of lesser shows.

NBC weighed in with *Meet the Press* and *Philco Television Playhouse* on Sunday nights, *The Texaco Star Theatre* with Milton Berle on Tuesdays, and a large number of musical, news, panel, and quiz shows of lesser note.

CBS launched *Studio One* and *Toast of the Town* with Ed Sullivan on Sundays, newscasts five nights a week at 7:30 P.M., *We the People* on Tuesdays, *Winner Take All* on Wednesdays, and a variety of sporting events. And though William Paley and the CBS brass were still consumed with their negotiations with Jack Benny and the other NBC radio stars, they were also watching the extraordinary public following that kept developing for one of their *own* radio stars: Arthur Godfrey.[1]

It is the morning of November 23, 1948, and *Arthur Godfrey Time* is set for its usual 10 A.M. start on the CBS Radio network. The morning show is at its peak of popularity, sold out, and fast becoming an American entertainment staple. Godfrey had been right: he had an important and unique format to bring to network radio. And with less than one percent of American homes owning television sets, network radio is still king in 1948.

With many hours to fill each day on its fledgling television system, someone at CBS has come up with the idea of broadcasting *Arthur Godfrey Time* each morning on radio *and* television. Godfrey isn't very comfortable with this idea, which they call simultaneous broadcasting, or "simulcasting." His morning show is freewheeling, low-keyed. The talent dresses casually. Arthur often wears a headset and has Mug at his side to hand him the paperwork. The audience is right up close.

The format is working well. Television could undo all this.

But CBS has persisted, and so today, Studio 22 in the basement of East 49th Street is not only filled with the usual cast and crew members and a buzzing audience of some 50 people seated on folding chairs, but with additional crew, additional equipment, and huge spotlights and floodlights that are needed to create a good "image" on the early cameras, but that raised the temperature considerably. On stage left is the countertop that Godfrey uses as his desk. Behind it is his chair, and the chair next to it is for Mug. To the right of the desk are a stand-up microphone and two rows of folding chairs. Already seated are singers Janette Davis and Bill Lawrence.

In the center, toward the rear, is the orchestra. Guitarist Remo Palmier and bass player Gene Traxler are shooting the breeze with the other band members. Stage right is a music stand and stand-up microphone where announcer Tony Marvin is rereading his script, ready to introduce each of the four 15-minute segments. Behind him is a blowup of the label of the first sponsor, Nabisco Premium Crackers. And positioned in front of the desk, the chairs, and the orchestra are three huge television cameras mounted on wheels with cameramen behind them. The men wear headsets and are receiving instructions from someone somewhere outside of the studio. Camera cables sprawl all across the floor.

The men in the cast are wearing ties and jackets. Janette Davis wears a sweater and pearls. Mug is in a tailored suit. Godfrey arrives ten minutes before airtime in a tweed sport jacket and tie. He is greeted by applause from the audience—some 40 women and 10 men. He waves, smiles, and goes to his desk where Mug and several technical people are waiting. He puts on his headset and settles into his chair.

At exactly 10 A.M. EST, the band strikes

up "Seems Like Old Times," Godfrey chimes in with his whistled version, and Tony Marvin begins his usual introduction: "It's *Arthur Godfrey Time* with Arthur Godfrey and all the Little Godfreys. And here's that man himself, Arthur 'Nabisco Good' Godfrey!" The band ends its refrain simultaneously, and the audience applauds generously. Arthur speaks:

Good morning. We're back again with a whole hour of entertainment...brought to you by the miracle of radio. [pause] *You know, it may not be long until we come to you through the miracle of television.* [pause] *This morning, we've got lights all around this place...and they're driving us crazy. They said, "We'll come in, Arthur, and you won't even know we're there."* [He makes a face, thumbs his nose at the camera. The audience laughs. Then he addresses the radio audience.] *For a penny post card I'll explain that laugh to you folks.... We're having what they call a "dry run." Dry? After an hour under these lights for heaven's sakes there won't be a dry guy in the house!... But it's worth it. Just think how wonderful it will be when we get this show on television. You folks at home will be able, just with the flick of a switch, to be transported from your dull humdrum living room through miles of space, through the miracle of electronics...to this dull hum-drum basement.... The first thing you'll see is Tony Marvin.... Television may be the answer—or may not. Seeing is believing.*[2]

And with that highly skeptical view of television, Godfrey and the cast move into the show. Janette sings. And then Arthur goes into a plug for Nabisco. He takes a bowl of crackers and begins crunching them up with his fingers. "Listen to these crackers...Hear how crispy they are! And to go with these dainty little crackers today, we have an eighty-pound turkey!" The sponsor, he explains, wanted to present the turkey to Arthur and the cast in advance of Thanksgiving Day.

The crew delivers the turkey on a large serving tray and places it in front of Godfrey. The camera cuts to a close-up. "Look how they've fixed it up. ... And *look* what they've put on top—par-sa-ly. I know just what to do with this par-sa-ly," he says, grabbing a bunch. "I know *exactly* what to do with it!" He stuffs it into the backside of the turkey. The audience roars. Mug smiles in disbelief. He shakes his head. "I think you'll agree that's the proper place for par-sa-ly." The camera cuts to a close-up of the stuffed turkey. "Gee, that's gonna look pretty on the film isn't it?" Then, to the radio audience: "If you folks can guess where I shoved the parsley..." The audience roars. The camera lovingly pans over the turkey. "Let's go on here and be serious.... That's a *very* pretty bird.... And I thank you Mr. Nabisco for giving me the bird."

The Mariners, relaxed and jovial, are at the music stand and sing their song. Bill Lawrence, with his grown-in crew cut, tie and jacket, sings. Back to Arthur, who tells about calls coming in from listeners in New York City who also own television sets, wondering why they can't get the show on those sets. He explains it is only a test being filmed. During the third segment for Chesterfields, Jeanette sings "You Made Me Love You" in a soft tempo. When she finishes, Arthur decides to try it himself with the band in an upbeat tempo. He sings from the desk, one hand on his face, the other hand holding a cigarette. More talk. The winner of last night's *Talent Scout* show sings. Arthur sings with the Mariners. Janette sings again. The show ends.

Although it would be another three years until simulcasts of his morning show would appear on the CBS network, within six weeks all the Little Godfreys would begin appearing on CBS television—every Wednesday night. The format would end up being different than the morning show. But the cast would be basically the same—with Godfrey, as unpredictable as ever, as host.

In November, pressure was also building to bring cameras into the *Talent Scouts*
show. The fall launches of *Toast of the
Town* with Ed Sullivan and *Studio One*
had been particularly successful. But it
was an NBC talent, Milton Berle, who was
the surprise hit of the season. Berle, an
old vaudevillian, had been starring in his
own successful radio program on NBC for
several years. But his move to television
proved phenomenally successful, and although there would be no Nielsen ratings for two more years, it was clear that
his show, *Texaco Star Theatre*, broadcast
Tuesdays at 8:00 P.M., was the runaway
hit of the season. Indeed, thousands of
Easterners were setting aside Tuesdays
as the nights to visit friends with television sets, or the nights to get to the local
tavern to catch a glimpse of Berle and
his slapstick brand of comedy. Thanks
to Berle, NBC was out in front in the
television sweepstakes, gaining most of
the national attention, press, and viewer-
ship.

All the more reason to move Godfrey
on to television. Arthur was skeptical. "In
the beginning I thought television was
going to be a medium strictly for motion-
picture actors. When the Lipton Tea folks
had first approached me on the question of
televising the *Talent Scouts* show I had
said, 'If you think it's fit television fare to
photograph my radio show, go right
ahead—provided you keep your cameras
out of sight and don't interfere with the
broadcast. I'm a radio man, not a movie
star.'"[3]

And so, with that agreed, on December 6, 1948, at 8:30 p.m., *Arthur Godfrey's
Talent Scouts* was broadcast simultaneously on CBS radio and CBS television.
And the show was little changed in the
move.

Most commercials in 1948 were produced live. In part, this was a carryover
from radio. Besides, filmed and animated

spots, though not uncommon, were expensive to produce. Few sponsors had the
money of a Gillette Razor Company to
pay for quality filmed commercials, and
few ad agencies were geared up to produce such a product. And so, Milton
Berle's show featured the singing Texaco
servicemen and a vaudevillian named Sid
Stone who sold the products, and the
Kraft Television Theatre showed you in
detail how to use cheese in all of your
recipes.

From the first *Talent Scouts* television
show, it was clear that Arthur Godfrey
could sell on television every bit as well as
he had on radio. Lipton's sponsored the
television version as well, and now Godfrey not only spoke to the virtues of the
product, he could show you how to make
that pot of tea and mix that instant soup.
Variety published a rave review:

Whatever the indefinable quality that has skyrocketed Arthur Godfrey into coast-to-coast
bigtime as Columbia network's $5,000,000
billings baby, it's been captured in spades on
video....The premiere televising of Godfrey's
Talent Scouts on Monday can be chalked up as
perhaps the first surefire AM-television simulcast in the commercial program sweepstakes.
... As far as Lipton's, the sponsor, is concerned,
this one's in the tea bag.[4]

The television version would prove a
boon to the performers. Now, they not
only got a chance at network radio, they
got their first television experience, and
credits as well.

Among the earliest winners were a female barbershop quartet called the Chordettes. The show took place on September
26, 1949, during opening week of the new
season on both network radio and television. CBS has touted Godfrey's return with
a glowing press release:

Refreshed after a two-month vacation, America's most listened-to personality, Arthur

Godfrey, resumes his strenuous radio and television schedule on CBS.... He will be in front of the microphones and cameras for 7¾ hours weekly.

During his vacation, Mr. Godfrey took a one-month, 18,000-mile tour of South American countries as the guest of Captain Eddie Rickenbacker, President and General Manager of Eastern Air Lines.[5]

After the opening, Godfrey takes his seat at his ever-present desk, arrayed with Lipton products and signs, makes himself comfortable, and looks around. "Gee. Isn't the place all lighted up nice for television and everything." Then, to the studio audience, "How do I look, OK?" Then he fills them in on his "53 hours in one of Eddie Rickenbacker's Constellations, 30 days in South America, a month lying around Miami and Puerto Rico, and down on the Farm in old Virginny." He is glad to be back where you can get a good cup of tea.

He introduces Ted Rauh, from Hasbrouck Heights, New Jersey, a Western Electric plant inspector. "That's my home town," he tells Rauh. "Everybody talks about it, Arthur," Rauh responds. " Why?" quips Arthur. "I paid off the bills. They don't have to talk anymore.... Any hobbies?" he asks. "Barbershop singing," replies Rauh. "I'm president of the SBEPSQSA, Inc." "I'm a member of that group too! Manhattan chapter," says Arthur, his interest rising. "Never been to any meetings though. ... What did you bring for talent? Not a barbershop quartet?" "Not a men's, a ladies'," replies Rauh. "Ginny's father is president of the SBEPSQSA." "Done anything professionally?" "Traveled around the country."

And with that Godfrey introduces the Chordettes, who sing "Ballin' the Jack," a cappella. When it ends, Godfrey is visibly

pleased. But the Chordettes have some competition that evening. The next performer is a young silversmith named Wally Cox, who has been appearing at the Blue Angel and the Village Vanguard. "What's his act?" Godfrey asks the talent scout, who is Cox's neighbor. "He is a comedian." "OK, then, the Lipton Spotlight falls on your discovery, Wallace Cox!" Cox, who would go on to fame for many years as television's *Mr. Peepers*, has the audience rolling. When he finishes and the applause dies down, Godfrey comments, "My jaws hurt so much I can't talk!"

But when the final reprieves had ended, the audience applause indicator had declared the Chordettes the winners. And they went on to become regulars with Godfrey for the next five years, and had several hit records too, including "Mr. Sandman."[6]

Over the next ten years, *Talent Scouts* would provide many young entertainers with their first network television exposure, including Al Martino, Connie Francis, ventriloquist Shari Lewis, Steve Lawrence, pianist Marian McPartland, Robert Goulet, Leslie Uggams, Pat Boone, the McGuire Sisters, the Diamonds, Roy Clark, and Patsy Cline.

But all that lay ahead. For now, the big news was that Arthur Godfrey was on television. For many avid listeners, it was their first chance to *see* Arthur. For Lipton's it was another step toward dominating the tea industry. For CBS, it was a clear sign that they were going to be a leader in the now burgeoning business of television. By October 1950, the television version of *Talent Scouts* was the eighth-highest rated television show in the country; by the following year it had nudged Milton Berle out of first place and was America's number one show.

17

Everything a First

ON THE HEELS OF THE SUCCESSFUL television launch of the *Talent Scouts* show, CBS fired another volley in the great rush to television: the new musical variety show *Arthur Godfrey and His Friends*, which premiered on Wednesday evening, January 12, 1949, at 8 P.M.

The show's producer was Larry Puck, who had joined the Godfrey organization the previous year. Puck was a veteran of more than 30 years experience as a producer and director in stage, radio, and television, with expertise in talent scouting for vaudeville, having worked early on, in the Loew and B. F. Keith offices. He knew just about every major artist of the day, and that boded well for the new Godfrey vehicle since guest performers soon became a major feature of the Wednesday night show.

Also on board were morning regulars Tony Marvin, the Chordettes, Jan Davis, Bill Lawrence, and the Mariners. Archie Bleyer headed the orchestra and the

musicians were the same *Arthur Godfrey Time* radio group, although they were soon augmented by other CBS staff musicians to add strings and more brass. Chesterfield picked up sole sponsorship for the live hour.

The first shows were intentional attempts to recreate the successful morning show approach, with more time for performance and a chance to be more visual. But early on the critics were cautioning that it wouldn't be enough. "There's no animation in the show," complained *Variety*. "While Bill Lawrence is potentially a promising singer, he doesn't know how to move in front of the lens.... Janette Davis cannot move either, handles herself poorly, and although she boasts a fair enough voice, she needs plenty of coaching.... All of which means that Lawrence stands still, Miss Davis stands still, the quartet stands still, the orchestra sits down and so does Godfrey. Besides, something or somebody has to stand off those slow

92

ballads with which the vocalists persist. It's all too much radio."[1]

Puck responded on the third show by bringing in a guest, comedian Guy Raymond, who livened things up a bit, and by having Godfrey move over to the second piano for a lively duet with his pianist. Godfrey's response to the criticism was not as practical. He took time out during the program to explain how much work went into the show, and at one point stuck his tongue out at the critics. "The sniping," reported the *New York Sun*, "did not seem calculated to keep the program in the second place it won in the last television Hooper report or to retain for Godfrey the admirers who like him for good humor."[2]

But the show did succeed. Over the spring, guest artists of note began showing up regularly, including a July appearance by legendary lyricist Oscar Hammerstein II. The regular cast, along with well-known guest vocalist Betty George, offered a number of Rodgers and Hammerstein tunes. Well-known cartoonist of the day Ham Fisher also appeared on the program and during conversation took time to point out the importance of racial tolerance, pointing to Arthur's recent stand when he had refused to have his cast perform at a Daughters of the American Revolution concert at Constitution Hall in Washington after he had been informed that the DAR would not allow the integrated Mariners group to appear. Godfrey then read the lyrics to "You've Got to Be Taught," written by Hammerstein for the hit Broadway show of the time, *South Pacific*.

Arthur Godfrey and His Friends was now on track. By Fall 1950, it was running at a very respectful 18th each week, commanding a Nielsen rating of 35.9 percent of all American television households.

Puck had gone to work and the results were much more polished shows. On November 8, 1950, Godfrey, fresh from a Hawaiian visit the previous summer, imported a number of his friends from the islands and held a Hawaiian night featuring Duke Kahanamoku, an internationally famous swimmer of the day, beach boys Splash Lyons and Chick Daniels, plus three winners of a ukulele contest which Arthur had judged during his visit to Honolulu. From the Lexington Hotel's Hawaiian Room came Momikai and her hula dancers and vocalist Haleloke, who would soon be a regular on the show. The show received high ratings and set off a whole series of Hawaiian-oriented shows in the series.

Over the following two years, guests included Berrah Minevitch and his Harmonica Rascals, a young vocalist named Marion Marlowe who also became a Godfrey regular, comedians Morey Amsterdam and Jerry Colonna, concert singers Helen Traubel and Patrice Munsel, entertainer Harold Lang, gospel notable Mahalia Jackson, and a comedy musical group called the Vagabonds, whom Godfrey had "discovered" in Florida and who proved extremely popular visitors on numerous occasions.

The Wednesday night show not only became a place for guest entertainers to perform, but afforded viewers an opportunity to meet these people. In the first year, guests included singer Pearl Bailey, young comedian Lenny Bruce, stars of the big Broadway shows like Lisa Kirk and Vivian Blaine, vaudeville acts, baseball stars. In addition, Puck scheduled notable stage actresses like Helen Hayes and movie stars like James Stewart and June Allyson, who came not to perform but to talk with Arthur. Arthur proved to be a superb interviewer. *Arthur Godfrey and His Friends* became a place to see the personal side of the stars and the character actors from radio and television. Early on, in February 1950, long-time actress Gertrude Berg (whose own program, *The Goldbergs*, about a middle-class Jewish family with middle-class problems, had been a favorite on radio for twenty years and then a big hit on CBS-TV beginning in 1949), stepped out of character for a visit with Godfrey. It was probably the first opportunity for millions of her followers to meet her.

The Wednesday night show was the only place on television for such relaxed talk. Ed Sullivan's *Toast of the Town*, for all its showcasing of the stars, was a stand-up performance show. So were Milton Berle's *Texaco Star Theater*, *The Colgate Comedy Hour*, *All Star Review*, *The Admiral Hour* and the Jack Benny and Red Skelton shows that soon followed. Dramatic anthology shows were all scripted. So were the detective shows and early sitcoms, including *I Love Lucy*. For that matter, all the leading radio shows, including Bob Hope and Bing Crosby, were all rehearsed. Whether CBS or Godfrey or his producers were aware of it at the time or not, they were blazing the trail for a whole new genre of television programs—the television talk shows. It would be 1954, five years after Godfrey's *Friends* show premiered, that *The Tonight Show* picked up on the approach. Prime time talk would not happen on network television for a dozen years or so, and then only on tape.

Television critic John Crosby was one of those taken by Godfrey's ability to lead guests through conversation. "I was on his shows several times and I was awed by the tremendous professional ease with which he handled singers, guests, audience and above all, the *time*, which is the essence of television. Time slipped by imperceptibly on his shows and all of a sudden—it always seemed much too soon—there he was saying goodbye and God bless you. (He was always God blessing us.)"[3]

When Arthur took time off for vacations or military training, CBS brought in well-known stars of the time, including actress Celeste Holm, comedian Victor Borge, and a popular tenor from the thirties and forties, Frank Parker, who soon joined the Godfrey cast on a regular basis.

In the process, Godfrey became a believer in the importance of providing a more professional show for evening television; it took much more effort than he had first envisioned. Many years later he would say, "We were trying to ... keep you interested, and we figured that in order to do that, we had to change it every week—every day if we could. Always dreaming up something new, the theory being that in order to live, to last any length of time, one had to grow in stature.... If you didn't watch yourself, you got typed and presently people would tire. We fought to keep the bill of fare changing all the time. And that was why, I suppose, we were quite successful.... The reason for it was that you never knew what you were gonna see on the Godfrey Show. Very simple reason for that—Godfrey didn't know."[4]

In May of 1952, Godfrey and several cast members did a few turns on the ice during a production number. It was so well received that he decided to do a more ambitious program. And so, on December 17, 1952, *Arthur Godfrey and His Friends* presented the first of a series of live ice shows, the first to appear on television. CBS press releases touted how the show had been in preparation for seven months, "probably the longest 'rehearsal' in television history. For seven months [the cast took] ice-skating lessons from professional Fritz Dietle atop Madison Square Garden in New York. Some of the cast, Janette Davis and Marion Marlowe, had never skated before. Haleloke ... had never even seen ice outside of a refrigerator. During the months of lessons there were falls and bruises. Mariners Jim Lewis and Nat Dickerson got banged up in tailspins. But ... all are ready now."

Building a 1,600-square-foot rink on-stage at the CBS-TV Playhouse "was a triumph of production know-how, speed and ingenuity. Two nights before the program, ice specialist Everett McGowan and a crew of fifty began construction, which called for waterproofing the bare stage, bordering it, and installing refrigerating pipes connected to an ice-making truck outside the stage door. When ice was not ready on Tuesday evening for final rehearsal, Godfrey and company motored to Great Neck, Long Island, and at a late hour took over the rink for practice. On Wednesday, they did their finals on ice, rehearsing almost up to airtime. Arthur was quoted as saying that the skating session sometimes made his legs stiff and sore, but that he enjoyed skating, and felt it helped his legs."[5]

The show was also a challenge for director Bob Bleyer and cameramen, who were not familiar with televising live ice events or, for that matter, ice events of any kind.

In the end, it was an unequivocal success. Included in the cast were two female professional skaters who did solo numbers and skate-danced with Arthur. Following the broadcast, an avalanche of calls, telegrams, and letters poured in. Even Godfrey was overwhelmed. The show hit a 49.0 rating and a 73.7 share of those watching television, a new high in Trendex ratings.

There would be additional ice shows in the years ahead, all of them live. The show experimented in many ways. As early as April 1950, Godfrey hosted the show live from Chicago, where he was performing with Perry Como and Bing Crosby at the National Association of Tobacco Distributors' Convention. The rest of the cast was in New York. The director switched back and forth between the two studios, though it was hardly perfect. Each time the cable was switched, there was a split second of blank screen. But with Godfrey's strong presence and with Perry Como as guest for the second half, the show came out fine.

"You have to remember," Godfrey later explained on his final television appearance in 1981, "and it's very difficult, I know, unless you were living at that time and old enough to watch, to remember what it was like without television, and when television first came along ... everything we did was ... a first. For instance, we did the first underwater show.... We built a big glass cage and put the camera inside and the cameraman alongside of this camera in the tank, and lowered the tank into the water. And the poor guy was scared to death because ... if a wave had come along and put some water down in there, he knew he was gonna be electrocuted, and maybe the camera [would] blow up or something. But none of those horrible things happened, and we were able to show America for the first time what it looked like underneath the water, live—we didn't film anything. We just didn't have any underwater equipment then."[6]

Sometime in the late 1940s, Godfrey began to visit Miami Beach. Air travel was still out of reach for most Americans. Those who traveled to Miami and Miami Beach were still doing so by train or, if they were willing to make the demanding trek, by car. Yet Miami Beach had already become, in 1940s terms, one of the nation's premier resort locations, a place that every American had heard of. Though most Americans still only had a picture postcard impression of southern Florida, it was a place that many an Easterner, caught in the grip of ice and snow each winter, dreamed of visiting. It was Arthur Godfrey who was going to make those visits a reality by bringing the Beach right into their living rooms.

For Arthur, Miami Beach was the perfect vacation retreat, offering him, fishing, swimming, golfing, sailing and most of all, warm sun to help relieve his constant pain.

In 1949, a young publicity man named Hank Meyer became the first full-time public relations director of Miami Beach, a job he would retain for 27 years. Meyer was highly entrepreneurial, determined to make Miami and Miami Beach even greater tourist attractions.

Godfrey was already coming to Florida for vacations, including regular visits with his wife Mary and his attorney and manager, Leo DeOrsey, and DeOrsey's wife Helen. DeOrsey owned a piece of the Kenilworth Hotel at Bal Harbour where they stayed. When he returned to his radio and early television shows, Godfrey would wax poetic about the state, and the Beach in particular. His comments did not escape Meyer, and he arranged for a meeting during Godfrey's next vacation there.

The two hit it off immediately. Godfrey couldn't say enough about what the Beach had to offer. And Meyer saw him as a potentially wonderful promoter for the area. When Arthur talked about how much he'd like to share his Beach experiences with his viewers, Meyer suggested originating some shows from Miami Beach. "We can't do that yet," Godfrey told him. "We've been trying since 1948 but it's very expensive to ship a show out and besides, the coaxial cable only reaches as far as Atlanta from the network headquarters in New York." "If I can get the cable extended down here, would you do some shows?" Meyer asked. "I'd be down here in a day," Arthur responded. Meyer set to work to obtain the backing. He succeeded and nine months later, DeOrsey called Meyer with the news: "Hank, you have yourself the first network radio and television programs to come out of Miami Beach."[7]

Indeed, the shows were among the very few telecasts produced outside the New York studios of CBS, NBC, Dumont, and ABC.

"The first show was done out of the Kenilworth Hotel in the winter of 1953," Meyer later recalled. "It was a balmy night at the Beach, and Arthur and the McGuire Sisters were placed on a boat just offshore. As the show opened, they jumped off and swam to shore." The orchestra and the rest of the cast of Little Godfreys were already stationed around the pool and the adjoining beach area where floodlights provided "live" sets. Godfrey proved the perfect host, regaling Florida and the Beach and all its attractions. Before the show was over, Godfrey, sitting on the sand under a palm tree, with the surf breaking behind him, implored his viewers, "Don't take my word. Come on down. Experience it for yourself." For Eastern viewers, trapped in the cold, the black and white images and conversations were riveting. Arthur was there. Why not them? "The phones rang off the hook," according to Meyer. "From that point on, Arthur owned the Beach."[8]

One can only imagine the stir Godfrey's plans to televise out of Florida must have caused at CBS. In radio, live remote broadcasts were common throughout the 1940s. During World War II in particular, Kate Smith and others took their entire shows on the road for weeks at a time to sell war bonds. But television was a different and much more complex and expensive challenge. Arthur's entourage of performers, producers, writers, directors, cameramen, technicians, instruments, and technical equipment must have required enormously complex transportation and production logistics, let alone the costs of hotels and food. But Godfrey pushed the envelope on the technology of the time and his ratings soared even higher. His sponsors were more than satisfied.

In the years that followed, he returned

Arthur Godfrey and His Friends travel to Cheyenne, Wyoming, for an early telecast and are welcomed in a public parade. Phyllis and Chris McGuire of the McGuire Sisters are in the top front seats; singer Janette Davis and Frank Musiello, assistant producer, are facing the camera. (Doreen Partin Roberts collection.)

regularly to do his Wednesday night television and morning radio and television shows from the Beach.

In 1953, the *Friends* team experimented with an original musical score and lyrics by Joan Edwards and Lyn Duddy, tailored to the talents of the cast. Entitled the "TV Calendar Show," it featured different numbers for each month of the year. The response prompted a cast record album.

But on many of the more routine shows, there was still a lot of the relaxed Godfrey. "He was [basically] doing the same thing he was doing on the morning show," explained guitarist Remo Palmier.

"He'd show up in the middle of rehearsal unless he had something to do in it like a little dance routine.... We would rehearse all these different numbers ... and about three of the things were never used. Arthur was one of these guys who just went by feel. He felt [things] going in a certain direction and he felt [something] was superfluous, he would just leave it out. But we rehearsed it. We had a CBS staff drummer named Howard Smith, a terrific drummer, who could do anything. He was put on the Wednesday show to do this number. He came in one week and we didn't do it. We did everything else we had rehearsed but that one. That was left out. He came in the next week and it didn't get in again. So Howard looks at Archie [Bleyer] and says, 'Archie, is it all right if I just send in my picture next week?'" [9]

The Wednesday night show was notable for another breakthrough: it was the first television series to present an integrated singing group on a regular basis. Godfrey's first radio network show had featured the Jubilaires, an all-black group that specialized in spirituals and gospel. But now, for television, Godfrey had hired on the Mariners, a quartet composed of two black men and two white. If that in itself was not unique on the tube, the fact that the group not only sang their own songs but also joined the cast in singing and dancing routines was, in the late 1940s and early 1950s basically unheard of.

Each Christmas, the Wednesday night show would become a family event, with the children of each of the cast members on stage with Arthur. Among the children were the young daughters of Jim Lewis and Nat Dickerson. Arthur would gather them all together, introduce them to the audience and the viewers around the country, talk with them, and give them each presents. In a time still prior to integration in the United States, the image was riveting. Godfrey was sending a clear message. As one magazine article put it, "The four fellows who put their voices together to make sweet music are living examples of a bigger kind of harmony."[10]

But in the South, the message and the visual impact did not go down well with some. In particular, the governor of Georgia, Herman Talmadge, who, after three years of the *Friends* show and a Ken Murray variety show where a mixed children's group sang Christmas carols, had seen enough. On January 5, 1952, writing in his political newspaper, *The Statesman*, Talmadge charged several national shows with violating the spirit of the South's segregation laws. "We are speaking of a complete abolition of segregation customs in these shows which are beamed to states of the South." He pointed to the Mariners, saying, "Negro men frequently are seen mixed up in the dancing ensembles." He promised to prohibit the show in the South as a stage presentation. He called for congressional action.

CBS was quick to retort. "The Mariners have appeared on the Godfrey show for four years. We never have exploited the fact that two of the singers are white and two are Negro," the statement said. "They are simply comprised of the best quartet Godfrey could find." It described the Godfrey show as a little "League of Nations," with performers of various creeds and from various sections of the country, including Hawaii.

Godfrey's response to the Associated Press was even more pointed:

I am sorry for His Excellency, Governor Talmadge, but as long as I'm on the show the Mariners are going to stay with me.

The Mariners served together on a Coast Guard ship during the war. That's where I found them. We also have some colored boys fighting in Korea. I wonder if the Governor knows that.

It's a pretty tough place where human beings can't sing together. In such a place liberty is going to collapse.

I'm sorry about the Governor's segregation laws. I don't know why he wants to separate one human being from another human being. It just doesn't make sense.[11]

Within nine months of the premiere of *Arthur Godfrey and His Friends*, NBC responded by launching its own variety show in the same time period. Entitled *Four Star Review*, it featured a rotating roster of comedians—Ed Wynn, Danny Thomas, Jack Carson, and Jimmy Durante. Though the show would continue for three years, bringing additional comedy stars to television for the first time, including Martha

Raye, Olsen & Johnson, Spike Jones, Victor Borge, Bob Hope, the Ritz Brothers, and ventriloquist Paul Winchell, it was no match for the Godfrey show. It moved to Saturday nights after just one season.

Arthur Godfrey and His Friends had won out not only because Godfrey was so popular, but because the show itself was a breakthrough prime-time format. With its stock company of performers, it became the model for a whole new breed of variety shows. Soon Garry Moore, another of CBS' early daytime personalities, was offering a nighttime version of his show featuring his own little company, including vocalists Ken Carson and Denise Lor and announcer-comedian Durwood Kirby. The show was the predecessor of Moore's hour-long show that ran for nine years from the late 1950s until 1967, and by then had added comediennes Carol Burnett and Marion Lorne as regulars. Burnett then spun off her own successful variety show with her own cast of regulars. Throughout the 1960s, all three networks offered their own versions of such variety shows, the most notable being Lawrence Welk.

The show's influence was also felt at NBC when it launched its late night talk/variety show, *Tonight*, in 1954. There was the desk for the host (Steve Allen) that Godfrey had made so familiar, the announcer (in this case Gene Rayburn), the band (Skitch Henderson), the vocalists (Steve Lawrence and Edie Gorme), the patter, and the occasional guest. "Arthur Godfrey did not do what the typical vaudeville comedians like Milton Berle were doing on [early] television," points out Steve Allen. "He had a remarkable naturalness. Right away he seemed like a human being. He had that in common

with one other person out of radio in the early fifties, Dave Garroway. Godfrey spoke exactly on air as he did in person—low key, thoughtful, grammatically correct. Those two guys made it possible for the talk show hosts who came after to be acceptable—Steve Allen, Jack Paar, Johnny Carson. ... We didn't have to explain [to the network officials] why we wanted to speak informally on our shows."[12]

A year after the launch of the show, Godfrey was on the cover of *Time* magazine, which at that time hardly ever gave such attention to entertainers, let alone broadcasters. He was now a superstar in two mediums—well before that label came into common use. During the 1951-52 season, his evening television shows, *Arthur Godfrey's Talent Scouts* and *Arthur Godfrey and His Friends*, held down 1st and 6th spots in the Nielsen ratings. The following season they were in 2nd and 3rd place behind the new *I Love Lucy* show.

America was in a postwar boom. Incomes were rising. And the list of new products available to consumers was multiplying by the month. Frozen foods, instant foods, new grooming aids, new medications, pills, plastic, aluminum wrapping. American families, many now moving out of the cities to the suburbs, were beginning to consume goods and services in quantities unimaginable just a few short years before. From household appliances to frozen foods to travel and entertainment, the engine for this consumer frenzy was television. And the pied piper was a man named Arthur Godfrey. A 1951 magazine called *Godfrey the Great* could boast, "Arthur Godfrey's voice is heard by more persons each week than anyone in the history of the spoken word."[13]

All the Little Godfreys

CARMEL QUINN IS A SLIGHT woman with sparkling blue eyes, an infectious smile, and carefully coifed red hair that falls to her shoulders. She is unmistakably Irish and when she speaks she literally transports you to her homeland. Her voice is warm and surprisingly deep and she speaks thoughtfully and in melodic tones, holding onto words for emphasis.

After 45 years in show business, she is still performing in the U.S., England, Canada, Australia, and Ireland. Her brochure promotes The Carmel Quinn Super Show with her longtime musical director, Jimmy Martin. Based in New Jersey, she is on the road regularly doing concerts, TV and radio, clubs and cabarets, festivals, and special events. She has several CDs out and has been nominated for Grammy awards three times. She is the only artist ever to appear at Carnegie Hall for 25 consecutive years.

On stage, she has clearly mastered her craft. You expect to hear Carmel Quinn the singer, but you are surprised to experience Carmel Quinn the humorist. She tells funny stories about family and growing up Catholic, about Irish relatives and the differences between men and women. "Men don't talk much after age 45. Isn't that right, sir?" she says to a white-haired man as she roams the audience. "Yup," he says, confirming her thesis. And she often begins her show with a reference to Arthur Godfrey. "I'm sure he is in heaven because he would talk his way in."

How did I become a part of the show? It was dead luck. The first night I arrived in America, my friends took me to a bar called Connie Hurley's at 50th Street near the NBC studios. I noticed a television set up on a shelf. This was a great novelty for me as we didn't have television yet in Ireland. My friend mentioned to Connie that I had done a bit of singing in Ireland and wasn't bad. "Well," replied Connie, pointing up to the television set, "There is the show for her." It was *Arthur Godfrey's Talent*

Scouts. The name Arthur Godfrey meant nothing to me. A few weeks later I went to CBS and asked for an appointment for an audition, but was told there was a six-month wait. "Sure we could all be dead in six months!" I said. "Well, I'm here now and I might as well sing a few songs." If I knew then what I know now, I would never have said these words. But thank God I was naïve. I was invited inside to audition. I sang without music. There was a panel of five people inside a glass booth who just stared at me. I sang an obscure Irish song a cappella and the panel just continued to stare till one of them said, "Have you another song?" And I sang another one. By now the panel had their heads in their hands, so I switched to a popular song I remembered hearing [recording star] Jo Stafford perform. "We hear these songs all the time, dear, sing another Irish song." I offered "How Can You Buy Killarney?" One of the panel, Jack Carney, came out and said they were putting me on the show the following Monday night.

I had no idea that it was such a big show. I thought maybe it was a local show. But not knowing this was the best thing for me, Monday night arrived and I found there were two other competitors who proved to be excellent. They were talented and polished. My turn came, I clumped out, sang my song and clumped off. When I was called out for my reprieve, I couldn't hear the music because the applause from the audience was deafening. I was stunned. I never sang a note, just looked out at the audience and started to cry. Then I walked off. Arthur was shouting "Come on out! Come on out! You are the winner!" But I stayed backstage crying and laughing at the same time and never went out. Arthur told the audience, "You'll see her tomorrow on the morning show."[1]

Carmel Quinn. (Courtesy of Carmel Quinn.)

She was with the show for six years.

"Arthur reminded me of my father in appearance. It wasn't just the thick head of auburn hair and the blue eyes, it was his manner and quick sense of humor, and that sly understated way of saying things. He also had great insight into people. He understood women, especially the housewife and mother."[2]

Godfrey was taken by her naturalness and her wit. She had no compunctions about speaking up on the show. "When he would tell a joke and everyone would laugh, he would look at me to see if I was laughing. If I wasn't he'd say: 'You didn't think that was funny, Carmel?' And I would reply, 'To tell you the truth, I've

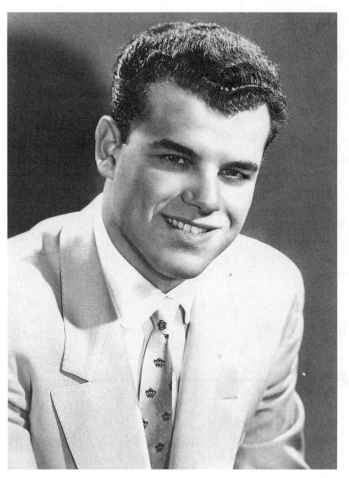

Julius La Rosa, one of early television's first singing sensations. (Library of American Broadcasting, University of Maryland.

heard better.' He would love this and laugh."

And he loved her spunk. She mirrored his "I'll try anything" spirit. "Arthur took the whole Wednesday night show to Coney Island for a live broadcast. Arthur wanted a volunteer to go on the parachute jump. At times like this some of the cast would develop severe headaches, but in me he found a willing soul. So we were strapped in our small seats…and up we went into the sky. So very high. It was a lovely night and Arthur and I (both miked) were supposed to chat and exchange witty remarks. He said, 'Isn't it beautiful, Carmel. Look down at New York City.' I was petrified and forgetting that my mike was on, just kept repeating, 'Dear God help us,' over and over. This was going out over the air to all our viewers. Next thing we dropped fast, flying through the air. I'm screaming 'Ah God, please.' We stopped a few feet from the ground…the blessed ground. I felt like kneeling and kissing the ground. But before I could undo my belt Arthur said, 'Did you enjoy that, Carmel?' I was feeling proud of myself by now and said, 'Oh yes, it was grand.' Right then, Arthur said, 'Take us up again!' And off we flew.

"I loved him for letting me be myself. He would say to me, 'Carmel, if I could fly you back to Ireland each day after the Show, and fly you in next morning, I would.' He'd stop me in the hall and say, 'You're going to be a big star. I just want to tell you to save your money. Fame is fleeting.' He said he feared I would 'change,' become different because of all the attention I was getting. I remember when Patsy Cline was on the show and I found her crying in the bathroom, desperately lonely and despairing. The producers and directors had told her, 'You're wonderful, beautiful, but now change.' Everyone had to change. But Arthur said, 'Don't change.' At one point he issued an order to 'leave Carmel alone.'"[3]

Carmel Quinn was just one of a surpassingly young group of vocalists, most in their early twenties, with whom Godfrey surrounded himself through the years. Their professional experience ranged from a lot to a little to none. Some, like Carmel Quinn, the Chordettes, and the McGuire

Arthur constantly encouraged Carmel Quinn and her career. "I loved him for letting me be myself," says Quinn. (Courtesy of Carmel Quinn.)

Sisters, came to him by way of the *Talent Scouts* show; others, like Julius La Rosa, Marion Marlowe, and Lu Ann Simms, he discovered himself. He was old enough to be their father and most called him "Mr. Godfrey." It was twenty years before Pat Boone could feel comfortable calling him Arthur—it was always "Mr. G." There were exceptions. Frank Parker, for example, was about the same age as Godfrey.

For many of them, it was a long run. Janette Davis was with the shows from 1946 to 1959. Some chose to stay on until they were let go, like Haleloke, or fired, like Julius La Rosa. Others, like Pat Boone, left on their own to pursue their careers.

Their talents varied considerably, but most viewers and listeners saw them more

as family members than as independent professionals, and they were held to a more relaxed standard. The shows were so popular that each performer had fan clubs. Though viewers and listeners had different favorites, they tolerated everyone.

The fact that some members of his group, such as Pat Boone and the McGuire Sisters, went on to become stars, was not unrelated to his bringing them on to his shows. He knew the formula he wanted, and he knew who would fit in. And fitting in often meant adjusting to such Godfreyisms as not having agents and taking lessons.

Godfrey was very good to them. He coached them. He had others available to train them with their singing or in many cases, their finances. In most cases, he

Many of the Little Godfreys became good friends, including cast and secretarial staff. A wedding shower for singer Lu Ann Simms (seated and holding gift). Seated: Chris McGuire (2nd from left), Marion Marlowe (4th from left), Lu Ann Simms, Dorothy McGuire. Standing: Haleloke (third from left). (Doreen Partin Roberts collection.)

helped them get recording contracts and work beyond his shows. He flew them in his planes and took them to his farm, and on trips to Florida or Hawaii where they were to perform, he usually picked up the tab for their spouses and children. Many developed lasting friendships with other members of the cast. Several married within the larger family of musicians and producers.

At the time nobody's programs were watched more or listened to more than Godfrey's. So even if you only got to sing one song a show or even if he never got to you that day, it was worth it. The pay was extraordinarily good, but there was little security; few in the group ever had con-

tracts. You were on the show until you were told your services were no longer needed. They all understood that. Later on, it was the press and the public who assumed, every time someone was not asked back, that he or she had been fired.

Godfrey looked for "wholesomeness" in his cast. And hard work. He seemed to play out *Pygmalion* over and over with both his female and his male cast members, bringing to them fame and riches far beyond what talent alone would have brought them. In return, Godfrey demanded loyalty. And most of the Little Godfreys were delighted to give it to him.

There is no program or series on radio or television today that has a cast as large,

Opposite: The McGuire Sisters (top to bottom: Christine, Phyllis, and Dorothy). Their careers took off after winning the *Talent Scouts* show. (Library of American Broadcasting, University of Maryland.)

that performs together as often, and has been together for as long, as the Little Godfreys. By 1953, Godfrey was literally running a company within a company, a virtual subsidiary of CBS. In all, there were about 45–70 people, depending on who was included: the performing cast, the orchestra, his writers, producers, directors, engineers, secretarial staff, and attorneys.

The first time the McGuire Sisters met Arthur Godfrey was when they won on the *Talent Scouts* show December 1, 1952.

If the Andrews Sisters were the sweethearts of America during World War II, the McGuire Sisters stole our hearts in the fifties. Though their predecessors, the Chordettes, were good, they lacked the attractiveness and energy that the McGuires projected on the television screen. Besides having a terrific, well-projected sound and the ability to sing ballads or upbeat songs with equal agility, they were pretty, animated and exuded youth.

Christine, Phyllis (the lead, but the youngest), and Dorothy grew up in Miamisburg, Ohio, where their mother was a minister. Taking to music early on, the girls worked their way up to the staff of WLW Radio in Cincinnati, then began doing club dates across the state. They soon decided to try their luck in New York. They gained their first television exposure with an eight-week stint on the early Kate Smith show. But winning the *Talent Scouts* show was their big break. Within two days they met with Godfrey in his office, and two days later they were made members of his cast. At the time, Phyllis was 22 years old.

The sisters were hard workers and constantly rehearsed, something that Godfrey always found very appealing in his cast members. Like Carmel, Phyllis and her young sisters looked on the demands Godfrey made of them as opportunities—to learn to skate, swim, travel, fly. And to become big recording stars. Between 1954 and 1961, the trio had 17 Top-40 hits, including two number one songs, "Sincerely" and "Sugartime," which are still played on air today. Other hits were "Picnic," "He," and a number of early rock 'n' roll songs. The group still comes out of retirement to perform now and then.

"They were all very warm, very welcoming," recalls Julius La Rosa, who joined the show in 1951. "They were all as helpful as they could be, as supportive as they could be. I have nothing but wonderful memories…. And the bandleaders. And the people in the band. There was a wonderful camaraderie among the cast. We all liked each other. …We all realized we were lucky. We're on national television! This is the big leagues!"[4]

It was shortly after Remo Palmier, then Remo Palmieri, was named by *Esquire* magazine as America's top guitarist for 1945, that he was hired for the new *Arthur Godfrey Time* radio show. He and Arthur would work together for the entire 27-year run of the radio series and on all of the Monday and Wednesday night shows on television as well. Remo is a slight fellow, with a ready smile, who speaks softly and thoughtfully, usually with that wry sense of humor many musicians carry with them. His spacious Riverside Drive apartment on the Upper West Side of Manhattan also serves as classroom most weekdays for students who learn the fine points of guitar playing.

"Arthur never learned to play a regular guitar. He was used to the four-string ukulele, so I made him a four-string guitar. He was very aware of chords and sounds. He had to work hard at learning the guitar, but he did it."[5]

When Remo talks about Godfrey one gets the feeling that although they spent many hours together practicing ukulele and guitar for a quarter of a century, their relationship had a certain distance, a distance that allowed Remo room to remain first and foremost one of the band, and a distance that allowed him to observe Arthur from a special angle. And if Godfrey had the stardom, Remo had the insight. He seems to have been able to see the vulnerable Arthur and the reasons why he got into so much trouble. "Arthur was always trying to explain his feelings [on air]. But he was so honest," he begins to chuckle, "He'd say things the wrong way.

Arthur Godfrey and Janette Davis. She was often linked romantically with him during her early years in the shows, though in those days no one pursued that kind of gossip. (Courtesy WTOP.)

"He was very impulsive. He'd say things and do things and an hour later he'd be sorry. One time he balled out [orchestra leader] Dick Hyman on the spot in front of a whole group. So Dick walked out. He wasn't going to take that. Afterwards, Arthur asked me why Dick left. I said 'Arthur, you just humiliated him.'"[6]

The Mariners were each accomplished singers in their own right. Jim Lewis, the baritone, grew up singing in Birmingham, Alabama, graduated from Talladega College as a sociology major and planned to study law. But singing assignments for extra cash soon turned into a full-time occupation. Tenor Tom Lockard, from Pasadena, California, studied music and dramatics at Pasadena College and UCLA and did some concert and radio work before going into the service. Tenor Nat Dickerson was born in Georgia, grew up in Philadelphia and was a well-known soloist by the time he was in high school. He eventually studied at the Juilliard School of Music in New York, later appearing on Broadway in *Porgy and Bess* and *Finian's Rainbow*. Baritone Martin Karl, from Missouri, started out to be a violin player, switched to singing, and performed leads with the American Light Opera company on radio and television.

The four joined up in the U.S. Coast Guard, sang on Fred Allen's show at the end of World War II, and joined *Arthur Godfrey and His Friends* as regulars when the show premiered. They also appeared on the morning shows each day. Certainly their Coast Guard backgrounds gave them something in common with Godfrey.

"I defied anybody for telling me where to put my blacks alongside of people in the show when we did a number together," Godfrey recalled in 1982. "Once we were invited to a ... big auditorium in Washington, and they found out [about the Mariners]. They said I couldn't bring the show to that auditorium if I had the two

blacks in it. I had a few words to say about that on the air.... It was a thing that I felt within my soul, that I must get rid, if I could, of the hypocrisy, of the bigotry that was in the country.... Those are the things we care not to remember...we try not to recall too frequently, but they were milestones. We passed them, and if I had anything to do with...dispensing with them, I'm happy about it."[7]

Janette Davis' ideal singer was Dinah Shore, one of the most popular post-war vocalists. And she sounded a lot like Dinah, though in some ways Janette's voice was richer and warmer. She was born in Memphis, Tennessee, and grew up in Arkansas. Somewhere along the way she developed a sexy, slow Southern accent. At age 14, she won an amateur show and a radio contract in Memphis, and commuted there to sing and play the piano on her own show. The local station paid for voice lessons, and in time she worked her way to Chicago and WBBM where she became a regular on a number of shows.

Slim, with brown eyes and auburn hair, she was not unattractive. She fit right in with the others as homespun and dependable. She was often linked romantically with Arthur, though in those days the press never pushed to find out. In later years, she married Frank Musiello, one of the band members, and retired to Florida after producing both *Talent Scouts* and the Wednesday night show in the late fifties.

Lu Ann Simms was another alumnus of the *Talent Scouts* show. Only 20 at the time, with no professional training at all, it was her all-American looks and sweet subdued voice that had appealed to the audience. At the time, she was selling phonograph records in a department store in Rochester, New York, for $33 a week. Like Carmel Quinn, her appearance on the *Talent Scouts* show was serendipitous. In New York for a visit, she stopped in to the popular Lido Restaurant where her aunt was the chef, joined a trio of musicians who were performing, and impressed a diner who submitted her name to the *Talent Scouts* staff. She was invited for an audition, then the show, and then was named to the Wednesday night cast.

Janette Davis was one of the first to welcome Haleloke to the Little Godfrey group in 1950. Arthur and his family had traveled to Hawaii that summer and Haleloke, a regular performer on a radio show *Hawaii Calls*, had been chosen to entertain for him. Arthur was impressed with her voice and style and invited her to appear on the Wednesday night show. In her mid-twenties at the time, she was not convinced at all that she should pursue the offer, but ultimately did. "This is Haleloke," said Arthur to the rest of the cast during a rehearsal. "She's going to be a member of our family."[8]

Clean cut, smooth singing Charles Eugene (Pat) Boone became a major singing star in the late 1950s, second only in popularity to Elvis Presley. He joined the Godfrey cast after winning on the *Talent Scouts* show in 1955 while still a student at North Texas State College. When he was asked to join the cast, he transferred to Columbia University and moved east with his wife, Shirley.

Pat Boone was the heir apparent to Julius La Rosa, who had left in 1953, but there were distinct differences between the experiences of the two. When Boone joined the Godfrey cast he was already recording for Dot Records and had a hit record, "Ain't That a Shame." His approach to pop music was clearly defined. In 1955, black artists were begin-

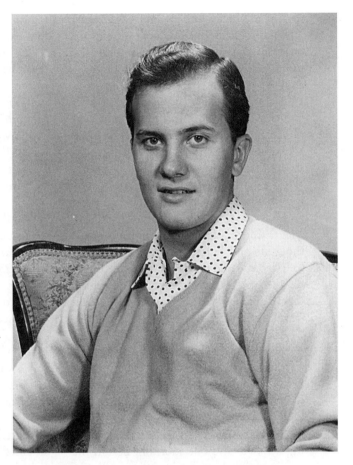

Pat Boone became one of the most popular singers of the 1950s. His friendship with Arthur Godfrey spanned 25 years. (Courtesy of Pat Boone.)

ning to make inroads into pop music with rhythm and blues. Pat began "covering" their R&B hits and bringing the tunes into the mainstream. For disc jockeys across the country, his "sound" was more familiar, and playing his versions of the songs also helped them to reach larger numbers of young listeners—the up-and-coming Baby Boomers.

Busy with other engagements, he was not dependent on Godfrey and his weekday morning and Wednesday night shows, though the television exposure broadened his following tremendously and helped sell lots of records. For Godfrey and the producers, Pat was a way to embrace the rock 'n' roll music and its young followers. The more Pat Boone's records were heard on radio and sold to young listeners, the more audience it brought to the Godfrey shows.

Arthur and Pat hit it off from the start and though his tour on the program was less than two years, he always felt he owed a great deal to Arthur Godfrey. Pat would study Arthur's approach to broadcasting. "He'd even let long pauses go. And if you were scanning the CBS dial you'd go right on by it 'cause nothing was going on! He was taking his breath and gathering his thoughts and letting his audience reflect for a second, and he was looking at the letter and just taking his time. And nothing was happening! But it was *hypnotic* if you were listening!"[9]

And when Boone was out on his own, he "would always try to emulate Arthur. Particularly if I was going to a commercial or appearing before a live audience, I would always try to talk to one person, to keep it very personal.

"[Years later], I was in New York making a movie and one morning he did me the incredible honor of having me come in and host the show. And having watched him so much I thought, 'I can do this.' But…when that light came up and I had to ad-lib and read mail and do the stuff he did for an *hour*, I sweat blood." Boone had asked a song-plugger friend who he considered to be very funny to come on the show that day, and "it fell so flat. And I came to an even greater appreciation for Arthur who could make *any* hour seem substantive, enjoyable, personal, and seem so effortless."

Boone was always appreciative of the opportunity to work with Arthur. On the trip to Lake Placid for the ice skating show, he remembers that "Some of the others were griping. I'd say to myself, 'Gee, I got a wife and a baby coming along, why complain?'" He got to introduce his hit

records on the show. And it gave him his first experience on television.

Pat never got more than scale. And he never had a contract with Godfrey. "Arthur would just say, 'See you on Monday,' and you knew you were still going to be around."[10]

Pat went on to have 38 Top-40 hits between 1955 and 1962, including ten Top-10 hits such as "Ain't That a Shame," "I Almost Lost My Mind," "Long Tall Sally," "Love Letters in the Sand," "Friendly Persuasion" and "April Love." He made a number of films like *Bernadine* and *State Fair* and had his own television series from 1957 to 1960 on ABC. In later years, he turned to gospel music and continues today to make recordings and do live performances around the world.

Six feet tall, dark-haired and good-looking Tony Marvin, announcer for Godfrey's shows over a 13-year period, was originally planning a career in medicine, but dropped out after two years of medical school to pursue a career in singing. He appeared on Broadway, but after serving as chief announcer for the 1939 World's Fair, he got a job with CBS as a staff announcer. As a staff man, Tony did everything from daytime serials to symphonies and in 1946 joined *Arthur Godfrey Time*.

And on the Godfrey show, he did everything as well. Godfrey considered him a cast member, not just an announcer, and so Tony was expected to sing, dance, and skate as well. And he was able to do all these things with ease. He had been an equestrian rider, so horseback riding was easy. Singing was easy. And he had a way of finding humor even in the dancing lessons where he had to wear ballet slippers along with the rest of the cast. Tony was a good sport about it all.

For the famous Lake Placid broadcast, he was asked to come down the toboggan chute with the current Olympic champion and describe the whole thing over the air.

Singer Frank Parker, a visiting CBS official, and Arthur share some good humor between scenes of *Arthur Godfrey and His Friends*. Arthur repayed an old debt of assistance and resurrected Parker's career. (Joan Zacher collection.)

During rehearsal, he was given the wrong size helmet and it fell over his eyes as they came down the slide at a fantastic speed. But trooper that he was, he narrated what he could.

On a show from Miami, he was asked to dive from the high tower in full dress and top hat and cane. He did. That same trip, Tony saved Godfrey's life. They were in Miami rehearsing and Arthur was in a pool. Apparently Arthur got a cramp in his leg and started to go down. Tony jumped in and rescued him.

He saw the shows as an adventure.

They never knew what they were going to do from one week to the next.

He was loyal to Godfrey until the shows ended in 1959. Arthur sent him a letter, and Tony never considered himself fired. He went back to news and became the Mutual Network's chief newsman.[11]

It was in 1935 when tenor Frank Parker and Arthur Godfrey first met. Frank was appearing in Washington, D.C., in the opera *La Traviata* and was already a name star on network radio. Godfrey attended the show, was impressed enough to plug

Orchestra leader Archie Bleyer, Carol Bushman (one of the Chordettes), and Leo DeOrsey when all were still among the Little Godfreys. Bleyer was a brilliant musician, and his guidance on what audiences wanted most from Arthur Godfrey was lost when he was fired. (Doreen Partin Roberts collection.)

Frank's performance on the *Sun Dial Show*, and the rest of the performances sold out. They met when Frank came to the station to thank Godfrey. During Godfrey's attempts to make it on the network radio, Frank introduced him to important people in New York.

Trained for opera, Frank preferred vaudeville and musical comedy and starred on Broadway. In the early thirties, he joined the *A&P Gypsies,* one of the very first successful network radio shows. The Gypsies began as a small six-piece orchestra, playing exotic music sponsored by the Great Atlantic and Pacific Tea Com-

pany. Over time, the orchestra grew, and a quartet, which included Frank, was added. Throughout the thirties and forties, classical, operetta, theater music and light classical music concerts were a radio staple, and Frank was a regular on these shows, often sharing the stage with soprano Jessica Dragonette, one of radio's legendary personalities. He was the singer on Jack Benny's summer show in 1934 and Bob Hope's first series in 1937, appeared briefly with Burns and Allen in 1938, with columnist Louella Parsons on her musical variety show, *Hollywood Calling,* in 1938, and was a frequent guest around the dial.

Then, tired of singing, he retired to pursue other interests.

Later, down on his luck, Frank tried to return to radio but found he was considered a has-been at 47. In 1950, he contacted Godfrey, whose career was booming, and Arthur invited him on the Wednesday night show. Soon after, he became a permanent member of the cast about the same time as young Marion Marlowe, and the two became immediate audience favorites, the most popular singing duo since Jeanette MacDonald and Nelson Eddy. Their voices were a perfect blend, and the two looked like lovebirds as they sang, though behind the scenes Frank had little affection for Marion.

For Marion, on the other hand, becoming a regular on the Godfrey show provided her with her first full-time job. With long, jet-black hair and a stunning figure, she had pursued a career as a singer. Unsuccessful, she had given up and become a housewife. She happened to stop in to the Kenilworth Hotel lounge in Florida while she and her husband were on vacation. Friends there asked her to sing with the music. The owner was taken with her and asked her to return to sing three songs one night for $50. Godfrey was in the audience that evening, and was duly impressed with her voice and her beauty. Playing talent scout once more, he invited her up to New York for a guest appearance on the Wednesday night show. Calls and letters after the show convinced him that she should become a regular at the age of 21.

Julius La Rosa loved Frank Parker's wit. He remembers a Thursday broadcast in the fall when Arthur was talking about his

Frank Parker was a familiar voice on radio throughout the 1930s. (Library of American Broadcasting, University of Maryland.)

upcoming weekend on the farm: "And Mr. Godfrey was saying something about all the leaves turning this wonderful amber but 'I miss the green.' And Frank said, 'Why don't you count your money?' He was the only one who could say anything like that 'cause they were contemporaries."[12]

Probably the most significant Little Godfrey of all in the early years was orchestra leader, composer, and arranger Archie Bleyer. Like Parker and many of the band members, Bleyer had strong musical credentials in place by the time he joined *Arthur Godfrey Time* in 1947.

But it was Bleyer's ability to understand

what the audience wanted from Godfrey that made him so important during the forties and early fifties. Archie realized that people identified with Arthur and admired him for always trying new things, be it dancing or skating or tasting a new food. And they expected him to screw up now and then.

"Archie had terrific perception about what people enjoyed watching," recalled long-time band member, guitarist Remo Palmier. "He'd tell Arthur, 'People know you're not a professional. Just do it! People will love it.' But Arthur was always trying to perfect himself. If he danced, he wanted to be Fred Astaire! Archie would tell him 'that's not important.' Arthur would fight him every inch of the way. But Archie was right because all week long after we did a show, that's all you heard people say. 'Did you see Arthur, he screwed up this,' and so forth. That was the most entertaining part of the show.... Archie was the monitor, someone who kept [Arthur] in line and kept him focused on what he was supposed to be doing. Arthur would put on people and talk about aviation and so forth and Archie would blow his top.

"Even though Arthur would fight him, he would succumb to the idea that Archie was dreaming up because it was always successful—even though he didn't like it. When he recorded the record 'Too Fat Polka,' that was Archie's idea. Arthur hated it, hated every word of it! But you see it was successful!"[13]

Another who gave Godfrey sound advice was Mug Richardson, his assistant. "Mug kept him in line," recalled Remo. "She was always reprimanding him when he'd be rude to someone."[14] Chuck Horner, who was the chief writer for Arthur during the early television days, agreed. "She was the one, when they walked into a room, who knew the phonies."[15] She would steer him to the people he should spend his time with. She was his compass. Unfortunately for Godfrey, Mug would not be around for most of the television years. She retired in 1950 after 16 years with Arthur and his shows.

Actually the Little Godfreys went through three evolutions. There was the original cast, then the larger cast that grew in the early fifties for the Wednesday night show, and then, after the La Rosa affair, there were many newcomers and replacements. When Godfrey returned to radio after his cancer operation in 1959, he eliminated all the regulars, developing instead a stable of entertainers who regularly appeared on his radio shows throughout the 1960s and early 1970s, including jazz legend Eubie Blake, ragtime king Max Morath, singers June Valli and Ethel Ennis, and pop singer Richard Hayes.

19

Selling Products, Building Companies

"I WAS SITTING WITH HIM ONE day," recalls legendary talkmaster Larry King, remembering one of his frequent appearances on *Arthur Godfrey Time* in the 1960s. "He was doing a commercial.... 'My next sponsor,' he says, 'You know, I hope they never sell another product again. I hope that the company goes into bankruptcy. My prayer is that no one will ever, ever have to use this product again. Because that will mean we've cured the common cold. Until then, all we have is Contac.' That was the whole commercial. That was thirty years ago. Every time I'm in the store and see Contac, I remember that. I don't remember their thirty-second spots, their flashy television spots. I remember Arthur Godfrey. He said the name of the sponsor once and built me up to listen to it by saying he hopes they go out of business. It was great broadcasting. That's a great broadcaster! "[1]

"I called it shock power, " Godfrey explained in 1982. "How can you make people remember? I had eighty-some sponsors a morning. How the hell is anybody gonna remember one of those products, or *any one* of 'em, unless I shock you into remembering it. And the way I would do that would be, for instance, Kellogg's Bran. OK, Kellogg's Bran. And the way they sold it was for 'regularity,' wasn't it? So I used to say, 'If you eat a couple of tablespoonfuls of Kellogg's Bran every morning, you will be known throughout the neighborhood as a regular fella.' That's the kind of kidding that I did. I did something to make you remember the *name* of the product.

"Lipton's chicken noodle soup? I used to say, 'Chicken noodle soup. There's plenty of noodles in it. Chicken? I didn't see any, but maybe one walked around the pan or somethin'. Somehow they got the

115

Godfrey at work. (WTOP collection.)

flavor in there. It's delicious. But I'll call it 'Noodle with a chicken flavor' if I were you. Cause you're never gonna get very far on the chicken that's in there.' People would say, 'Did you hear what that clown said about that Lipton's soup?' And [they'd] go down and buy it and look and say, 'By God he's right. It's all noodles.' But it was delicious and it sold like wildfire."[2]

By 1953, Arthur Godfrey was bringing in $27 million a year to CBS Inc., representing 12 percent of the network's total revenues. Though inflation over the years now make the dollars seem somewhat unexceptional, no one individual in broadcasting, before or since, has ever come near that ratio of 12 percent. And Godfrey truly brought in those dollars himself. He picked his sponsors and personally delivered every message. And he did it live, rarely using a script. Larry King, Johnny Carson, David Letterman, Oprah Winfrey and others who went on to great popularity never undertook nor achieved what Godfrey did. For to equal his performance, they not only would have had to perform on the air, they would have had to personally deliver all of the commercial messages on their programs *and* do so successfully.

Much of his success in selling was Godfrey himself. His informal style was disarming. His voice was unique. But those who worked with him credit him with much more than luck or charm or a good sense of humor. Arthur Godfrey worked at selling products and he knew exactly what he was doing.

"I guess I was nine or ten years old," recalled Larry King. "And I was home from school, sick. And Arthur Godfrey was doing a commercial for Peter Pan Peanut Butter. And he said, "I know you're not supposed to do this, but I'm gonna eat this peanut butter on the air.' ... He put it in his mouth, and naturally when you put

peanut butter in your mouth, you can't talk very good, so he was saying [King imitates Godfrey trying to speak with peanut butter in his mouth], 'Aw, this is good!' Well, I went nuts. I ran to the cupboard. We had no peanut butter. And with a fever I got dressed—no one was home—went to the store and bought a jar of Peter Pan peanut butter and brought it home. I could taste that peanut butter. I had to have that peanut butter. Arthur Godfrey *sold* me that peanut butter![3]

"It's hard to convey how outrageous he was…just by being *honest*," King observed, recalling another Godfrey original sales pitch. "Jingles then were on (phonograph) record 'cause you didn't have cartridges or tapes. And the jingle went:

> Pepsi Cola hits the spot
> Twelve full ounces, that's a lot,
> Twice as much for a nickel too
> Pepsi Cola is the drink for you!

"Commercial finishes. He says, 'You know, everywhere *I* go, it's seven cents.' And he broke the record. He smashed it! He says, 'I've been drinking Pepsi downstairs for the past week, and it costs *seven* cents. The bottles are seven cents. It's seven cents in the grocery store. It ain't a nickel. It's a great *drink*, it's worth *more* than seven cents, but it *ain't* a nickel.' That was wild. But it put Pepsi in my mind and it had me sing the jingle to you now."[4]

Pitching an egg-and-milk shampoo, he once told listeners, "If your hair is clean, you can always use the stuff to make an omelet."

Part of his success was that kind of spontaneous humor. You listened to his message because you knew each one was an original. He was creating it as he went along. And you might learn something or you might just find some humor in it. It was the same as anything else he said on his shows. The word today is *seamless*;

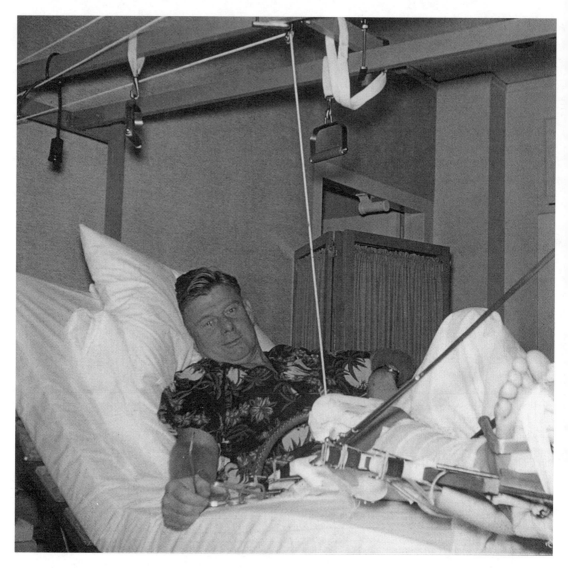

Arthur in one of his famous Hawaiian shirts following hip surgery at the Massachusetts General Hospital in Boston, June 7, 1953. CBS President Frank Stanton took the photo during a visit to check up on the network's biggest money earner. (Gift of Dr. Stanton to the author.)

Godfrey's commercial messages were not an interruption at all.

He also had a very clear picture of who he was talking to. In the mornings, it was the woman of the house at home. In his mind's eye, he could see her cooking, cleaning, moving around the house. In those days that was a true picture of what the great majority of American women *were* doing at that moment. "He under-

stood women," explained Carmel Quinn. He'd say, "When your husband gets home and he's cranky, give him a big kiss. And if that doesn't work, put your coat on and go out and have a good time." And they'd roar at this. He understood what women went through. Women would write to Carmel and explain how they would watch and listen while they worked. They'd say, "I've got a television on downstairs [because in those days everyone only had one and it was downstairs] and I'd be upstairs making the beds and I'd have the radio on. I'd hear Arthur tell Carmel, 'That's a nice dress. I like that.' Then I'd fly down and look at the dress on the television and then go back up." "It was part of their life," Quinn added.[5]

Godfrey also knew that on Monday nights and Wednesday nights there were many men watching and listening as well. He had an innate ability to know what kind of twist to add to his sales pitches.

"He was always making these double-meaning jokes on the air," remembers Remo Palmier. "For instance, he was talking about the different uses for Lysol Spray. He says, 'You can even spray your pet's area, you know.' And then quietly in the microphone he says, 'Did you ever spray your pet's area?' They loved it. 'Cause you know, whatever he sold … the sales of the product went just sky high. There was another commercial for Ban roll-on [deodorant]. And he started talking to the guys. He says, 'You guys out there, get yourself some Ban roll-on. Just because you're a man doesn't mean you have to smell like one!' Which to me was a great commercial!"[6]

Pitching Johnson's Glass Wax when it was still a relatively new product on the market, he'd say, "You *rrrrub-it-on*…and you *rrrrub-it-off*." Listeners could digest that any way they wanted to.

"He never read the copy they'd send him," recalled Palmier. "He'd look at it, he'd read maybe three or four sentences, and he'd read it with this real sarcastic— always making fun of the copy, you know. And he'd say, 'Now don't listen to all that junk! You should get this because of this and this and this,' and go into his own terminology about why the product was good."[7] His favorite way of starting out was to say, "It says here…." And you

knew he was not going to read what it said there.

"I never razzed the products; I never made fun of the product," Godfrey said. "I kidded the shirt off the vice president of the company and the idiot agency that wrote the scripts because they wrote some of the—as they do today—the most awful stuff to ask you to swallow, and I would often take them apart. But I never did anything to belittle the product because I [wouldn't] represent a product if it isn't everything they say about it."[8]

Even companies that were not his clients often got the benefit of a Godfrey plug. In 1953, following his hip replacement surgery, Godfrey returned to the air and filled the audience in on his surgery and recovery. He told them he had been in a lot of pain but they had given him this wonderful new product that killed the pain and didn't upset his stomach. "It's called Bufferin and I'm told you can get it at your drug store." Within days, Bufferin was on its way to be becoming the best-selling pain reliever in the country.

In the years following his cancer surgery in 1959 and his subsequent recovery, he told the story of the nurse at the hospital who gave him cranberry juice to drink each day. He had questioned why she wasn't giving him orange juice. She told him that she had had been diagnosed with cervical cancer and that the prognosis had been grim. But her mother started giving her cranberry juice, he told his listeners, and a year later, all her symptoms were gone. He would point out that there was no medical proof that the cranberry juice had been responsible for the recovery, but he said he believed it had helped him as well. It wasn't long before Ocean Spray Cranberry Juice became a regular sponsor on the program. And he would tell that story again and again during their spots.

Throughout all of this there was the ability to convince the audience that he knew the product, had tested the product, and used the product!

"He's so sincere he even sells off the air," CBS's Chairman told *Time* magazine in 1950. "One time at a conference he started selling me on Johnson's Wax. And I went right home and asked my wife if she'd ever used it."[9]

It was not unusual for Godfrey to visit the manufacturing plants of the sponsors. He often attended Lipton sales events. And he was often a speaker at conventions and conferences of his sponsors or the sponsors' industry. In later years, when he was doing spot commercials for Chrysler cars, Godfrey walked through a plant demonstrating Chrysler's special attention to safety.

If he got mad at a sponsor he made them pay for it on the air. Upset at the Chesterfield people for some reason, he once avoided doing a commercial through the entire program. Just as he was about to sign off, he said, "Oh, and today we're brought to you by Chesterfields. They're cigarettes." That was it. The Chesterfield people were far from happy; they wanted their money's worth. On another occasion they sent an advertising agency rep to the studio to time their commercials. As *Life* magazine reported it, Godfrey got wind of the visitor, "told his audience about this indignity," and then "confined his commercial to the words, 'Start your watch. Chesterfield. Stop the watch.'"[10]

"It says here," he began a cosmetics commercial, "that this lipstick comes in several alluring shades including blackberry. ... Blackberry alluring? ... It's revolting. ... Come to think of it, it doesn't taste bad at that. If you really feel naked without lipstick, girls, you can't go wrong on this stuff. The junior size is only half a buck and the regular size a buck. For two bucks they'll probably pipe the goo right into your boudoir."[11]

During the late 1950s a tuna fish scare developed after several people opened cans of bad tuna, ate it, and died. The press had spread the news and sales were down everywhere. Godfrey thought of an old friend of his on the West Coast, among whose products was Breast o' Chicken tuna. Godfrey knew the company and had been through the plant. He knew their quality controls. So he called his friend to ask how things were going with the scare. "Oh, Arthur; we're about to close up." Godfrey convinced his friend to buy a ten-minute participation or exclusive segment on his radio show each week. Within 60 days, sales were up 115 percent.

"How did I get him out of the hole? I faced the facts right square in the puss. I said, 'Been eating any tuna fish lately? No, huh? Why not? Ooooh, you got scared, huh? Now let's stop a minute and think.... For 30 years Breast o' Chicken has had the Good Housekeeping Seal of Approval. They've got mine too.... You be brand conscious and you'll never worry. You get all the tuna fish you want to eat.'"[12]

When Charlie Wilson, the head of General Motors and a friend of Arthur's, wanted him to sell Chevrolets, Arthur said, "Hell Charlie, you sell lots of Chevrolets. Give me something you really need help with." At the time, GM owned Frigidaire and sales were slow. Godfrey emptied the warehouses.

Dr. Frank Stanton, the long-time president of CBS, remembered that some time later, Charles Wilson went to Godfrey offering him a proposition: he wanted to buy *all* the commercial time on *all* of the Godfrey shows, making GM the sole sponsor. Godfrey thought it was a wonderful idea. But sighting the danger of putting all of the CBS eggs in one basket, Stanton nixed the idea.[13]

Godfrey was always thinking from the buyer's point of view. And he'd make up arguments as he went along. One day he departed from the script he was handed for a Chesterfield ad and said, "You know what? Don't buy 'em by the pack. Buy 'em by the carton. It's probably cheaper." Six months later, the Liggett & Meyers Tobacco company had to build a new factory to produce them. They couldn't keep up with the demand.[14]

"He invented that soft sell [approach]," added Remo Palmier. "If you watch the programs after that, everybody was trying to imitate it. They'd have people doing commercials in a chair like [he did]. But it wasn't informal in the same way. He'd say to me, 'When somebody's doing a commercial like that, people just tune out. They're not listening. Just speak to them normally, like you would your next door neighbor.' And he was right, you know. 'Cause everything he touched like this, the sales soared."[15]

On a January afternoon in 1952, a young radio comedian from the West Coast named Steve Allen, who had recently joined CBS-TV, received a panicky phone call from one of the CBS program people. "You've got to go over to Arthur Godfrey's theater as quick as you can. Arthur is in Florida. He planned to fly back for his *Talent Scouts* show tonight, but there's a terrible snowstorm along the way. He can't get back! We need you to substitute. Can you fill in?"

"I'd seen the program only a few times but agreed to replace Godfrey and ran over to the studio." Arriving at the theater in the early evening, Allen began getting his instructions from the show's producer for the live show that would air at 8:30 P.M. There was the entrance, the opening remarks, the introduction of the Talent Scouts and the banter with them, the introduction of the performer, the applause meter, etc. And, pointed out the producer, Steve would have to do the commercial messages for Lipton's. There was the plug for the hot water heater, the tea bags to be taken out of the box, and so forth.

"I never got it all down before airtime. And yet it turned out to be the luckiest thing that ever happened to me up to that point. Arthur had #1 and #2 shows at the time and millions were watching. I was in the relative obscurity of daytime television.

"It turned out to be hysterically funny." Unintentionally, Allen "screwed everything up. Eventually I just got into it. I put the tea and the noodle soup into the hot water and poured it into the ukulele." He was exhibiting the kind of zaniness that would soon become his trademark on the *Tonight Show* and later on his Sunday night shows. The audience loved it. So did the industry daily *Variety*, which reported the next day, "One of the most hilarious one-man comedy sequences projected over the television cameras in many a day.... The guy's a natural for the big time. He rates kid-glove attention." And so did Arthur. Television producer Marlo Lewis later recalled, "Steve was so hilarious on the show that five minutes after it was over Arthur Godfrey called to say that he had laughed so hard he still had tears in his eyes."[16]

There was always a long waiting list of sponsors. But even when spots opened up, he accepted no sponsor whose product he or his staff or his family hadn't tried and approved. He would ask for samples and give them out to others, with the assignment to let him know what they thought. Long-time office manager Doreen Partin Roberts explained that "Many times we would have to try out the product. One time somebody wanted him to do some dog food commercials. And he had a lot of dogs [on the farm]. He took the dog food home and the dogs wouldn't eat it! And he wouldn't take on the product.

"But when he *did* take on a product, he

was *fervent*. For example, Angostura bitters. The only time I used them was when they used to make that horrible drink, Manhattans. A group of us went to his house for dinner one night and he said, 'Now this stuff is good on *everything*.' And he was putting the stuff on everything. We even had ice cream the maid brought in. 'Put it on!' It was terrible! He wasn't being funny. He was sincere. They had told him it was good on everything and he [wanted] to believe it."[17]

When Godfrey stopped smoking in 1953, he told his long-time sponsor, the Chesterfield people, "I can't sell your product when I don't believe in smoking any more. I think it's a terrible thing."[18] Millions of dollars left CBS' balance sheet that day. But Godfrey had to be true to himself and his credibility. "He did a very brave thing," believes Andy Rooney. "He had espoused their cause for so long. He was very much associated with Chesterfield Cigarettes. He realized he had been wrong...and he didn't want any more part of them."[19]

He would say, "I was not on the sponsor's side. I was on your side."[20] Yet, working with the sponsors, Godfrey gave many products their first exposure on the burgeoning medium of television. Toni Home Hair Permanents, introduced by the Gillette Company in 1950, was one dramatic example. The product became an overnight sensation.

Through the years many celebrities have endorsed products. But no one has ever put his reputation on the line with the public as often as Arthur Godfrey. He did it every day with his endorsement of dozens of consumer products.

He was an odd mix of entertainer, host, and salesman. But it was clear where his loyalty lay. "One day when we were on the air," recalls Larry King, "I said to him, 'What does it say on your driver's license under occupation? Broadcaster? Television

host?' He said, 'Salesman. And that's all we are, Larry. I'm just honest enough to put it down.'"[21]

In 1964, *Sales Management* magazine took stock of Arthur Godfrey the salesman in a cover story entitled "Arthur Godfrey: First You Have to Sell Yourself":

He doesn't easily fit a slot; he's so readily classified as an entertainer that his sales prowess is sometimes overlooked. Yet by his personal persuasion he has probably helped more manufacturers move more merchandise than any man in sales history. [22]

When they asked Godfrey if he had a formula, he said what the driving force was in his salesmanship was doing whatever it took to make the listener remember the name of the sponsor. So the first thing that counted was acceptance of the salesman by the listener. Using a headache remedy as an example, he pointed to the fact that "There are 50,000 of them on the market. People are bombarded with them. So... you'd have to [convince] a personality whose integrity is unquestioned [to] sell it. If he believes in it, then he can...say—as I do—'I'm like you. I'm so sick of claims and counterclaims I can't see straight. But the people representing this new brand came [to me] and said...here's what we did in the way of research.... And you know what? I looked into it and I found out about it and by golly, they're right! And it is my personal recommendation that you give it a try.'" He talked about his confidential tone. "I want them to listen to me," he explained.[23]

No broadcaster before or since has ever achieved the success in selling that Arthur Godfrey did. Indeed, his form of personal endorsement selling is hardly ever heard or seen on the air today, in large part because there is no one able to combine recognition, popularity, integrity, ad-libbing, and powerful sales arguments all in a period of 30 to 60 seconds. Godfrey was the master. And he did it only for CBS. He reveled in telling people that by the time CBS's chairman William Paley got up for breakfast in the morning, he (Arthur Godfrey) had already paid all of the network's expenses for the day. As critic John Crosby put it, "He *was* the profit margin at CBS."[24]

20

Life at the Top

IT WAS THE 1952-53 BROADCAST season, and Arthur Godfrey at 49 years of age was at the zenith of his broadcasting career. His two prime-time television shows were running second and third in the Nielsen ratings, *Talent Scouts* having been bumped from the top spot that fall with the premiere of a new situation-comedy entitled *I Love Lucy*. Interestingly enough, Godfrey's popularity had contributed significantly to the launch of Lucille Ball's classic show, reinforcing a key strategy for the networks. Looking for an ideal time slot for the new series, CBS chose 9 P.M. surmising that many of the millions watching *Talent Scouts* at 8:30 P.M. would stay tuned to sample Lucy and become regular viewers. The overnight success of *I Love Lucy* became the ultimate example of the "lead-in" strategy and it has been a central consideration in the launching of just about every new series since.

In September of 1951, the coaxial cable was completed, making delivery of network programs possible coast to coast. For the first time, television viewers on the West coast could watch New York-originated network programs live, experiencing them simultaneously with the rest of the country, or see them later that day at a more timely West Coast hour via a live-to-film process called Kinescope.

And more television stations were on the way. With the release of the Federal Communication Commission's historic Sixth Report and Order in April of 1952, a four-year freeze on all pending applications for new television stations ended, and during the following two years the number of television stations viewers could tune to more than doubled in many communities. Over 15 million sets were now in use and production roared on.

Radio was still the country's most available electronic medium, particularly in areas outside large cities where television reception was still sporadic at best. And for many Americans, a television set—costing several hundred dollars, minimum—was still out of reach, though clearly at the top of their wish list. Portable radios had become big sellers and made that medium even more accessible. But though the four radio networks continued with a full schedule of news, nightly entertainment shows, daytime soap operas and the rest, national advertisers were abandoning the medium for television at an alarming rate—even faster than listeners were. CBS and NBC did their best to keep their radio enterprise intact, introducing new breakthrough radio shows like *Dragnet* and *Gunsmoke*. Many stars, like Bing Crosby, refused to go on to television at all. Others, like Jack Benny, continued to do both television series and separate radio series. But, despite sweeping cutbacks in radio advertising rates, the bottom line for network radio shows was getting redder and redder. Any hopes that the public and the advertisers would value both mediums equally were proving overly optimistic: network radio was dying.

The exception was Arthur Godfrey. *Arthur Godfrey's Talent Scouts* continued to be simulcast each week, and Lipton was delighted to sponsor it on both mediums. And *Arthur Godfrey Time*, the morning show, was still the number one daytime radio program, a big winner for CBS both in audience and revenue.

Yet the siren call of television, especially the enormous investments that advertisers now appeared willing to make in the medium (to no small degree because of what Godfrey was able to do for *his* sponsors), became the preoccupation of CBS's executives. When NBC rolled out a full schedule of new morning television shows, CBS counterattacked. On January 7, 1952, a little more than two years after the initial tryout, the second 15-minute segment of CBS Radio's *Arthur Godfrey Time*, from 10:15 to 10:30 A.M. EST, premiered on the CBS-Television Network as a simulcast, bringing to 3 and a half hours each week the time that Godfrey was on television. With no added production values—no sets, no costumes, no vocalists reading lyrics from music stands—this was the only way Godfrey would allow the show to be televised, and an inexpensive way for CBS to counter its television competitor. And television exposure meant increased revenues for the sponsor, Lever Brothers.

CBS now estimated that Godfrey's weekly audience was hovering around 40 million people, and boasted that he "goes into more homes in America every morning than the milkman."[1] As a result, whatever Godfrey wanted from the network, Godfrey got. And reflective of that power, there would be no television simulcasts on Fridays. Arthur was home in Virginia on Fridays. Fridays was strictly radio, with Godfrey in his den while the cast performed from the New York studios. CBS would have to find something else to put on television that morning.

Again demonstrating who was really in charge of Arthur Godfrey, after only one month of television simulcasts had occurred Arthur took a four-week vacation to report for active duty at the Naval Air Training Station in Pensacola, Florida, to qualify as a carrier pilot. Today, it was would be unheard of for a television star to take leave of his or her daily or weekly, live or taped show(s) at the height of the broadcast season. But Godfrey's contract with CBS allowed for just that kind of thing.

His absences always called for a reshuffling of personnel—there were live shows to do every day. This time, comedian Joe E. Brown substituted for Godfrey on *Talent Scouts*, Frank Parker took over the Wednesday night series, and Robert Q. Lewis, one of CBS' bright young performers, spelled Godfrey on the morning show each day on radio and on

A party at the Stork Club with (left to right) Arthur's attorney and advisor Leo DeOrsey, whom Arthur later would blame for poor investments; Mug Richardson, his loyal assistant for 16 years as he moved up the ladder at CBS; Godfrey; and affable CBS vice president in charge of Arthur Godfrey, Jim Seward. (Doreen Roberts collection.)

television. Worthy of note was the fact that his audiences continued to tune in record numbers, even without Godfrey present, which could only have befuddled the other networks even more.

It was that ability to bring in the audiences, even in absentia, that gave Godfrey the power over CBS. Apparently, they were scared to death of losing him, willing to put up with any request, demand, or complication he might generate. "So important was Godfrey to the CBS profit pump in those days," wrote author Robert Metz, "that James Seward, an avuncular CBS vice president, became more or less offi-

cially vice president in charge of Arthur Godfrey. Seward, a cordial man with a voice and manner startlingly reminiscent of actor Jimmy Stewart, had other duties as well, of course. But his prime responsibility was to keep mercurial Arthur happy."[2]

To further insure its investment, CBS hired Peter Lind Hayes, another of their young program hosts, who was paid just to stand by in case Godfrey took ill. "At one CBS stockholders' meeting," critic John Crosby once explained, "stockholders raised the roof because Hayes had been paid a quarter of a million dollars in one year for what turned out to be about nine hours on air."[3]

One thing no one at CBS was worried about that year was overexposure for Arthur Godfrey. When he returned from summer vacation in September of 1952, CBS extended his morning television time to three-quarters of an hour Mondays through Thursdays. He was now before cameras *four*-and-a-half hours a week. For those who still couldn't get enough of Godfrey, he was on the radio every Saturday night with *Arthur Godfrey Digest*, with taped highlights from the weekday morning shows. He seemed to be everywhere. His recording career continued. In 1951 he recorded two beautiful Alec Wilder pieces on Columbia Records with Mitch Miller directing the orchestra. "What Is a Boy" and "What Is a Girl" caught the essence of childhood and Godfrey's readings of the two essays was not only a welcome departure for him, but met with solid sales success.

His workday was fairly predictable. Doreen Partin Roberts, who was his office manager for almost eighteen years, explained: "He would come into the office around nine o'clock. Before that the writers would pick out items from the newspaper and write some gags about it. And he would look at this material, make notes on it, etc. After that, he'd get material ready for the show." Remo Palmier would stop in for a brief go-through of any song he was to play the uke on. "Then he'd go down to the studio." It was always last minute. "Like two minutes to ten he'd walk in and do the program!"[4] After the program, he'd come back up to the office for appointments.

A likely visitor would be Seward, the V.P. in charge of Godfrey. "He was a very sweet man," Roberts remembers. "I think they picked him because he was so easy going and low key. He was a liaison, maybe there to keep an eye on Arthur. I

don't think it did much good. But he tried! If CBS thought Arthur was going overboard, Seward would talk to him. I [also] remember seeing Frank Stanton, Ed Murrow, but not very often. He didn't seem to me to be chummy with the CBS brass."[5]

There would be a number of appointments with sponsors or advertising people. Godfrey's attorney and financial advisor, Leo DeOrsey, might come up from Washington. DeOrsey was a big tax lawyer and also represented stars like Marlene Dietrich and Gene Autry.

He rarely went out for lunch; it was usually brought in for him and the secretaries from the dining rooms. If he had a show that night, he'd have the barber up and the manicurist. Tuesday afternoons there were rehearsals for the Wednesday shows. "He was amazing. If he had a show that night or a rehearsal, he could take a nap in ten minutes. He'd say, 'I'm gonna lie down.' I'd say, 'You [have to] leave in fifteen minutes.' 'Well that's all right. Just call me in ten minutes.' And he actually would [wake up] rejuvenated."[6]

On off nights, he would meet friends for dinner. But by early Thursday afternoon he was on his way to Virginia.

When Roberts (then Doreen Partin) first went to work for Arthur Godfrey in 1947, bags of unopened mail lay on the floor. The office staff consisted of Mug Richardson and her secretary, both of whom worked with Arthur on the programs. Arthur had a personal secretary but there was no one available to open or sort the hundreds of letters, telegrams, post cards, and packages from listeners across the country that were flooding the office each day—let alone answer them. "They were just more or less overwhelmed. It had to be opened and read." Roberts went to work on the mail "and then it just escalated from there. We ran out of office space, we had so much mail. So we moved across the street from 485 Madison to the Studio

Fred Hendrickson, producer (far right), and other production personnel discuss last minute details just before the evening's show while Margo Kingsley, Arthur's makeup specialist and manicurist, readies him for television. "My routine," he explained, "is normally pretty hectic." (*The Saturday Evening Post.*)

Building [where we had] a full floor." Soon she was overseeing a staff of eight women just handling the mail. Roberts reported directly to Godfrey.

The first time I met him (I'd heard about him and all but I'd never seen him) he came up to the office and walked in and he was bigger than life. "Where the hell's Mimi [Mug's assistant]. I need Mimi." I was all shaking. I said, "Oh, ah, Mr. Godfrey! Just a minute. She's in the ladies room. I'll get her." "Oh for Christ's sake," he said. "Let the poor girl take a pee." And that was my first meeting with Arthur Godfrey!

Arthur was very interested in his mail. He was very concerned. He felt that if people took the time to write, every letter should be read and if possible acknowledged. We used to write letters and send out pictures, but it got to be

thousands of dollars! I used to take piles of letter home at night. I used to fall asleep at the kitchen table reading the mail, trying to get caught up.

Originally it was probably important because it showed CBS executives how popular he was. But [later] he liked to use some of the letters on the program, so going through the letters [we'd look for] something funny, interesting. Some of them were very insulting. And he *loved* to read insulting letters on the air!"[7] [One letter read: "My wife feels it's unfortunate that we here in St. Louis receive your program late. I feel it's unfortunate that we receive it at all."[8]] "Others were provocative. Others were about the products.

Later on, particularly with the television shows, I used to make reports up for him. He liked to know what people liked, what they didn't like. Every week after the Wednesday night show I would make reports.

Doreen Partin Roberts straightens up Godfrey's office. His desk and walls were filled with memorabilia of his great passions outside of broadcasting: flying, fishing, hunting, sailing, music, and travel. (*The Saturday Evening Post*.)

There were a lot of medical questions. He was a great source of encouragement to people. When he had that hip replacement, a very new surgery at the time, we got all kinds of letters from people around the country. Would that help them? We'd have to tell them where to write. And then of course when he had the cancer surgery and came back and went on and performed. So many people who had cancer in those days would write to him and many times he would write back, "Just keep fighting it," to encourage people.[9]

Some wrote for advice, like a young girl from New York State going to Florida for her vacation, who asked him to recommend a place to stay. "We'd feel more secure if you selected the hotel." One day there was a letter from an Army officer in Korea with a 25-dollar money order asking him if he would be "kind enough to

purchase a present for my wife? Our anniversary is coming up next week, and I can't be there to buy it for her in person." Godfrey arranged for a nightgown and a bottle of perfume.[10] People also wrote for program tickets, personal and business advice.[11]

By 1953, the office was receiving 60,000 pieces of mail in an average month. Besides letters, more than two thousand gifts a month arrived—from baby chicks for his farm to patchwork quilts to boiled lobsters to fancy underwear. There were hundreds of invitations a week inviting him to "family weddings, christenings, bar mitzvahs, graduations, and home-cooked spaghetti dinners," reported *Collier's* magazine in a five-page article devoted completely to his fan mail. When he mentioned "how long it had been since he had eaten real

It took seven full-time secretaries to handle the 60,000 pieces of fan mail and two thousand gifts that poured in to the Godfrey office every month. (*The Saturday Evening Post*.)

homemade bread," hundreds of loaves arrive the next day. When he swatted at a fly in the studio, the next day 5,000 fly-killer gadgets of all kinds arrived for the office staff to unpack. Nearly 4,000 tea bag rests of all shapes and sizes arrived after he couldn't find a place to put a tea bag during his *Talent Scouts* show.

After championing the cause of truck drivers and their courteous ways, a Cadillac arrived from a group of trucking companies. After his hip surgery, they were flooded with canes, crutches and wheelchairs. The office turned them over to hospitals, along with a set of surgical knives that had also been sent.

"When you fly somewhere in your DC-3," wrote a man from Chicago, "I feel like I'm listening to some neighbor who made good but still is one of us and comes back to tell us about the glamour-world. There's one woman on our street who says you're bragging. We don't feel that way.

We know how you left home at the age of thirteen, how you slept on piles of newsprint and how you got smashed up in auto accidents. To us, you're the average man who overcame great handicaps and made good. You make us feel that maybe we, too, can overcome our handicaps and make good in the same way, and that's why we live so vicariously in everything you do."[12]

Godfrey's influence continued to extend far beyond the products he sold. If he mentioned going to a Broadway show the night before and enjoying it, ticket sales would increase immediately. His listeners and viewers were so tuned in to his every word that if he mentioned a book or sang a song he had recorded, sales jumped immediately.

In 1949, a young CBS radio producer named Fred Friendly, who would later go on to become president of CBS News, had been fiddling with tape recorders and an idea to take great speeches from history and make a record album. An agent friend named Jap Gude lined up Edward R. Murrow to do the narration. In assembling the materials, which included FDR's speech to Congress and the nation the day after Pearl Harbor was bombed by the Japanese and Winston Churchill's wartime call for courage in England, he included Godfrey's 1945 coverage of the FDR funeral. With an advance copy of the record, called *Hear It Now,* in hand, Gude went to see Godfrey and, as a courtesy, played him his excerpt. Apparently Godfrey had never heard the narration since the day he delivered it. When the piece ended, he was in tears. Wiping his eyes, he canceled a lunch appointment and asked Gude to play the entire record. Then, over the next few weeks he talked about it frequently on the air. "He plugged it and plugged it," Gude later told a CBS chronicler, Robert Metz. "And it became a runaway best seller. I would guess that Godfrey was responsible for at least half of the records sold." He wasn't paid a penny for the plugs or his part on the record. [13]

When a devastating flood hit the Netherlands in the early fifties, CBS newsman Walter Cronkite came up with an idea to rally the American people to help the battered country. He arranged with his friend Rex Smith, the vice president for public relations of American Airlines, to have their ticket offices used as collection points for donations of clothing and blankets. He then got one of Godfrey's writers, Andy Rooney, to convince Arthur to agree to interview General Anthony McAuliffe, who pitched for donations during the next Wednesday night show.

The following day Cronkite was awakened by a frantic phone call from American's Rex Smith: "What have you done to us?" he shouted. "Our ticket offices are inundated. Some of our people couldn't even get into their offices—stuff was piled in the doorways before they ever got to work." With the help of the Association of American Truckers, much of the material was moved from American ticket offices to a New Jersey pier for shipping to Amsterdam, and the operation was deemed a great success. But he and American had yet to experience the full impact of the Godfrey broadcast. The coast-to-coast coaxial cable was not yet in place, so, six days later, the West Coast audience still hadn't seen the show or the appeal for donations. That would come the following evening. Cronkite, fearing a repeat of the previous week's audience response and American's inability to handle the load, called Rooney and begged him to convince CBS to drop the segment before it aired. Instead, CBS agreed to end the repeat broadcast by saying that the need had been met. "That didn't stop the West Coast donations," reported Cronkite. "But it kept them within acceptable bounds."[14]

Godfrey's influence didn't hurt the ukulele industry either. From the time he first appeared on his Wednesday night shows in 1949, audiences began making a connection between Godfrey and the instrument. When he premiered a short 15-minute series of ukulele lessons in 1950, public interest began to mount. Uke sales had been holding at about 5,000 a year for the previous 20 years. Soon, stores began selling that many in a week's time and, according to one source, in the first six months of his television appearances sales had risen to 1,700,000 instruments. In Chicago, the *Herald-American* newspaper began to offer a free ukulele with every two subscriptions and the subscriptions rolled in to the point where the governor of the state of Illinois, Adlai E. Stevenson, along with the mayor of Chicago, sent Godfrey a ukulele embossed with a letter of appreciation for making Chicago and Illinois "uke conscious." Godfrey received no pay for any of this. The fad only grew bigger over the next several years, reaching the point where music publishers began adding ukulele chord notations to sheet music.

Along with his love for and promotion of Florida came an equally strong affection for Hawaii. During his short visit there in 1944 on his way to and from Saipan, he had spent enough time in Honolulu to fall in love with the islands. The people and the views of Waikiki Beach in Honolulu Harbor with Diamond Head in the background made an indelible impression.

At that time, he was unknown there, but when he returned six years later in July 1950, he was welcomed as a hero. By now, he was a famous CBS network radio star and though television had not yet reached the islands, his face was already familiar. He had spent hours and hours on his various shows talking about Hawaii and singing its native songs, and had just finished up his two-month special television series on how to play the ukulele.

His impending arrival was headline news a week before. "Record Aloha Scheduled for Godfrey on Sunday," was the front page headline on the *Honolulu Advertiser* of July 26. "One of the biggest aloha welcomes in Honolulu's history" was expected to take place. "Musical groups, dancers and representatives of Hawaii's racial communities would take part in the ceremony." The huge welcome of 5000 people was "intended to show the appreciation of the people of the islands" for "his aid on behalf of Hawaiian statehood and a growing interest in Hawaii and its people."

When the United Air Lines Stratocruiser did land with the Godfrey entourage—including Arthur, Mary, his oldest son Richard, Mug Richardson, his manager-lawyer Leo DeOrsey and his wife Helen, and Rose Bigman, a family friend

and Walter Winchell's secretary—it was six hours late, delayed on takeoff from San Francisco. Still, it was one of the largest welcomes in history, with crowds estimated from 5,000 to 15,000 people greeting the party. Godfrey emerged from the plane "wearing a coconut hat, aloha shirt and carrying his 'dearest possession,' his ukulele." The party was swamped with leis and friends, well-wishers, civic officials, photographers, reporters, and the general public "crowded around to get a glimpse of the man who...helped make Hawaii famous." There was an official welcome at the terminal, gifts, and then 45 minutes of entertainment from hula dancers, musicians (including a 20-piece ukulele band), and costumed representatives of racial communities. Then Godfrey entertained the noisy crowd with two of his own Hawaiian numbers on his ukulele before he and the others were whisked off to a private home where they would be staying during the month-long visit.

In the weeks that followed, Godfrey made four official public appearances. He was the guest of honor at a luncheon of the Honolulu Chamber of Commerce where 600 local leaders heard his recounting of his first visit: "I didn't know a soul. One evening I wandered out to the Willows [a restaurant and entertainment spot], spotted a ukulele lying on a piano, grabbed it, and started playing and singing." Soon he was joined by the band and "the jam session continued till 7 A.M. the next morning." One of the highlights of the visit had been the ukulele lessons local entertainer "Squeeze" Kamana had given him during that visit. He told the Chamber audience how he returned to the States and began boosting the islands, and how interest in the ukulele had surged on the mainland. In the Chamber audience was Capt. J. E. Whitebeck, now the Coast Guard commandant of the Hawaii district, who back in Baltimore in 1929 was the officer who had arranged for Godfrey to get out of the service early so that he could take up his radio chores full time. "That man," said Godfrey, pointing to Whitebeck, "was really responsible for this career I'm in now." The event was carried on three radio stations.

Later, he judged the semifinals and finals of a ukulele contest, with the winners invited to New York to appear on his shows. There were *luaus* (feasts), a fishing trip where he hooked a 240-pound marlin, and continuous praise. The Honolulu city and county councils adopted a resolution to name the next thoroughfare in his honor. When he appeared on a broadcast of *Hawaii Calls*, the islands' most popular radio show, he was kiddingly bestowed with the name Ke alii nui o na ukulele I ka poo ehu haolaha Hawaii, or "the chief of the ukulele players who has red hair and who loves the Islands." Then, officially, he was given the name Mino aka, or "Smiling Arthur."[15]

"Everybody should learn to fly," Godfrey would say regularly on his radio and television shows. "It can't be too hard. After all, if I could learn, *anyone* could." It is impossible to know how many private flyers were first encouraged to pursue that dream by Arthur Godfrey or how many families took their first flights on a commercial aircraft after he had expounded on the virtues of flight. But by 1950, old friend Eddie Rickenbacker, the World War I flying ace and president of Eastern Airlines, thought it was time to recognize Godfrey for his efforts on behalf of the commercial and private aviation industries. "Arthur has done more to make the public air-minded than any single person since Charles Lindbergh," is the way another top aviation executive had put it. Rickenbacker gathered a group of aviation executives, and arranged for one of Eastern's silver fleet DC-3s to be completely re-outfitted and given as a gift of appreci-

ation to then U.S. Naval Reserve commander Arthur Godfrey for his own personal use.

Originally designed to carry 21 passengers, the twin-propellered DC-3 had been one of the standard workhorses of the post–World War II Eastern fleet. It was delivered to Godfrey on June 26, 1950. The cabin had been transformed into a living room, with a card table and chairs, an observation lounge with couch and coffee and large windows, a desk, a telephone, a built-in television set, a fully equipped galley, and several divans that doubled as full-length beds. Just about everything else was completely replaced, from the flight equipment to the tires. Godfrey would go on to log over 6,000 miles with the aircraft.

Many of Godfrey's absences from the studio were to pursue his military career. He was fascinated with jets. And in 1950, shortly before the outbreak of the Korean War, Brig. Gen. "Rosie" Grubbs of the Air Force invited him to fly in a two-place jet trainer. "I never enjoyed anything so much in my life," he later recalled. "No noise, scarcely any vibration, speeds previously undreamed of!"[16]

Afterward, the Air Force boys ribbed him, encouraging him to quit the Naval Reserve and join the Air Force. "We'll let you fly anything we've got." Godfrey spread the word to the Navy that he was giving serious consideration to the Air Force offer. And in short order, Secretary of the Navy Mathews was on the phone. Godfrey explained that he wanted his wings, that he'd flown thousands of hours in the air. He disputed the Secretary's concerns about his age and his hips. Relenting, Mathews arranged for Arthur to fly to Pensacola, Florida, where he convinced another skeptic, Vice Admiral John Dale Price, that at age 47, though twice the age of the average cadet, he was physically suited for the training course that would qualify him as a naval aviator. When he told Price he had only two weeks to complete the course, Price protested again: "You can't learn anything in two weeks. Even our instructor's refresher course takes six weeks." Godfrey said he would fly nine hours a day instead of three, and though Price was sure he couldn't do it and would have to return at a later time to complete the course, he gave Arthur the go-ahead. Two weeks later, Commander Arthur Godfrey (Ret.) had his wings.[17]

On a return visit in January of 1951 for jet training, Admiral Price told him why he was so accommodating. "We're getting a lot of letters from irate mothers, wives, and sweethearts, giving us hell for turning these kids loose on jet planes. People seem to think jets are lethal—that only supermen can fly them. But if they find out an old phoof like you can fly jets, they'll think anyone can do it."[18]

When Arthur returned to his shows in early February, he told his audiences that it was safe for our boys in Korea, Europe, and in the States to be flying jets, and with that, the outpouring of concern to the Navy ended. One woman wrote, "I read it in the papers and I heard experts say it, but I never felt reassured about the safety of my son until you told me so this morning."[19] His impact would not be forgotten by the military.

Within the next twelve months, Godfrey went on to qualify as a carrier pilot, went through the Navy Instrument School in Texas, and in October of 1952 returned to Pensacola and completed a course in helicopters. His stamina was nothing less than amazing.

In the summer of 1951, Godfrey joined his long-time friend, financier Bernard Baruch, on a trip to Paris to see General of the Army Dwight D. Eisenhower, then head of SHAPE, Supreme Headquarters Allied Powers Europe. Baruch, an advisor to both presidents Roosevelt and Truman, had apparently been asked by Eisenhower to visit with him and, if he liked, to bring several influential broadcasters with him. The financier invited a famous radio team of the time, Tex McCrary and his wife Jinx Falkenberg, and Godfrey.

It is unclear when Baruch and Godfrey first met, but whenever it was, Baruch, according to his biographer, "was astounded at the depth of his thoughts and the breadth of his questions." For his part, Godfrey had "admired Baruch's dignity and wisdom and had fired queries at him on economics and military affairs and politics in the broadest sense."[20] The two men had become close friends. But it was now Godfrey's *influence* that led Baruch to invite him to the meeting with Eisenhower. "Baruch did not have an air and television audience of some [forty] million people."[21]

As Jinx Falkenberg remembered the meeting with Ike, Baruch led the conversation, Tex asked questions, and Godfrey listened. Eisenhower needed the nation's help to fight against communism in Europe and America. At the end, Eisenhower said, "Arthur, you need to go back and be a Billy Sunday." Apparently awed by his visit and the seriousness and importance of the message, Godfrey returned to New York and did what Ike had requested. He talked about the trip and told his listeners and viewers that if we didn't give Eisenhower the support he needed through mobilization and controls, "by golly, we'll lose the war here before we even fire a shot." As with his advertising messages, as with his messages to the relatives of the young airmen flying jets, his points hit home.[22]

Yet there was criticism. Just as entertainers often criticized Bill Paley for having such a "no-talent" personality on the air, military experts and others criticized Baruch. "Baruch had had his pick of brains, they argued. Why had he taken Godfrey to sit in at the conference?"[23] But, like Paley, Baruch knew why he had done what he done.

Godfrey's influence was further apparent as the 1952 presidential campaign heated up. A great admirer of FDR, Godfrey's political leanings were now influenced more by his military experiences and the corporate executives he was meeting, men like Charles E. Wilson, the head of General Motors. Wilson was a leading Republican of the day and active in the party's efforts to insure that they would be successful in occupying the White House when Truman retired the following January.

Like Baruch, Wilson was well aware that by now Godfrey was as influential an American as anyone. His impact on his listeners and viewers was becoming legendary. Add to this his red-white-and-blue patriotism, and he seemed a natural to help in the effort on behalf of the Grand Old Party.

Certainly, Godfrey was flattered by the increasing amount of attention being lavished on him by the likes of Eisenhower, Wilson, Baruch and others. So when Wilson asked him to join him in meeting front-runner Robert A. Taft, senator from Ohio, and Eisenhower, who was now back in the States as president of Columbia University, he was quick to say yes. Andy Rooney recalls Godfrey telling him one day, "We're looking for the right guy."[24] Eisenhower won the nomination in the summer of 1952 and that fall, Godfrey launched a Get Out and Vote campaign on his shows that included his morning gabfests as well as his Wednesday night show. With the Korean War still festering, with Eisenhower the popular hero from World War II promising to visit Korea himself if elected, and with his opponent being Adlai E. Stevenson (divorced and often appearing to be effete and overly academic), the polls showed that a majority of American women were clearly in the Republican camp. But would they vote? The party needed a media blitz to get the women out to vote, and who could do it better than Arthur Godfrey? "Just the way he sold soap, he sold candidates," observed Remo Palmier.[25] Though Godfrey never mentioned the candidates, when the dust had cleared, women had turned out in record number and Ike had been elected in a landslide. Whether it had been Godfrey's idea or Wilson's or Baruch's or Eisenhower's, his efforts had made a remarkable difference in the election and it only increased interest in him and his influence by politicians and big business.

21

Trouble in Paradise

AFTER FIFTY YEARS OF CONSTANT activity, from horseback riding and flying to dancing and ice skating, Godfrey, now approaching age 50, could no longer laugh off the pain from his damaged hips. He had often said that, when he was pieced back together after his accident in 1931, "some of my bones didn't quite fit the way the good Lord originally intended." But the pain wasn't funny.

In his Washington days following the 1931 car accident, the hip wasn't much of a problem. "He just had a little limp," recalled Granville Klink.[1] But as the years rolled on they took their toll. Now, by the time he would begin the *Talent Scouts* show at 8:30 in the evening, "he was in excruciating pain," recalled Remo Palmier. "I know this from being on rehearsals with him and [when] it started to get late at night, he would favor this pain.... The show would start and he'd walk out and move to the desk. And the next day I would hear 'Boy, did you see Arthur last

night? He was so drunk he couldn't even walk....' He never drank whiskey. He had maybe a couple of glasses of wine with dinner, but that was it. He wasn't a drinker."[2]

Writer John Crosby, who at one time was America's most prestigious television critic, remembers Godfrey's ability to ignore his problem. One time he spent a weekend with Arthur, Mary, and the kids in Jamaica. "I'd get up at 6 A.M. and go for a swim in the ocean. There would be Arthur ahead of me on the beach, hobbling painfully up and down, inspecting every seashell with that insatiable curiosity which was one of his characteristics.... One thing I will never forget about that trip. I was snorkeling, something I had done very little of, and I was not in very good condition. There was a strong current running which swept me much further from the boat than I had planned. I started to swim back and suddenly I was struggling with that current and not making any headway. It was Arthur on the boat who first noticed. He dove right in, gimpy legs and all, swam to me, and pulled me back to the boat with those powerful big arms of his. I never forgot it."[3]

"He didn't complain about it," Klink recalled. "He was that kind of a guy. Never complained."[4] But years later he would admit in the *Saturday Evening Post* that he had had "plenty of emotional and mental stress—in addition to physical agony." His left leg was an inch shorter than the right and his right hip was locked so that he couldn't lean forward. "I couldn't even put my shoes on without help."[5] It was worse than that. He usually had to be helped in and out of the cockpits of planes.

For years he had been asking doctors what could be done and had been told over and over that there was nothing to help.

Then in the spring of 1953, his family physician heard about a Dr. Marius N. Smythe-Peterson, in Boston, whose specialty was hip arthroplasty. He had designed a new kind of vitallium cup to be used as a replacement hip socket and had been having good success with it. Godfrey went to see him.

He told Dr. Smith-Pete, as he was called, that he was not a patient who just wanted pain relief. "I want to skate, and I want to ride, and I want to tie my shoes." "This is April," said the doctor. "By January I'll have you skating."[6] They would do both hips. After 22 years, relief was finally in sight. Godfrey returned to CBS and announced that he would be leaving for an extended period to undergo the surgery.

The news was released to the press by President Frank Stanton and then by Godfrey himself on his morning radio program. The public was shaken. To his millions of fans, it showed his vulnerability, and they worried if it would affect his long-term well-being. When he announced the news to his audience, three thousand letters poured in.

Typical was a note from a woman in Massachusetts: "I was deeply saddened this morning to learn that you face major surgery. I feel as if one of my own family were going to the hospital to be operated on. I cried. I couldn't help it. I hope and pray that the good Lord will make you well and strong again, and that you'll be off your crutches much sooner than you expect."[7]

"This was a soap opera," notes Andy Rooney, who was a writer for Godfrey throughout the 1950s. "And he did it very well. He took his listeners right through it with him. They knew the orthopedists, etc. [These people] became characters in the broadcast."[8]

CBS, of course, was also faced with a challenge: filling Godfrey's shoes for five and a half hours a week on radio and three and a half hours a week on television. For the Wednesday night show, they signed up a glittering array of substitute hosts: in May it would be comedian Jackie Gleason, Perry Como, Ed Sullivan, and George Murphy; in June, Jerry Colonna and Robert Q. Lewis; in July, Gloria Swanson, Gene Autry, and Helen Hayes. Many would not only host the show, they would do the commercials as well. For some who signed on, they were coming to the aid of CBS and Arthur; for others, like Swanson and Murphy, it was a chance to try to revive fading movie careers by trying out a new medium.

Standing in on *Talent Scouts* would be Garry Moore, already busy with his daily hour variety show. And the five-day-a-week television and radio stints on *Arthur Godfrey Time* would be taken on by Robert Q. Lewis, who also had an hour-long variety show each afternoon on the network.

Godfrey traveled to Boston and checked in at the Massachusetts General Hospital in May 1953. The adjoining room was also commandeered and became headquarters for his private secretary. On May 14, he underwent surgery on his hip. The operation took four hours. Afterward, he went into shock several times. "He almost lost me," he later recalled, referring to Dr. Smythe-Peterson. His personal physician, who was at his side during surgery, admitted later he thought Godfrey was "gone for sure."[9] His wife Mary was also there and appears to have considered him close to death. He had a number of transfusions.

But he got through it and America, kept informed daily by Robert Q. Lewis on the morning shows, breathed a sigh of collective relief. Within days, several members of the CBS brass flew up from New York to make a state visit to his bedside, including CBS president Frank Stanton, who snapped a color photograph of him with his right leg suspended from an elaborate sling.

The operation appeared to be a success. "They picked my right leg up and moved it around. They could bend my knee up against my chin. They could swing it out away from the other leg." Dr. Smythe-Peterson was pleased and said they would operate on the other leg shortly. But Godfrey reneged, saying he wanted to wait until he was out and about to see how the leg functioned. "The leg you operated on doesn't feel like it's attached to me any more. I don't want two legs like that."[10] This was on the sixth day of his hospital stay. Two days later, Dr. Smythe-Peterson had a sudden massive coronary attack and died. His partner, Dr. Otto Aufranc, agreed that under the circumstances the left hip surgery could be delayed.

Godfrey went home to Virginia to recuperate over the late spring and early summer. It is estimated that every week he received 40,000 cards and letters wishing him well. In churches across America, people lit candles and prayed for his speedy recovery.

At CBS, the show went on without him. Of the Wednesday night stand-ins, the most interesting proved to be Ed Sullivan, who had hardly ever met Godfrey. Arthur's shows consistently bested Sullivan's weekly outing in the ratings. Sullivan surprised everyone by casting off his stiff personality, laughed, sang and danced a production number with the Little Godfreys, sang a duet with Frank Parker, accompanied Haleloke and Frank Parker on a zither, and did a soft-shoe dance. Said *Variety*, "Why Sullivan can come on in strange surroundings and enjoy himself and yet appear so uncomfortable on his very own show is something of a [mystery]. It's to be hoped that some of the gold dust carries over from that Wednesday night to Sundays."[11] It never did, but within a year Ed Sullivan and Arthur Godfrey would be at loggerheads.

Film legend Gloria Swanson sang with the McGuire Sisters, commented on clips from her old silent films, and reprised her telephone scene from *Sunset Boulevard*. The commercials, however, were handled that night by Julius La Rosa, and *Variety* observed, "Interestingly, La Rosa seems to have assumed Godfrey's sincerely informal mannerisms for delivering commercials by osmosis. When giving the intro pitch for Toni [Home Permanents] and Chesterfield [Cigarettes], La Rosa scratched his head, rubbed his nose, and gestured in the little-boy manner of his seemingly ingenious boss. Whether he was posturing or not intentionally, the selling trick came off effectively."[12] But in general regarding the commercials, Godfrey had nothing to fear from any of his stand-ins. *Variety* reported, "The one art in which [the subs] can't equal Godfrey is that of kidding the...commercials."[13] Only Arthur could get to do that right.

His absence from radio and television continued. CBS, desperate to get their leading money maker back on the air, worked out an arrangement with Godfrey whereby he would not only be able to broadcast his radio shows from his farm, but his television shows as well. The job fell to Godfrey's old engineer from WJSV/WTOP days, Granville Klink.

"To get the program back to the network, we put up a 144-foot television tower for the microwave antenna. And that was right out beyond the barn. And that was microwaved into Garden City (N.J.) which was the AT&T terminal for the network. We had our equipment [cameras, lights, etc.] in part of a large barn….We didn't have to bring equipment down with us…. We ran the microphone circuits and the camera circuits out to the various parts where we needed to pick up….We had a professional electrician because of running the voltage around the area. We didn't want to take responsibility for that. We were given almost a free hand on all that material. And if we needed another piece of equipment we bought it. Charge it to Godfrey! And that was the magic name. Anything that Godfrey wanted, we got. That was a real good way to go in early television. Now of course things are a lot different. I don't think they get that kind of service in television."[14]

CBS and AT&T spent a reported $100,000 over three months to build the tower and install the equipment. And as would be expected, Godfrey's return to his three shows was heralded as if it were the Second Coming.

On July 27, 1953, he returned to his *Talent Scouts* show and *Variety* was as riveted as the nation was:

Seated barefooted in front of his Beacon Hill farm, swathed in a Truman style, dappled sport shirt and exhibiting an extra coating of freckles, Arthur Godfrey was back. Except for a few extra worry lines cross-hatched under his eyes, he looked fine. His return was obviously an occasion freighted with human interest, and he made the most of it in what may have been the most moving performance of this career. Once again, he demonstrated that he is unexcelled as the informal showman versed in the seeming artlessness of playing on mass emotions, as though creating a tone poem of sympathetic rapport.

By use of the split-screen technique, he was able to communicate with the scouted talent who appeared in CBS-TV's Studio 50 in New York…. But the performers were entirely subsidiary to the spectacle of seeing the extraordinary Godfrey in action as a man just seeming to act like himself.

He skimmed from one mood to another with consummate ease. He was the fellow eager to confide about his operation: "I'm recuperating wonderfully, but I can't climb the stairs yet." He was the gossip, apologizing for his haircut given him by the barber down the way who also runs a garage: "Holy catfish! I look like a grease-ball!" He seemed close to tears as he thanked his thousands of votaries for praying for him. "I know what prayer will do—it works." He appeared profoundly touched as he mused that it was the first full day in three years when not one of our Korean boys faced death: "Gee, that's wonderful."

It was good to have him back.[15]

That night Arthur received one of the biggest shares of audience in the history of television before or since: 91.4 percent of those watching television that evening tuned in to *Talent Scouts*. "By contrast," CBS was quick to report, "only 4.4 percent of the audience were tuned to the next highest-rated program."[16]

His Wednesday night return that week was even more dramatic. Sitting on a patio chair in Hawaiian shirt, barefooted, his crutches lying on the grass next to him, he again talked to the audience about his recovery. Then, he moved to the pool. Shedding his shirt, he walked on to the diving board, the spotlights capturing him against the black sky. And he made the most of the moment. He straightened his swim suit, slowly raised his outstretched arms toward his head, and leaning forward with the New York studio audience aghast and murmuring, he plunged into the pool to sustained applause that continued while he swam to the edge where a microphone was waiting. Looking in the camera—eye to eye with his viewers—he said slowly, "You know what I believe? I believe in God. And I believe in the power of prayer. And I believe in…fundamental goodness."[17]

As critic John Crosby later put it: "It was all a bit too much." *Radio-Television* magazine commented, "The deification of Arthur Godfrey has been in progress for some time. It's only a matter of time before the second syllable of 'Godfrey' will be forgotten."[18]

CBS celebrated his return to his morning show, *Arthur Godfrey Time*, the following week, by not only broadcasting from the farm, but announcing that for the new season his television time would be expanded to 90 minutes a day on Monday and Wednesday mornings and to 75 minutes on Tuesdays and Thursdays. In addition, two long-time Wednesday night sponsors, the Toni Company and Chesterfield Cigarettes, were added to the morning roster.

Looking back, one wonders how Godfrey could have agreed to such a work increase at a time when he was just coming back from surgery. It could hardly have made his recovery easier. He was a workhorse and possibly was feeling his oats considering how he had pulled through on his surgery. But it seemed premature.

By August, Arthur was back in the city. And the stress began to show. He began by doing something that probably has never been done before or since on national television: on a day's notice, he canceled his own scheduled live show and substituted another. At the dress rehearsal before his weekly *Talent Scouts* program, he apparently found the talent sub-par. So, on a day's notice, he canceled the talent and the scouts and went on the air with a hastily assembled last-minute version of his *Friends* show with Frank Parker, Janette Davis, the McGuire Sisters and Marion Marlowe, explaining to his audience that the planned *Talent Scout* show just wasn't up to par.

Ironically, though many calls came in to the CBS switchboard, there were no complaints about the change. Most of the calls were trying to get word to Godfrey that they had talent and wanted to help him out.

The cancellation was hardly business as usual, even for Godfrey. But it apparently brought no rebuke from the executive offices. They knew that criticizing Godfrey usually backfired. He could be cocky. And he usually didn't take criticism well. Back in 1949, when Bill Paley told him he thought the new Wednesday night television show "lacked movement," Godfrey brought out a line of hula dancers for the next show and leered in to the television camera: "Is that enough movement for you, Bill?"[19]

According to Remo Palmier there was always a war going on between Godfrey and the top brass, but "they feared that he would leave. So they weren't about to dismiss him."[20]

His unparalleled success as a salesman was never questioned by CBS. But that did not make him a favorite of Paley and the others. They respected his sales ability, but loathed his arrogance. As Andy Rooney pointed out in an insightful article in *Look* magazine in 1959, "Godfrey's answer to any complaint broadcasting executives have ever made is 'Am I selling the stuff?'" Advertising executives got no better. "If they put up with his 'go to hell' attitude,"

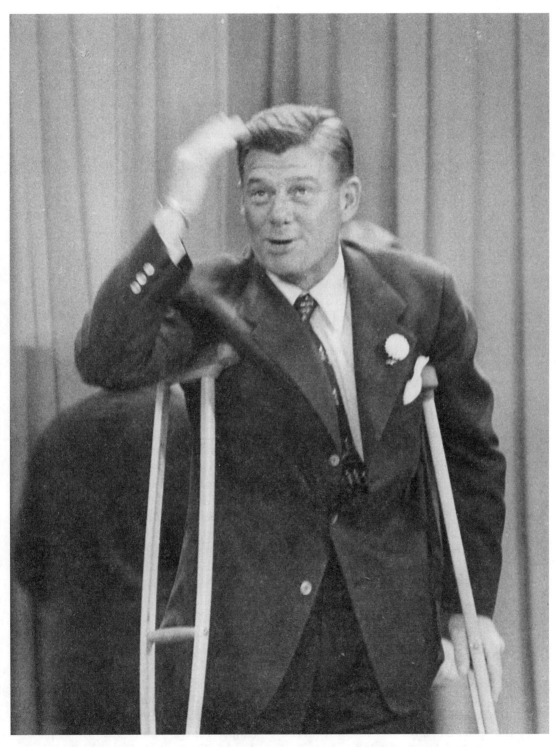

Returning to air following his hip surgery in 1953, Arthur received one of the biggest shares of audience in television history: 91.4 percent of those watching television that evening tuned in to see him. (Joan Zacher collection.)

explained Rooney, "it is only because he makes money for anyone connected with him."[21] CBS president Frank Stanton was once quoted as saying, "Never again will CBS allow itself to be so dependent on one man."[22]

For all of the deification, Godfrey's temper, his rudeness, his arrogance were already legendary around the organization. Gene Rayburn, who later became a popular master of ceremonies and host, was part of a morning radio team in New York in the early fifties when he went to CBS to discuss a possible television show. As he approached an open elevator to take him to his appointment, he was confronted by Godfrey who was alone inside the elevator and insisted that he (Rayburn) take another; that he wanted to ride alone.[23]

And there was the famous Godfrey temper that had flared as far back as high school and later when he quit WMAL in 1934. "Somebody would call up and say, 'Arthur, we want to use a particular thing and we want to use so and so.' And he'd practically rip their head off. I couldn't understand what he was doing.... Then he'd get off the phone and tell me what happened. It was self-destructive."[24]

Palmier recalls how Godfrey was always saying things that could get him in trouble. "He was a very emotional person. He'd react emotionally to anything."

Sometimes it was comical. Once, on the birthday of one of the famous composers, Gershwin or Kern, Godfrey told the producer he was going to call out songs the composer had written and that he wanted Cy Mann, the pianist, to play about eight bars of each. According to Palmier, the show began and "he called out about six tunes, and Cy played each one of them just beautifully." Afterward, Arthur "was mad as a hornet." He called the producer into his office and bawled him out. "I thought I told you that I wanted this to be *spontaneous*," Palmier recalls Godfrey saying. "And Peter says, 'Well, it was.' 'What do you mean?' says Arthur. 'Everything I called out Cy played like he'd been rehearsing all morning.' I had to explain to Arthur that Cy never touched that music. 'He never went over one piece. As you called them, that's the way he played 'em. That's the kind of piano player you have downstairs.' He thought that they had [rehearsed] the whole thing.

"When he handed out assignments, he'd gather the group. 'I want this done, that done.' When it didn't get done he'd be furious! I told him, Arthur, when you want something done, point to one guy. When you tell four guys, each one assumes the other will do it."[25]

Peter Kelley recalls years later when Godfrey was filming a spot for Colgate. He was so used to ad-libbing and doing commercials live he couldn't get it done in the allotted time. It was either too short or too long. The secretary had a squeaky voice and she would announce to the producer after each take how much time it ran: 68 seconds, 54 seconds, and so forth. This went on for hours, and Godfrey was getting hotter and hotter. Finally, the producer decided to end Godfrey's ordeal before it went too far. "'But Mr. Prager,' said the secretary, 'It's 61 seconds.' 'Good,' said the producer, 'We'll make a special out of it. Now let's try it one more time.' Arthur burst out laughing."[26]

Though Godfrey had an uncanny ability never to use foul language on-air, off-air he swore like the ex-sailor, lumberjack and bouncer he was, or at least had been. "There were moments of vulgarity," recalls author Ralph Schoenstein, who knew Godfrey in later years. "And moments of temper. He was very human. It was paradoxical. One minute he could be vulgar and the next he'd be looking up [difficult] words in the dictionary."[27]

He could be difficult to read. Producer Peter Lassally, who was Godfrey's radio show producer throughout the 1960s and president of Arthur Godfrey Productions, found getting along with Godfrey a continual challenge. He sensed that in many of Arthur's relationships, the entertainer "was very enthusiastic at the beginning, but soured two years later. He'd find people he'd fall madly in love [with] and then it was only a matter of time." Peter and Arthur flew together often. Many times Arthur would invite Peter to go on trips with him. "I took the advice of Bob Carmen, a producer before me. 'Don't get too close to Arthur. If you do, he'll eat you alive.'"[28]

Godfrey spent many hours with male friends like Morton Downey, Scoop Russell, LeMay, and Baruch. But as Andy Rooney recalls, "He was more at ease in the company of women…it was probably good taste on his part."[29] He respected women of accomplishment like Lady Bird Johnson and others who worked hard to accomplish something meaningful. Several of his staffers remember him as way ahead of the times in his support of women's rights. But his fondness for *young* women went far beyond respect, creating yet another paradox.

He liked to tell the story of a bandleader who asked every woman he ever met to sleep with him. Most always, he was rejected. Asked by a friend why he would want to put up with so much rejection, the bandleader replied, for every 100 who said no, there would be at least one who would say yes. A female vocalist who went on to appear regularly on his radio shows in the sixties reported that when she first sang a duet with him on the show, "He had his tongue in my ear and his hands all over me." Reported another, more seasoned vocalist, "When I first sang on the show, one musician advised, 'Better get your roller skates on.'"

The press could not have been unaware of his temperament. But their public reporting was always positive at best and overly fawning at worst. Jack O'Brian, a columnist for the *New York Journal American* and syndicated to many newspapers around the country, was possibly the worst offender. In a series of articles on Godfrey in 1950-51 that was later incorporated into a thin book called *Godfrey the Great*, there wasn't a critical word to be found. Indeed, he went out of his way to explain away any possible misinterpretation of Godfrey's activities. A description of a trip home for the weekend, with Mug Richardson accompanying him for the Friday morning show, included specific references to be sure the reader was left with no ambiguity about their relationship. She had her own apartment in Washington, "does not go dateless," and as the Sunday evening return to New York approached, "Mug was powdering and packing or saying so-long-for-now to some anxious young man" while Arthur "kisses his wife goodbye [and] tousles the hair of his children."

O'Brian had visions of being Godfrey's official biographer. But Arthur was never very comfortable with people whom he sensed had their own agendas with him, and over time had made it clear that he was not in O'Brian's pocket no matter how flattering his reporting. O'Brian, along with the rest of the press, appeared to be biding his time, waiting for Godfrey to fall from grace even a notch or two before he took a more critical approach. Considering Godfrey's imperfections, it seemed only a matter of time.

22

The La Rosa Affair

THE WORD *HUMILITY* IS A FAMILIAR one in today's American vocabulary. But back in the early 1950s it was a seldom-used description of human character but one that was always in Arthur Godfrey's lexicon. Asked in 1950 by *Time* magazine what were his most important attributes, Godfrey mentioned three: honesty, interest, and humility. Within three years, however, another mention of that word by Godfrey would lead to a dramatic fall from power and public esteem and would haunt him the rest of his life. And it would become the biggest public story in the history of broadcasting.

Julius La Rosa was born in Brooklyn in 1930. His parents, Lucy and Salvatore, had immigrated to America, and Salvatore had begun a radio servicing business, earning a modest income to support Lucy, Julius, and their younger daughter, Sadie. Julius had always loved to sing. As early as the first grade he had formed a quartet with two other boys and a girl, entertaining at class functions. The quartet lasted until high school split the group up. But La Rosa, still without any formal training, continued singing.

Julie, as he was known, was a fair student, but after high school, in 1947, he decided to join the U.S. Navy. His father had been a Seabee, and sea life appealed to the younger La Rosa. After boot camp, he took up electronics and was assigned to the aircraft carrier USS *Wright*. There, he continued to sing, primarily at the enlisted men's club and the Officers' Club, to "get myself out of various kinds of boring duty," as he later put it.[1] With dark curly hair and an easy smile, Julie was easy to like. He was soft spoken and respectful. And his voice was smooth and warm.

When Godfrey went down to Pensacola, Florida, Naval air station in September of 1950 to finally earn his Navy wings, his arrival in the area was known to all the men. A friend of La Rosa's put a note under Godfrey's door at the

144

Bachelor Officer Quarters, suggesting that he come hear Julie sing. "I was at sea that one afternoon and there's a telegram," La Rosa recalls. "'Be at the enlisted men's club and Godfrey will audition you as your shipmates requested.' So I did. I sang 'The Song Is You' and 'Don't Take Your Love from Me.'" Godfrey was impressed and after returning to New York, he arranged with the admiral for La Rosa to be given leave so he could come up and sing on his shows. Julie traveled up, appeared for three mornings on radio and on that week's Wednesday night *Friends* show. "[I was] terrified, scared to death. And to their everlasting credit, his whole staff couldn't have been warmer, more encouraging." He kept in touch with Godfrey and later that year was invited to be on the Wednesday night Christmas Show.[2]

"He had a pleasant voice, although nothing outstanding," Godfrey later told Pete Martin and the *Saturday Evening Post*. "He was awkward and amateurish...but he had a nice quality, and I guess the thing which appealed to me most was the fact that he was in a Navy uniform." Before his live national audience, Godfrey said, "Kid, when you get out of the Navy, you've got yourself a job with me."[3]

La Rosa was thrilled, though years later he had another view of the invitation. "I think he recognized that this unprofessional, unbusinesslike, totally unfinished product—with the natural manner and the innate shyness—was a perfect foil to his personality."[4]

When his four-year tour of duty was completed, La Rosa took Godfrey up on his offer. He stopped into the office, and just ten days after his discharge, he started on the morning radio show. It was November 19, 1951, and within a year Julius La Rosa was to become a national phenomenon—the first popular singer since Frank Sinatra to become the idol of a million American teenage girls and adult women.

"If there is an original Horatio Alger [story], that's it," La Rosa remarked in 1996. "I had been making a hundred and eighty dollars a month and all of a sudden I was making five, six, seven hundred dollars a week! Astonishing."[5] "Nobody can really understand how powerful a force television is," La Rosa told writer Max Wilk in the early 1960s. "In the years before television, you could work for weeks, months, years, pay your dues in night clubs and up on the bandstand, go up to the Borscht Circuit and work—*learn*. That's where all the old stars came from. Television wiped all that out overnight.... Kids like me...were discovered, shoved out in front of the camera, and were turned into public heroes overnight. Pretty heady stuff, if you don't know how to handle it...which I guess I didn't.... Oh, how I needed to learn. I had never been on a stage before—I'd never even had voice lessons, until after I got on the show."[6]

"I remember when Julius first arrived, the first day he walked in the office," recalled Doreen Partin Roberts. "He had his sailor suit on and he was holding his hat and he was all nervous and shy, putting his head down...and Arthur put him on the air. And all the girls in the office, of course, single girls, were crazy about him. He was just very sweet. He couldn't be nicer to you."[7]

La Rosa found Archie Bleyer to be particularly helpful. "I guess you could say he was a mentor. You know, we never sat down and he said do this, don't do this. He always let you go—well, again, he said early on, 'Don't ever abandon your instincts. You have wonderful instincts.' I adored him."[8]

Looking back, La Rosa found Godfrey of two personalities: "that wonderful folksy personality that was...a form of genius," and his off-air one. "It was like

Arthur Godfrey and singer Julius La Rosa. Their famous rift in 1953 had a negative impact on both of their careers. (Library of American Broadcasting, University of Maryland.)

he saved all his good for that camera and his not good when the camera was out. But we all do that. I call it party manners. His [Arthur's] party manners were always in front of the camera, as mine are.... You have company in the house and you don't scream at your wife or scold the kids. You know, you wait till the company's gone. His remoteness, his distance from the cast, despite what was projected on the cameras, was manifest the first day.... The show was over and everybody has a cup of coffee. And he just walked right through and up into his office." But through the years La Rosa found many in the business to be just the same. "That is not uncommon for people in the business to have one personality here and another [there]. About the only person I've ever met whose personality was the same on-air and off was Perry Como. He [Arthur] was the boss. And I don't say that with any hidden meaning. He had a producer [and] a director...and he endowed them with the authority.... There weren't too many times when he took issue with them. He seemed to know his limitations. If the director said, 'Well, Arthur, I think the light should be here,' or whatever, he more often than not deferred to their expertise. But he had those incredible gut instincts about something he felt was right or something he felt was wrong. And adhered to them."[9]

Two months after La Rosa joined the cast, Archie Bleyer and musician Lee Erwin invited him to join them in forming a record company. According to Godfrey, they came to him and asked him to join as well. "I had tried to interest Columbia Records in LaRosa," Godfrey later recalled, "Pointing out that the kid was catching on and would someday be a smash, but it was no go. Now Archie had become impressed with the way Julius was building, and they wanted my help." Godfrey declined, saying, "I'm a dyed-in-the-wool Columbia man." But he added that

he'd be glad to help them "by plugging their records if they were any good. And I told them I hoped they would make a million." A few weeks later, Bleyer and La Rosa showed Godfrey a contract and asked his opinion. "I didn't like it because I thought it gave Julius too small a share of the take, and I said so." At Godfrey's suggestion, they got his attorney, Leo DeOrsey to rewrite the contract.[10]

La Rosa's first recording for the new Cadence Record Company was "Anywhere I Wander," a Frank Loesser ballad written for the movie musical *Hans Christian Andersen*. The song had already been recorded by Tony Bennett and others but no one had had success with it. Godfrey, true to his word, had Julius sing it often on the show. His recording sold over a million copies. "Eh Cumpari," his third record, also became a best seller.

Godfrey's radio and television shows were now at their peak in popularity. The cast had expanded to include the young McGuire Sisters, who were also poised for stardom.

With stardom comes money, and money needs managing. Godfrey knew all this from personal experience. He understood the role that press agents and a personal managers play in show business, and that young performers "need wise counsel when Dame Fortune overtakes them early in their careers and catapults them into nationwide prominence. How in the world can a lad used to fifty dollars a week intelligently face a situation where he suddenly has a thousand?"[11] But Godfrey saw no need for *his* cast to have talent agents. He had personally hired each of them; they needed no representation in their negotiations with him. And he thought he had treated them fairly. In addition, as the demand for personal appearances in nightclubs and theaters increased, Godfrey assigned his own staff to work on behalf of the cast members. "I even hired extra people for the purpose, who saw to it that our performers were billed properly, got a fair amount of money, had proper orchestrations, and were presented to good advantage. I bore all of the expenses because having told them they needed no agents or representatives, I felt it was my responsibility. And we managed to get some whopping fees for those appearances."[12]

"Arthur told all of us that we shouldn't go out and get managers or an agent," recalls Phyllis McGuire. "Because if he had to deal with all the agents he would never get his shows on the air."[13]

Godfrey paid them scale. La Rosa, for example, had been hired at $200 a week. "But [Arthur] opened the doors," recalls Carmel Quinn, who joined the cast a few years later. "On Friday morning's shows he'd say, 'Now girls, what are you doing this weekend?' And the McGuires would say, 'We'll be in Chicago at the such-and-such a club.' 'OK,' he'd say, 'All you folks in Chicago, get out there and see these girls. And Carmel, what are your plans?' And I'd say, 'I'm going to be in Boston at Blinstrub's,' and he'd tell the Boston audience to come see me. You didn't need to clear the appearances with him. I didn't need an agent."[14]

"Up until the spring of 1953," Godfrey told Pete Martin, "Julius was coming along fine. I was quite fond of him, and what's more I'm sure he liked and respected me. He tried to do everything I told him to do. He didn't like the ballet work, but he even made a halfhearted try at that." Arthur and Mary had Julius down to visit on the farm with other members of the cast. "He was a lot of fun, and we all enjoyed his visit." But when Godfrey left the hospital after three months for his hip surgery, he detected a change in Julius. "He was a big shot now." [15]

Looking back, La Rosa could see that he had indeed been overwhelmed by his success. "Perhaps I had become a little

smart-ass. I was getting six or seven thousand fan letters a week and I was only twenty-three."[16] Falling on his head while attempting a cartwheel during a rehearsal one day, he said, "Who says there's only one star around here?"[17] Godfrey had set up ballet lessons for the cast. La Rosa missed a lesson and the next day he found a note. "Since you felt your services weren't needed at yesterday's dance class, we won't need you today."[18] La Rosa insists he had gone to see Godfrey to tell him he had a family conflict and that Arthur had seemed to understand but told him to try to get back if he could.

La Rosa was enraged. He went over to the Lexington Hotel, where Godfrey lived, and had the operator ring his room. He was told Godfrey was out. But Julius had seen his car on the street and decided to wait for him to come down to the lobby. Finally, according to La Rosa, Godfrey came down with two of his assistants and brushed by La Rosa without acknowledging him. "I said to myself, Okay. So I went and got a manager and…an agent."[19] The agent, Tommy Rockwell of General Artists, was one of the best in the business.

When Godfrey returned to the show on October 1, he described what he found as "something like what a sailor might find when he returned to his small children after a four-year voyage. I didn't have a cast any more—I had a galaxy of stars. Julius had fan clubs all over the country. He had been making personal appearances at $2000 and $3000 a throw, his job with me had become only a showcase…. The other kids in the cast were all burned up with envy; here was the newcomer sassing back the producers and directors, refusing to attend classes, ducking rehearsals." Then came the letter from Rockwell stating that in the future, all dealings with La Rosa would be handled through the agent's office. Godfrey later remembered reading the letter. "I couldn't have felt any worse if my own son had sent me a note saying, 'In the future, when you want to talk to me, see my lawyer.'"[20]

"Arthur was really hurt, I think," observed Doreen Partin Roberts. "I think that Arthur felt [La Rosa] was very ungrateful."[21]

As Godfrey told the story to Pete Martin, he was now convinced that La Rosa wanted to leave and he thought it best to let him go. Julius' CBS contract had five years to run. Associates told Godfrey not to give in and lose him.

"The truth is that Julius wanted to get out and Arthur let him out," says Peter Kelley. "He had been manipulated by Julius' agents to his advantage. According to what Arthur told me, he let [La Rosa] go *after* Julius, at a previous meeting, had asked."[22]

Godfrey was concerned about the release, and particularly about what he would say to his audiences afterwards. He sought out Stanton and Paley for advice. According to CBS President Frank Stanton, as quoted in the *New York Post*, Godfrey called him on Saturday night to discuss the problem. "We decided," said Stanton, "that instead of having a press conference to announce it, the best way would be just to tell everyone over the air. Maybe this was a mistake."[23] Godfrey and others always said the decision was made over dinner, with Stanton suggesting that since Godfrey had hired Julius on the air, he should release him on the air. Paley agreed. "It will be easier, everybody will hear."[24]

On October 19, 1953, Godfrey let La Rosa go on the air for what he later called a "lack of humility." And the walls came tumbling down.

That morning something unprecedented happened, live on radio, that has rarely if ever been equaled since. The morning show was simulcast as usual on both the radio and television networks, with its usual enormous female audience. La Rosa was scheduled for the 10:15 television segment, but as he later told author Max Wilk, "One of the ways Godfrey would discipline you would be to keep you sitting around there, waiting to go on. It was his show—he pulled all the strings. All morning I sit there waiting, I've got two different songs to do. Around 11:20 [ten minutes before the end of the broadcast and now only on radio] he calls me up. He announces me. I sing my song."[25]

With time running out, Godfrey's introduction was longer than usual. "When I first met Julie, I'll never forget when he first came here and went to work steadily, he said to me, 'Gee, I don't know, with all those stars on the show.' And I said to him, 'Julie…I don't have any stars on my show. In my show, we're all just a nice big family of very nice people.' And I would like Julie, if he would, to sing me that song, 'Manhattan'. Have you got that song?"[26]

According to Andy Rooney, "Julius went out, absolutely innocently and sang his little heart out as he always did."[27]

After the audience applause Godfrey added, "Thanks ever so much, Julie. That was Julius' swan song with us. He goes out on his own now, as his own star, soon to be seen on his own programs. And I know you wish him Godspeed as I do. This is the CBS Radio Network."[28]

"Julius walked off," recalls Rooney. "He came back in. He said, 'was I just *fired*?'"[29] Within minutes, all hell broke loose.

"It was one of the great broadcasting mistakes of all time," according to talkmaster Larry King, who later was to receive much support and national exposure from Godfrey. "What he did that day was to go against everything we had believed he was. He was our *uncle*. He was our *friend*. He was our *father*. He was *Arthur*! And suddenly, out of nowhere…on the air he fires his singer. That was unbelievable.

It was the biggest broadcast story ever. And his career was never the same. Because what he did that day was show the public another side that we'd never seen. A lot of people felt tragic that day."[30]

Godfrey went up to his office. And a little while later, La Rosa came by. "I did go up to the office, " he remembers. "And I thanked him for the opportunity he had given me." [31] Godfrey remembered that as well. "After the show was over, Julius had walked into my office. He sat there with tears in his eyes and said…thanks. You've given me two breaks…you gave me a break hiring me…and now you've released me.' 'I'm sorry to see you go, Julius,' I said. 'I'd have liked you to stay with me, but if this is the way you want it, OK. And if you ever need help, you let me know.' We shook hands and he walked out."[32]

Many years later Godfrey told Peter Kelley, "I said, 'Julius you're crazy. You shouldn't do this, you damned fool. You're not ready at all. You need a lot of training yet. If you're smart you'll stay right here and learn your trade…. Then go out and you'll amount to something. You don't even know how to walk out on a stage properly.'"[33]

According to Godfrey, it was a year before he found out what happened next. According to his receptionist, when La Rosa left Arthur's office, waiting for him there were his lawyer, Jack Katz, his agent, Rockwell, his press agent, and two members of the press. "[Julius] had tears in his eyes. They asked him what happened and he said, 'I don't know. I'm bewildered.' And [Arthur continued], Rockwell went over to the reporters and said, 'Of course he's bewildered. That son of a bitch fired him on the air today. He humiliated him.' The guy had just broken down and thanked me, you know!"[34]

Until that moment all that millions who had heard the broadcast knew was that La Rosa would not be on anymore.

Now the other shoe dropped. By the time the afternoon papers—plentiful at the time across America—hit the streets, there was no question why La Rosa was going off on his own—he had been fired.

'The audience was the mother," observed Remo Palmier, "Arthur was the father, and Julius was the son, and the whole psychological thing…was [that] the father had thrown the son out of the house."[35]

The next morning, according to Frank Stanton, Godfrey came into his office, bewildered. "What did I do wrong?"[36]

In his 1956 interviews for the *Post*, Godfrey mused, "It seems clear now that Julius was being advised by people who were smart enough to figure that if he was going to make any real money, it wouldn't be profitable just to let him part company with me on friendly terms. That wouldn't get him anywhere. If it could seem that we'd had a fight and he'd been given a raw deal, that would be different.

"Those in Julius' corner were smart enough to see that the next act in the real-life soap opera I'd started would stir up tremendous interest—if only there could be another act. They were right. Their scheme was a press agent's dream come true. Before they were through with their handouts, tips, inside stories, and 'low-downers'…interest in Julius couldn't have run higher if I'd kidnapped him, tortured him and held him for ransom."[37]

Soon the studios were crawling with reporters out to get the story. *Why* had Godfrey fired Julius? "Everyone who had ever worked for me was interviewed. I was accused of 'gagging' my loyal associates because they wouldn't talk. Press agents of former associates tried desperately to cash in on the bonanza by producing pictures of me with their clients in 'happier days,' before I 'fired them because they fell in love with so-and-so.' Reporters were found hiding in restrooms hoping to overhear something. Everywhere I went I was trailed, and so were others of the cast.... The elevator boys, bellhops, waiters, and even the maids at the Lexington...were accosted and bribes were offered."[38]

Jack O'Brian led the charge. Writing in his *Journal American* syndicated column, he implied that what had really led to the dismissal was a budding romance between La Rosa and Dorothy McGuire of the McGuire Sisters; that Godfrey had fired Julius because he was jealous.

With speculation swirling, Godfrey now felt compelled to hold a press conference to explain why he had let La Rosa go, a move he would soon regret. Rambling on over two hours, Godfrey, without notes and speaking off the top of his head as usual, Godfrey addressed O'Brian's charge, explaining that Dorothy's husband, Sgt. John H. Brown, was on duty in Korea and that she would hardly let a small fling with La Rosa "carry her away." At one point he lavished praise on La Rosa, but then talked about how he had changed. It was at that point that he said Julius had "lost his humility."

"Now talk about the pot calling the kettle black," observes Peter Kelley. "One thing you could never accuse Arthur of is having overly humble opinions. And they picked up on that. They nailed his hide to the cross for that one. And it was all downhill from that point on."[39]

The next day, it was the word "humility" that was in newspaper headlines. People across the country ran to their dictionaries. Songs called "Humility" were quickly composed and hawked to music publishers. "Humility" became a buzz word for comedians. But instead of letting go, Godfrey pursued the issue, now feeling compelled to explain what humility was.

By coincidence, he was to be the guest of Ed Murrow that Friday evening on his *Person to Person* television show. Each week, Murrow talked with celebrities in a live half-hour interview, with Murrow in New York and the celebrities at their homes. Conversing with Murrow from Virginia, Godfrey responded to Murrow's questioning about his promoting young talent and said that he was particularly proud of what he had done for Julius La Rosa. When asked by Murrow why he had dismissed him "so brusquely and on the air," Godfrey's rambling response seemed anything but helpful to his case. In an interview with the Associated Press and on his morning shows over the next week, he continued to try to explain the word "humility," give positive examples, and justify his action. It seems clear now that if he had only let it go, much of the damage would have been controlled. One can only wonder if things would have been different if Mug Richardson were still with him, providing him the sage advice he seemed so desperately in need of at the time.

Meanwhile, Ed Sullivan, who only a few months before had subbed for Godfrey on his Wednesday night show, wasted no time. The same day that La Rosa was released, Sullivan, with his uncanny eye for headline talent, signed him to a multi-year contract to appear on *Toast of the Town*, his popular Sunday night variety show. Though both were major stars for CBS, Godfrey and Sullivan had met only once several years earlier when CBS had asked Godfrey to make an appearance on the Sullivan show. La Rosa's appearances drew huge audiences.

And Rockwell went to work as well. La Rosa, who already had a $100,000-a-year guarantee from Rockwell and General Artists Corporation, took on club dates that by 1956 were paying $6,000 to $7,500 a week for singing two shows a night. "When a percentage arrangement is made, he earns more," explained a feature article in *Look* magazine that year. "In Las Vegas last November, for a three-week stint he made $37,500.... In the two months following his firing, he earned $85,000. His 1954 income was $360,000 and in 1955 he made $480,000. His last year with Godfrey he had made $35,000."[40]

Just about lost in all of this was the fact that within two days of the La Rosa firing, Godfrey also released his long-time musical director, Archie Bleyer.

Bleyer never discussed his dismissal publicly. It was left to the press and to Godfrey to explain it. They agreed on one thing: the precipitating event was a trip by Bleyer made that same week to Chicago to record a series of poems with Don McNeill. McNeill, the long-time host of ABC's *The Breakfast Club*, was fairly popular, but he was hardly a threat to Godfrey's popularity. Yet, for whatever reasons, Godfrey considered him a competitor.

The press concluded that it was another instance of Godfrey's jealousy, that as in the case of La Rosa, Bleyer was becoming successful beyond his work as a Little Godfrey.

Godfrey explained it differently: with Cadence Records established, Bleyer was losing interest in the Godfrey programs. In 1955, he used his eight-part series in the *Saturday Evening Post* to laud Bleyer for all the contributions he had made in the early years. He explained how he had confronted Bleyer directly about his decision to record McNeill. "'Why did you do that, Arch?' I pleaded. 'You asked for time off from your job so you could rest. You rested by going to Chicago to make records for your personal company with a competitor of the very programs and network which have promoted your record company from the start.' He just sat there defiantly and I knew he had gone beyond my reach. I told him he was forcing me into a spot where I'd have to fire him. 'Do what you like,' he said, shrugging his shoulders. I kept his job open for him for weeks afterwards.... I kept hoping one day

he'd show up in my office with that old, warm, friendly look on his face. He could have had his baton back just that easily. But he never came back and I have never seen him since the last *Talent Scout* show he conducted for me [eight weeks later]."[41]

"The whole band was shocked, actually shocked," recalls guitarist Remo Palmier. "Because to get rid of someone like Archie...he was the perfect gentleman at all times and really was doing a super job.... But for some reason, their relationship [Bleyer and Godfrey's] got to be a little strained.... A lot of things started to be blamed on Archie that weren't his fault.... As far as I'm concerned, I think the show went steadily downhill after Archie left. Because he was the brains behind all that entertainment and what made the show successful. You know, as colorful as Arthur was, Archie was almost like this monitor. Somebody that kept him in line, and kept him focused on what he was supposed to be doing.... It was almost like Archie was the dad, and he [Arthur] was the son.... Even though Arthur was older, he looked at Archie as if he was a parent, and the parent kept telling him not this, do this, this is what counts.... He'd say, 'OK, it's silly, but people will enjoy it.' Archie had a terrific perception about what people enjoyed watching. [And] even though Arthur would fight him, he would succumb to the idea that Archie was dreaming up. Because it always was successful, even though he didn't like doing it. Everything Archie touched was successful."[42]

In its Wednesday edition covering the dismissals, *Variety* reported, "According to those close to the scene, neither the La Rosa nor Bleyer axings came as too much of a surprise in view of 'strange things that have been happening since Godfrey resumed after his operation.'"[43]

Godfrey may have had a rationale for dismissing Bleyer, but without Archie he had lost another anchor, another compass, and a great interpreter for him of what the public wanted.

Archie Bleyer went on to record many Top-40 hits with his company, including "Hernando's Hideaway," "The Naughty Lady from Shady Lane," and many more with the Chordettes ("Mr. Sandman") and La Rosa. His most lucrative find was the Everly Brothers, who went on to huge success on Cadence with such million-record country-pop sellers as "Bye Bye Love," "Wake up Little Susie," and "All I Have to Do Is Dream." With a subsidiary label, he created albums for Chuck Mingus, Max Roach, Abbey Lincoln and other jazz greats. He remained married to Jan Ertel, one of the Chordettes, until his death in the early 1990s. He never spoke publicly about Arthur Godfrey.

Godfrey and La Rosa met only two more times in the thirty years that followed. In 1960, they bumped into each other on the street. La Rosa had left a doctor's office and was walking down Fifth Avenue. "About forty feet away, coming out of a building, I see Godfrey. Now I don't look so hot, harassed and uptight, but I know I'm going to run into him. So we come together, we both kind of looked at each other from the side—'Is it really him?' I could tell he had the same reaction.... I put out my hand, and he shakes it...I take his hand and mine over his, and now it's the four-hand shake. He didn't look older than the first day I saw him in Pensacola. 'How are you? You look great—how are you? Fine.' It's one of those quick, brief things, and I walk with him a few feet and then I said, 'We'd better watch it, or they'll make an item out of us for the papers,' and he says, 'Fuck 'em.' And we walk a little farther and then we go our own ways."[44]

Then in the late seventies they would meet one more time. It would be nice to conclude the La Rosa saga with a happy ending, but that was not to be. Peter

Kelley, Godfrey's agent from 1966 until his death, wanted to do a record album, a reunion of the Godfrey cast. Over dinner with Godfrey he introduced the idea. "You mean you want Julius La Rosa, Marion Marlowe and all those shits that were on the show?" "That's correct," said Peter. "You're crazy," replied Arthur. "You do not need that.... All you need is some of the good music that was there then.... Why should I give them another boost from what they've done to me over the years?" "It won't be that," Peter responded. "You're going to be the beneficiary of it." "Come on," said Arthur, "This fella La Rosa has been kept alive because every time I go to a strange town some punk looks in a book and sees that La Rosa was fired and comes and questions me about it." Kelley told Godfrey he was exaggerating and urged him to "let bygones be bygones." He called the album "a first step," with Godfrey's book to follow. Godfrey subsequently agreed and a meeting was arranged between the two men.

At the meeting, according to Kelley, they hugged and while waiting for a Godfrey staff member to arrive, they began to reminisce. "There's just one thing I don't understand Julius," said Godfrey. "You knew the truth of this thing. Why didn't you come out and make a public statement and get me off the hook?" According to Kelley, La Rosa began to explain about the notice on the board after he had missed a rehearsal and how he had come to the Lexington Hotel to try to straighten things out, and how Arthur had apparently rebuffed him. He told Godfrey how that angered him.

"At that point the famous Godfrey temper went blooey!" recalls Peter Kelley. "He blew up! And kicked him out of his office."

Afterwards, Kelley sent a letter to La Rosa, "not to apologize for Godfrey's tirade, but for putting Julius in that position. I told Arthur and he got angry and fired *me*! A few days later he reconsidered."[45] But that was the end of any possible reunion and the last time Godfrey and La Rosa would ever speak.

As for Julie La Rosa, after the Godfrey shows, he recorded more than 30 songs with Cadence, then signed a three-year contract with RCA Victor Records. But his later recordings never reached the same popularity as his first two. And slowly La Rosa faded from popular view. "I did some acting in summer stock. In the mid-sixties, I put together a show called 'An Evening with Julius La Rosa,' and took it on the road. It was not a success. In 1968, I hired a manager and got some new arrangements and opened in one of the lounges in Las Vegas." He then did an "apprenticeship" as a disc jockey at WNEW in New York and stayed on for ten years, earning $100,000 a year. Then "it was back to saloons and summer stock." By 1987, La Rosa, now 57, began appearing at jazz clubs in New York. He worked hard at his singing and began to receive serious attention from jazz columnists. Today, he is still performing and puts out occasional CDs that receive favorable reviews. His musical achievements pale, however, in comparison to Sinatra's, the man who was his model, or to Tony Bennett's, a contemporary.

"The Godfrey experience was central to my life. It still follows me." Over the years, Julius has been interviewed countless times on the subject. He has always been surprisingly candid, acknowledging what Arthur Godfrey did for him in his life. "People think I dislike him. God knows, I didn't love him. But I was never hateful of him.... I'll always be grateful to him, but he wasn't a nice man."[46]

Godfrey fared worse in many ways. The New York tabloids fed on the firing for months. In a twelve-part series, written by eight *New York Post* writers a month

after the dismissals, his life was examined from stem to stern under front-page chapter banners such as "Hard Times," "How to Make a Million," "Big Time Operator," "Godfrey's BIG Friends—the Brass," and "Godfrey Inc." Each chapter was accompanied by a bevy of photos of Godfrey and the cast and his family, gathered from public and private collections. The approach was clear: "Arthur Godfrey spends almost as much airtime dredging up small details from his pathetic past as he does complaining about the immense bite Uncle Sam puts on his current annual bundle of between $1,500,000 and $2,000,000 in wages," began one chapter. "Arthur fought his way to the top by biting the hands that fed him," begins another. He was referred to as "the earthy, sentimental rogue of the airwaves," "the Fort Knox of the radio and television world."

Surprisingly, once past the hyperbole, the articles contained a good deal of complimentary material and a mild approach to Godfrey's personal life. There were photos of Mary and Mug on the same page, Mug in a low-cut dress with a wide smile, Mary in a Hawaiian blouse with the subtitle "The Second Mrs. G.," but the tone was respectful. "The life of the second Mrs. Arthur Godfrey has been remarkably quiet, considering her husband's apparent obsession for being heard or seen.... Mary manages...Beacon Hill and tends to the needs of the two younger Godfrey children.... Mary's independence, which many consider is the quality that attracted Arthur in the first place, hasn't diminished, apparently." Regarding Mug, "Intimates...assert that the Arthur-Mug relationship was nothing more than a solid business partnership. They note that he met his present wife before Mug came on the scene—and married her afterward."[47]

The accusations and counter-accusations would continue, spurred on by further "firings." Indeed, from then on, no other event in Arthur Godfrey's life was so immediately associated with him as the firing of La Rosa. It hounded him for the next thirty years. In comparison to all of his achievements before and after, "he blew it way out of proportion" believes Kelley, though he could never shake off questions about it.[48] It was on the mind of every interviewer and, at the end, a major part of every obituary. In many a broadcasting book or program, whatever else is said about Arthur Godfrey, there is always mention of the La Rosa Affair.

In retrospect, the event and all the fallout could have been completely avoided. Both men had made mistakes: from Arthur feeling compelled to take hasty action for the shortcomings of a 23-year-old cast member, to Julius feeling compelled to take hasty action for a slap on the hand. The people they went to then gave them bad advice. Rockwell pushed La Rosa too far too fast. And Stanton's and Paley's advice to release Julius on the air never really made sense.

Though the press sided with La Rosa, most members of the cast and staff sided with Godfrey. They felt he had been a father to Julius and that Julius had been ungrateful.

Several years later, another young singer, Pat Boone, then a regular on the shows, came to Godfrey to tell him he had received a movie contract. Arthur asked him if he had done any acting. Boone told him no, except for a play in high school. "Arthur said, 'Well, what are they gonna pay yuh?' I told him. 'Are you the lead?' 'Yes sir. It's 20th Century Fox.' And he says, 'Well, go ahead. You ought

to try it. If it doesn't work out, come on back.'

"Now you see, instead of some of the others who would just have had a lawyer or an agent notify him that this thing had come up and they were just going to do it, he appreciated that I came to him and asked his advice.

"Then later I came to him after I made two movies and I said, 'Mr. G., ABC has offered me my own half-hour music show.' And he said, 'Well, I can see why you want to do it. But you know you're takin' a big chance. Here with me you can come in every morning. You're protected. You don't have to carry the whole show. And if you do good it's fine. If you don't do so good one morning it doesn't matter, you'll be back.' We went round and round. Finally I said, 'It's a good deal. And it's about a million dollars a year.' 'Well, why don't you go ahead and try it. And if it doesn't work out then you can come on back here.'

"A lot of folks think he was brutal and mean because he fired Julius on the air and did a lot of things that seemed arbitrary. But I found that if I would confer with him and bring him into the decisions he would bend over backwards to help."[49]

But La Rosa and Bleyer had chosen a different tack.

In historical terms, perhaps the biggest story was not even the firings or the effect it had had on the careers of the men involved, but the fact that a broadcasting story had riveted the attention of the American public for days and weeks. Not even Orson Welles' *War of the Worlds* radio show in 1938 had had that amount of impact. America's growing fascination with radio and television had spilled over into hard news.

In the Wake

THE FIRESTORM HAD ENDED, THE dust had begun to settle. And when a casual observer looked around, not much had changed for Godfrey and his shows. The daily routines of broadcasting went on as usual. *Arthur Godfrey Time,* now in its eighth year, was still on both radio and television each weekday morning and sprawling across the CBS schedule from 10 A.M. to 11:30 A.M. The McGuire Sisters were as effervescent as ever, the Chordettes, Frank Parker, Marion Marlowe, Haleloke, the Mariners, Janette Davis, and new young singer named Lou Ann Simms were all on hand, joined each week by winners of the *Talent Scouts* show. The orchestra was still intact, though Will Roland was now at the helm. Advertisers were still getting ribbed, letters pro and con were still being read. Godfrey's days in the office were business as usual. There were the Thursday trips to Virginia, then the Monday night show and the Wednesday night show. Audience figures seemed to be holding steady. The CBS brass was silent as ever. And as for the press, Godfrey never did quite understand why his actions in October had received so much attention.

But with almost fifty years of perspective now, something quite significant *had* indeed transpired during the fall of 1953. The growing medium of television—still somewhat of a novelty for most Americans—had shown, for the very first time, its ability to generate its own news and to dominate the American mind, superseding for a time concerns about or interest in government, business, sports, movies, television, newspapers, magazines, or even daily life. The Elvis Presley gyrations were still five years off, the Beatles' premiere, nine years, and the final episodes of *MASH* and *Seinfeld* lay way down the road of television, as did the entertainment magazine and gossip shows that came to fill the screen in the 1990s. A television star had fired a television star and that was

as important in the late October days of
1953 as just about anything else that was
going on in the world. Reporting on television itself would now be taken much
more seriously by editors and publishers.

But there was more. If Americans had
come to consider Godfrey as father, neighbor, and uncle, the firings had sent a clear
message: better think again. Like the Wizard of Oz when the curtains fell down,
what was revealed was a rather ordinary
human being with many of the same faults
and temperaments that we all display and
see in others whom we experience in the
flesh. Godfrey was not a god. And to his
credit, he had never set out to be one. To
its credit, CBS had not set out to create that
image for him either. It was the American
press and the American public that had
anointed him and then—surprise—had
discovered he was not much different than
their fathers, neighbors, and uncles during an off day.

There are those who say that Arthur
Godfrey ruined his career with the firings.
Others would say that unintentionally, he
had done himself and others a great good,
that he had deflated the hype and become
a more real human being to his audiences.
Godfrey may have played to his power
regularly, but he had never played to the
public's idolization. If he had wanted the
idolization, he would never have escaped
each weekend to his Virginia farm and
family, or spent as much time flying or developing young talent. Aggressive as he
was at pursuing his career, had that been
the end-all, he would have had a stable of
professional handlers, never venturing out
on his own. And he would have scripted
everything he said to be sure his messages
were always clear and successful.

Inadvertently he had also sent a wake-
up call to American journalists, the kind
that would not be seen again as dramatically until the Vietnam war and the
Watergate investigation when the press

learned to stand apart, to ask more questions and give more answers, rather than
kowtowing to authority. But the lessons
were not to be absorbed that quickly by
the public or the press or Godfrey.

On January 7, 1954, Godfrey's temper
flared again and a second round of Godfrey bashing began. That evening, with a
considerable crosswind blowing, just as the
air traffic controllers were changing shifts
at the Teterboro, New Jersey, Airport
tower, they received a request from the familiar voice of Arthur Godfrey. He was on
the runway in his DC-3, requesting permission to take off on runway 32, a short
runway facing west. His request was
against airport policy and was denied. Instead, he was routed to another runway
facing northwest.

As the tower chief Dan Kaplan later recalled, "About halfway down the strip, he
(Godfrey) flew at low altitude veering over
waiting aircraft and headed for the control
tower. The four men in the tower dashed
for the stairwell. We could have counted
the plane's rivets as it roared over the cab.
Asked by radio if he was in trouble, Godfrey replied, "that was a normal takeoff for
Teterboro."[1] For his violation, he ultimately had his license suspended by the
Federal Aviation Administration for six
months.

From the moment it happened Godfrey
denied any wrong doing. On the surface,
that made sense; it certainly wasn't characteristic of the man who had spent his
life promoting air safety to purposefully
buzz a control tower. He blamed the airport and the FAA, explaining that he had
no choice, that the crosswind, which he
said was at about 50 knots, kept blowing
hard against the wing, turning the plane
into the wind as he went down the runway.
That, he would explain, required him to
counteract by putting less power on one
side and holding down one rudder pedal
while trying to take off—a difficult job.

Twice he "weathercocked" and had to stop and start again. Each time, the Godfrey temper mounted. With his request denied for another runway where the wind would be angled differently, he said, "Okay, if that's the way you want us to take off, come on!" And that's when he buzzed the control tower as he went up.[2]

The newspapers were soon on the story and for the second time in less than three months, Godfrey was the subject of a very unsympathetic press. "Godfrey Cited as Wild Flier. Port Authority Files Charge," read one headline. A columnist for the *New York Daily News* dubbed him as "television entertainer, second only to Captain Video as television's most daring pilot." He was characterized as reckless and loony. Most notably, Ed Sullivan wrote in his column, "The flippancies of Arthur Godfrey, in answering charges of reckless operation of his DC3...are shocking. Godfrey is 50 years old—hardly the age for a hot-rodder...such fliers are as dangerous as a drunk with a loaded gun."

As he was wont to do, Godfrey took to the airwaves to tell his audiences what had happened and to give the FAA hell. In a theme he would play on throughout the years ahead, it was Godfrey against the bureaucracy. He told Frank Parker during one of his broadcasts, "I've learned the hard way...nothing. I tell them [reporters and photographers] nothing! That's the only thing you can do. If you say anything to them whatsoever, they'll foul it up."[3]

When this new storm subsided, his relations with the press had deteriorated even further. In some ways it was more natural—this mutual distrust—than the constant unquestioning adulation he had received before October. Rightly or wrongly, as long as he remained a star, he was going to be fair game whatever he did, wherever he did it, no different from Frank Sinatra and many other big-time celebrities.

Yet the buzzing only increased the gap that the public saw between his on-air personality and what now seemed to keep emerging as his other side. His image was just hardened that much more and though you could continue to respect him and enjoy him, it was certainly becoming more difficult to like him.

What became more unnerving, as Godfrey appeared more vulnerable, were long-smoldering charges of anti–Semitism. And like the La Rosa firing, this accusation dogged him the rest of his life. It still persists today, though disputed by the facts and by almost every one who knew him. It is yet another example of how stars like Godfrey can be stereotyped by the public.

The previous winter of 1953, when Godfrey had done his first live broadcast from Miami Beach, it originated from the Kenilworth Hotel in Bal Harbor, up Collins Avenue from the downtown area. Bal Harbor was greener and posher, the hotels were fewer and more exclusive and the Kenilworth sat between Collins Avenue and a magnificent strip of the beach, far beyond the madding crowds just ten miles farther south. There was an entry from the ocean into the Intracoastal Waterway just north of the resort, and the hotel provided complete privacy for its upscale guests. Like many hotels in that area at the time, the Kenilworth was restricted, meaning it "took" no Jews or blacks. "There were lots of pockets of discrimination in many areas of South Florida," recalled Hank Meyer, who was head of the Miami Beach Chamber of Commerce at the time.[4]

In the 1920s, the entire "Gold Coast," as the Beach was called, along with the city of Miami just to the west, became one of the most popular vacation destinations in the States. It drew wealthy socialites, not-so-wealthy retirees, and middle-class Americans to dozens of hotels built up and down Collins Avenue. The Jewish population of winter tourists, numbering in the thousands, congregated in a one mile-area that stretched north to 47th street and was filled with restaurants, shops, and an increasing number of luxury hotels surrounded by more modest ones.

Few Jewish people were interested in staying in Bal Harbour, but almost everyone was aware that the Kenilworth was one of those restricted hotels. It was Leo DeOrsey, Godfrey's lawyer and manager, who had introduced Arthur to the area and the hotel, of which he owned a sizable piece. Beginning in the late forties, Mary and Arthur would take trips to the Kenilworth with Leo and his wife Helen. Times were changing and walls of prejudice were beginning to come down, but many of his listeners and viewers found the Kenilworth representing an unexplained side of Godfrey: Why would he stay at a restricted hotel? Was he anti–Semitic?

To the contrary, Peter Kelley, Godfrey's primary agent for the last 20 years of his career, recalls that "Arthur wasn't anti-anything, except probably anti–Fascist and anti–Nazi."[5] He traced the charge in part to the way Godfrey talked. Godfrey grew up in an era of mass immigration when many Americans, including the immigrants, referred to or identified others by their race or religion. He was no exception. Writer Ralph Schoenstein, who later guested on Arthur's radio shows and years later attempted to help him write an autobiography, agreed that it was Godfrey's way, at times, to so identify people but that it was also benign. "I know guys like Arthur. He was like my father. The same kind of street talk."[6]

Though few of his singers were Jewish, his announcer, Tony Marvin and a number of his bandleaders, band members, producers and writers through the years were. Ironically, when these individuals traveled to Miami Beach to do the shows, they stayed at the Kenilworth along with

Godfrey. Jazz musician Dick Hyman, who was Godfrey's orchestra director in the late 1950s, along with dozens of performers who appeared with him through the years, saw no signs of anti–Semitism, no traces of any hostility. Nowhere in Bill Paley's memoirs or in biographies of the man does the charge emerge. Hank Meyer and his wife Lenore were often guests of Godfrey's when he was at the Beach. One time Arthur had been invited to a Bar Mitzvah and invited them to join him and the celebrating family for dinner. The Meyers once spent ten days as Godfrey's guests at the Virginia farm.

Non-Jews in the business such as Andy Rooney also dismissed the contention, as did Remo Palmier, who observed it would have been very prominent if it were true. Former CBS president Frank Stanton, who brought Godfrey to national prominence, never found truth in the rumors.[7]

Kelley also suggests that Godfrey wasn't aware of the Kenilworth's policies during the early stays there. As far as he knew, everyone connected with his show could go there. "But shortly after he bought a small interest in it, in the early fifties, he found out about the policy and within six months had the restricted policy removed."[8]

Ruth Ann Perlmutter, whose husband Nate was head of the Anti-Defamation League (ADL) in Florida in those days, corroborates that story. "Arthur got such a bad rap. We lived near him in Florida. People pointed to the Kenilworth as proof of his anti–Semitism. Except when he bought into it, he desegregated it. My husband and I used to defend him."[9] "The problem," says Kelley, is that when he changed the policy, "it made the back pages, not the front pages."

If Godfrey had traveled with the entertainment crowd in Hollywood or even New York, where Jews were prominent, it is unlikely the charge would have stuck.

Though financier Bernard Baruch was a close friend and advisor, most of his closest friends were corporate leaders and military men, few of whom were Jewish. Yet Jewish entertainers like Jack Benny did appear on his programs. Humorist Sam Levenson subbed for him regularly. In 1950, actress Gertrude Berg who played a popular character named Molly Goldberg on radio and television, appeared on his program. Then, two weeks later, he played himself on her situation comedy show, *The Goldbergs*. On that program, Molly brought in the neighborhood talent to "try out" for Godfrey and sent him off with "borscht, blintzes, and strudel." [10]

Yet the assumption persisted, undermining his credibility. Peter Kelley's understanding was that the nemesis was Irving Mansfield, the talented producer for CBS in the 1940s who created the *Talent Scouts* program. It was common knowledge that Godfrey and Mansfield hated each other and that they carried out a constant series of slights or worse. It's said that Godfrey would purposefully fill the half-hour of his *Talent Scouts* show till the very last seconds so that there wouldn't be time to run Mansfield's credit. According to what Kelley had been told, Mansfield began to spread the word about the Kenilworth being restricted and Godfrey being anti-Semitic

Others dispute that account. Interviewing Irving Mansfied once, Larry King found him to be surprisingly positive about Godfrey. King, who was a reporter for the *Miami Herald* in the early fifties, was well aware of the Kenilworth policy. "If it had been me," he says, "I wouldn't have stayed there. But Arthur didn't think that way." [11]

On one occasion, the ADL was asked to look into charges that Godfrey was anti-Semitic. Arnold Foster, now a New York attorney, was national director of the ADL at the time. According to Gail Gans

of the ADL in New York, "the criticism of Godfrey dealt with his association with the Kenilworth Hotel. And the fact that he sometimes used an exaggerated Yiddish personal accent for comic effect." [12] At the time, Foster wrote: "I personally do not believe that Godfrey is any menace to Jews or to any other ethnic group. Or that any human relations organization ought to be concerned in any way about him. There's no evidence in our record that he has stepped over the line, so to say, with ill-advised humor in a long time and the Kenilworth has now for many years been open to Jews." [13]

Today, Foster adds that Irving Mansfield was a good friend of his. "Irving would say, 'I know [Arthur] better. An anti-Semite he's not. A loose tongue, yes. I would trust him on my life that he's not an anti-Semite.... He knows I'm an active Jew and involved and I tell you he's not an anti-Semite.' Walter Winchell and his secretary Rose Bigman also assured me he was not. I spent 60-odd years in the ADL including years as counsel, and I've looked under beds for anti-Semites. And if I concluded at the time that he wasn't, he wasn't." [14]

Yet for some who would define anti-Semitism broadly, and that does not include Foster, Godfrey is guilty as charged because of staying at the Kenilworth and apparent delays in getting the policy of the hotel changed once he took it over. Herman Klurfield, who was Walter Winchell's associate, acknowledges that Winchell's secretary, Rose Bigman, "was very fond of Arthur. Her sister worked for Arthur and he [Arthur] was fond of her." But he goes on to say that Winchell, also Jewish, became furious at Godfrey when he gained part ownership of the hotel that kept out Jews, and stopped writing about Godfrey. Though not suggesting that he or Winchell thought Godfrey anti-Semitic, Klurfield felt it was only under pressure that Godfrey changed the policy.[15]

Traveling east across the Julia Tuttle Causeway, from the city of Miami to the Beach, two huge green highway signs loom overhead in front of you as you approach the beach side. One directs you to Mt. Sinai Medical Center, the other points straight ahead to Arthur Godfrey Road, which then stretches for a mile all the way to the Ocean. "Arthur loved the Beach," remembers Hank Meyer. "When we renamed 41st Street Arthur Godfrey Road, he loved that too. But he had a great fear that someday people would say he was anti–Semitic and that the sign should be taken down. I would say, 'Arthur, they won't do that,' and he'd say 'It's not right, it's not fair, and it's not factually correct.'"[16]

The signs are still up on Arthur Godfrey Road. But the charge of anti–Semitism still comes up from many, some fifty years later, whenever the name Arthur Godfrey is mentioned. It is a chilling comment on how casually we often label people, especially our celebrities, based on few hard facts, no direct involvement, and a good deal of hearsay. The damage done can be devastating.

Novelists and book authors also had at the Godfrey story. This was long before the publishing industry was into "tell all" books by friends and associates. Had the Godfrey debacle occurred in the nineties there would have been at least a dozen such books. The most obvious take-off on Godfrey's life and career was a 1955 novel by a little-known writer named Al Morgan, who had worked for both CBS and NBC. Morgan's book, *The Great Man*, told the story of Herb Fuller, a wildly popular radio network star who dies unexpectedly in a car accident. In working on a memorial show, another employee of the network interviews members of his cast ("the Fuller Family") and the "common man,"

obtaining vastly different stories. He not only discovers a public that adored and idolized Fuller, but also unearths a marriage of convenience, a long-running affair with the girl singer on his show, and stories of Fuller's ruthlessness. Slickly written, it was also a story about the politics within the broadcasting business. The dust jacket stated that Fuller "exists only in the author's imagination."[17] In 1956 it was made into a movie, with Jose Ferrer starring and directing. Julie London played the singer and Ed Wynn his first boss. The preview trailer heralded it as "the most shattering, hard-hitting, daringly frank picture to come out of Hollywood" and said the film was about "a popular television star who was hated by those who really knew him." Surprisingly, both the book and the movie met with only mild success. Broadcasting had not yet penetrated the literary world.

In 1957, a far more compelling movie was written by Budd Schulberg, an accomplished author of the time. *A Face in the Crowd* told the story of a young guitar-playing hillbilly with an ingratiating personality who falls into a job at a local radio station, becomes a local phenomenon, and quickly rises to become a national television star. He allows others to shape his career, including network executives and corporate advertisers who fear him and use him, and he reaches a level of power where he is even considered for a cabinet post and reminds his cohorts, "I'm not just an entertainer...I'm an influence...I'm a force!" Directed by Elia Kazan, it featured Andy Griffith, in his film debut, giving a stunning performance as the singer, Patricia Neal, Lee Remick, and cameo roles by Mike Wallace, Walter Winchell and other media people of the time. It is considered by many to be an unrecognized classic. Asked in 1996 about the book, Schulberg denied that it was based on Arthur Godfrey's life; he said it was Will Rogers he had had in mind. Yet some of the most compelling scenes gave insights into not only Griffith's character, but into Godfrey's as well.

In 1955, Steve Allen, by now entrenched as the wildly popular host of *The Tonight Show*, wrote a book called *The Funny Men*. In it, he devoted an entire chapter to Arthur Godfrey. He reported that CBS had been continually uneasy about the future of their number-one revenue producer, an unease he said bordering on "contained panic." His message was that there was nothing to fear; that the La Rosa affair had only made him more human to his audiences, that his voice itself was a national treasure, that no one expected him to be a comic, that he had "a great power to move a great number of people personally," and that "Godfrey can be listened to painlessly....Godfrey doesn't make you think; he relieves you of the responsibility. He is a cup of hot milk, a sedative, a comfort in a noisy world." [18]

By June of 1954, *TV Guide*, acknowledging Godfrey's continuing hold on Americans despite all that had been happening off the air, was back to the American pastime of trying to discern just what the magic was. In yet another cover story (Godfrey would go on to appear on 16 *TV Guide* covers), with the provocative title "What's Godfrey's Hold on Women?" Dr. George W. Crane, a prominent Chicago psychologist and physician, explained that

"He creates a fatherly tone. Women are more apt to associate him with their fathers than with husbands or sweethearts.... Because of this, his career can survive incidents, such as the firing of several performers. Even his tiff with the Civil Aeronautics Authority...did not hurt his standing for any appreciable time. Father knows best." "Will Godfrey last?" *TV Guide* asked. "Certainly," said the doctor. "I've heard of fans getting tired of him. It's no reflection on his merits. You can get tired of too much sirloin steak too. His manner is permanently valuable. Any monotony comes only from...too many shows a week. Think of our lives in terms of music. As we grow older our tempo changes from a fox trot to a waltz.... Godfrey waltzes. A waltz is timeless." [19]

It would not be that simple.

When the 1953-54 season ended in April, six months after the La Rosa–Bleyer firings, there was cause for celebration. Godfrey's two evening shows, *Talent Scouts* and *Friends*, finished a strong 3rd and 5th respectively, suggesting that his audience pull was as strong as ever. *Talent Scouts*, not dependent on the Little Godfreys, had slipped modestly from second to third, tied with Groucho Marx's *You Bet Your Life* and commanding an impressive 43.6 rating. *I Love Lucy* and *Dragnet* were on top. Despite appearances by Julius, Ed Sullivan's *Toast of the Town* was a distant 17th on the list.

24

Transitioning

BY THE 1954-55 SEASON THE TELE-
vision landscape began to change dramatically. A third major network, ABC, had
emerged, and for the first time Godfrey
faced real competition on Wednesday
nights. ABC had come up with a real
heavyweight from 7:30 to 8:30 P.M. in the
person of Walt Disney. For the first time,
Disney was opening up his treasure trove
of feature films and shorts, including his
ever-popular cartoon characters, to television—in prime time and in color. *Disneyland* was clearly winning the ratings battle, and four months into the season on
December 29, 1954, Godfrey took action:
Larry Puck, who had been with the
Wednesday night show since it had begun
in 1949, was removed as producer, though
he would continue as coproducer of the
Monday night *Talent Scouts* show.

Under ordinary circumstances the press
would have seen this as a modest program
improvement move on Godfrey's part. But
it so happened that Puck, 55, had recently

become engaged to singer Marion Marlowe, 25, and the press saw it as another
cast member romance that was ending in
dismissal. Godfrey was back in hot water
again.

His first response was to deny that he
knew of the Puck-Marlowe engagement.
He publicly sent his "blessings and best
wishes to both of them." Things quieted
down.

But four months later, on April 15,
1955, Godfrey lowered the boom on nine
of his regulars: the Mariners quartet,
Haleloke, three of his long-time writers
(Charles Horner, Preston H. Mileas and
Charles Slocum), and—Marion Marlowe.
The press also reported on how the firings
were handled: according to Marlowe, the
singers were summoned to Godfrey's office
after the morning show and he read them
a statement:

"The heads of CBS Radio-TV have
decided to discontinue your services as
of now. We are going to use some other

people. Your services are no longer required." Marlowe told the Associated
Press she asked if this meant right now
and Godfrey said yes. Were there any
other questions? No, said Marlowe, and
then he thanked them for their coopera-
tion and said goodbye.[1]

Though their names were well known,
none of the performers had the kind of
major following that Julius La Rosa had
had. Indeed, many television critics had
been skeptical of their talents all along.
But it did seem odd to make the changes
with only six week left in the season.
What's more, the dismissals were poorly
conducted. And there did seem to be a
connection with the Puck-Marlowe romance.

So Godfrey found himself back in the
headlines—with one difference. This time
he began to let the columnists have it.
During his morning broadcasts, he called
Dorothy Kilgallen a liar, Ed Sullivan a
"dope," another writer a "fatuous ass," and
others "these jerk newspapermen" and
"muckrakers." *TV Guide* reported that on
one broadcast, "he labeled most news stories about himself as 'pure canard, pure
manufactured lies, no basis in fact at all.
It really amuses me what people do to try
to make headlines.... I don't give a [*pause*]
what they print!'"[2]

He told one reporter that all of his personnel changes were simply intended to
put *Arthur Godfrey and His Friends* back in
to the Top 10 again.

Once again, Ed Sullivan was waiting at
the door and immediately signed Marlowe
for his Sunday night show at $3000 per
performance. She had been making $1500
a week with Godfrey. "It's nothing personal against Godfrey," Sullivan said. "If
they'd fire him, I'd try to sign him up,
too."[3]

The 1954-55 season ended with *Arthur
Godfrey and His Friends* slipping from 6th
place to 22nd, despite remote broadcasts

from Virginia in the spring featuring
Arthur's horses and all the Godfrey farm
animals, a March fashion show, an April
visit from film star Jimmy Stewart to plug
his new movie *Strategic Air Command*, and
a one-hour origination featuring the entire
cast at Coney Island, all of it live. *Talent
Scouts* had also dramatically slipped from
3rd to 18th. Things had not returned to
normal.

The following October, a month into
the 1955-56 season, Godfrey let Puck go
from the Monday night show, along with
announcer George Ryan and the musical
conductor, Jerry Bresler. Puck had married Marlowe the previous June. Again,
Godfrey was combative. He told the Associated Press, "Do I have to give reasons?
It is my show and when I see it time to
make changes I make them."[4] The next
day he released singer Lu Ann Simms,
who had been on maternity leave. Once
again he handled things poorly with the
press. In a statement to *TV Guide* he compared Ed Sullivan to a buzzard flying
overhead after a jungle animal was killed.

Godfrey had always been his own person. He was being that now. And it was
clear that he was appallingly lacking in
tact and professionalism when it came to
managing change or working with the
press. There are reasons why broadcasting
organizations hire managers and public relations professionals: to let the talent do
what they do best. Godfrey was neither a
manager nor a public relations pro; no one
expected him to be. The problem was, he
wasn't about to delegate those functions. It
was this same attitude that always put him
at the helm in a boat or at the controls in
a plane or in the driver's seat in his own
limo. But when it came to managing public relations, he appeared unable to recognize or give in to his shortcomings. In
some ways, it was comical.

"Arthur was the number one controller
I've ever known," observed Peter Kelley,

chuckling. "I remember the first time that I ever got into his Bentley. He had a driver by the name of Neil, an elderly man, and I went to meet him at CBS. Neil's just bringing the car up and opens the door for me and I get in, and Arthur comes out. He opens the *front* door for Arthur. Arthur gets in to drive and Neil gets in and sits with *me*! Arthur hated to have anybody else drive, to have anybody else fly, have anybody else pilot the boat. He wanted to do it all. And [that included] writers writing commercials for him."[5]

As for his real reasons for the changes, Godfrey would maintain that change was the very essence of staying on top. Yet his impatience seemed to be growing with cast members who had contracts and other agendas.

In reality, it didn't really matter what he believed; nothing he said would be considered reasonable by most of the press and many of his followers who wanted only to see "the old Godfrey." Besides, it was no longer big news; explaining any of it this time would hardly be worth the effort.

By 1956, the television landscape had changed even more. In addition to the emergence of ABC as a competitor for viewers and advertisers, there was a dramatic move away from live television to film. ABC's alliances with Warner Brothers and other Hollywood film production companies were providing the network with an increasing number of its prime-time shows. While CBS was holding on to its big live entertainment shows like Jackie Gleason, Red Skelton, Ed Sullivan and Arthur Godfrey, most of the Top-20 shows were now on film and much of the production was being shifted to the West Coast.

And while live game shows like *I've Got a Secret* and *What's My Line* were still staples, it was the adult television Western that was all the rage. On Saturday, September 10, 1955, CBS introduced a new half-hour Western series called *Gunsmoke. Gunsmoke* had originated on the CBS Radio Network in 1952, and had quickly become one of the most popular radio network shows in years. The television series proved even more popular. In less than a year *Gunsmoke* became the seventh most popular television show in America. And it was quickly followed by ABC's *Wyatt Earp, Sugarfoot* and *Cheyenne*, NBC's *Wagon Train* and *The Restless Gun*, and CBS's *Zane Grey Theatre*. The westerns brought more violence to the television screen. And their impact was phenomenal: the number of westerns in prime time jumped from 9 in 1956 to 31 in 1959.

The costs of television production had risen with the quality and variety and it was becoming increasingly rare for a single advertiser to sponsor an entire program series. Moreover, sophisticated audience research methods were also coming into use and advertisers seeking to reach younger adults with more buying power were finding out just what shows they were tuned in to and pressuring the networks to provide more of them: especially situation comedies.

These winds of change did not bode well for Arthur Godfrey's approach to television: live, unscripted, a different theme each week, Godfrey doing the commercials, and, despite increasing efforts to take the show on the road, almost all of it coming from New York.

The two bright spots for Godfrey's shows were the arrival of Carmel Quinn, whose Irish brogue and quick wit seemed to bring new life to him, and Pat Boone, whose appearances brought younger viewers back for a time.

When the 1955-56 season ended, *Arthur Godfrey and His Friends* had fallen out of the Top-25 shows for the first time in its seven-year run. Some analysts quickly pointed to Godfrey's self-destructive firings

Well into his seventies, Arthur and one of his palomino stallions he named Goldie performed dressage, appearing at rodeos and fairs across the country. Arthur believed that with enough desire and discipline, one could become expert at most anything. (WTOP collection.)

and battles with the press. Others saw the *Friends* show, with its flavor of the week format, as an anathema in a dynamic, growing television market, with more choices, specialization, and faster paced, more sophisticated shows and productions featuring dozens of newer, younger stars.

Godfrey had now been at the television game for eight years. He had given it everything he could. But innovation on television was coming from other quarters, and audiences, younger viewers in particular, were finding many other choices on the dial. And as always, the Wednesday night shows required a tremendous

amount of his energy and attention. On April 20, CBS announced that at Godfrey's behest, they would discontinue the series.

It had nothing to do with his health. His energy had returned to normal and it was possible, for example, for him to accept a return engagement at the National Horse Show at Madison Square Garden and present seven evening and four afternoon performances of dressage with his seven-year-old Palomino stallion "Goldie" and still fulfill his morning and evening radio and television tasks. It exhilarated him. The study of dressage riding and the raising of fine horses on his Virginia farm was a labor of love and another fine diversion from the increasingly demanding world of broadcasting.

Dressage represents the highest degree obtainable in schooling a horse. It is one of the equestrian competitions of the Olympic Games and requires painstaking training, self-discipline and collaboration between horse and rider. Though the audience may not realize it, dressage requires the rider to exert strong leg pressure on his mount, something Godfrey had been unable to do until his hip surgery. Since then, he had taken up the sport with the same intensity he applied to any new venture and made numerous appearances at horse shows in the U.S. and Canada, drawing large audiences.[6]

Through all of the ups and downs Godfrey consistently kept his family away from public view. Mary, and sometimes Richard, would accompany him on trips, but they were kept completely apart from his broadcasting life. He worked very hard to let them have their own lives and protect them from the public. Both Michael and Patricia attended public school. Years later he was very upset to find out that one of his grandchildren had been reprimanded by a teacher at school who told the child that "that was no way for a Godfrey to act." He didn't want his family burdened by his fame. In later years he would say that, being in show business, he never should have had a family. "He was never in the traditional sense cut out to be husband and father," observed Peter Kelley. "Arthur was always on the go. He was always someplace else. He was the public's person. That's hardly conducive to a good family life."[7]

His mother went in and out of his life during the fifties. She had moved to Manhattan, traveled extensively, and found a supporter in popular classical orchestra leader Andre Kostelanetz, who often played marches and other music that she composed. She would visit the Godfrey set often and head right for the piano. She would have loved to have been on his shows regularly, though he did have her on for her 75th birthday. Carmel Quinn remembers her as "full of fire and fight. He was very proud of her. She wanted to perform desperately."[8] She would come to the studio rehearsals and play the piano. As a contestant on Groucho Marx's *You Bet Your Life* program she introduced herself as Godfrey's producer. "You are?" Marx said in disbelief. "Well, I'm his mother. I guess that makes me his producer, doesn't it?" she said. She grabbed her background card from his desk and proceeded to cut his name into it. "Wait a minute, you have my card!" he said. "Now I don't know what to talk to you about!" Ignoring him, she continued cutting. Groucho watched in speechless amusement.[9] She almost stumped the panel on CBS's *What's My Line* show with the same introduction. She was a guest on the Art Linkletter and Lawrence Welk shows, was written about in *Time* magazine, and got to know Jack Paar, Victor Borge, and other stars of the day.

Godfrey provided for her financially and at many times along the way for his sisters and brothers, though several were often bitter and envious of him. Max Morath knew his sister Kathy quite well. Kathy had had an extensive career on local television as, coincidentally, a talk show host. "She was very much like him, very vocal and very talented and very energetic. She was very good on the air." The last time Morath saw her she was in a Los Angeles hospital, totally bedridden, a progression of the polio she had contracted at age 18. "Arthur's paying for all of this," she told him.[10]

Though Godfrey's ability to dominate television had slipped away as the industry expanded, he was still a household name and America's most believable and influential salesman—two characteristics that soon led the country's governmental leaders to his door.

The Cold War was at its height in the mid–fifties and the threat of a nuclear attack seemed extraordinarily real. The Eisenhower administration had developed a vast and secret doomsday plan to insure the safety of the president and other key government officials in the event of a nuclear attack, and allow for the government to continue to function. A sizable bureaucracy was put into place to administer the plan, which saw government officials being evacuated to secret relocation sites around Washington. President Eisenhower and his cabinet were to be transported to a 265,000 square foot "Underground Pentagon" near Gettysburg, Pennsylvania, or to Mount Weather in Berryville, Virginia. Congress had its own top-secret relocation center buried beneath the Greenbrier resort in White Sulphur Springs, West Virginia. Hundreds of military officials and related personnel had secret assignments should the attack happen. An Emergency Broadcast System had been put in place to be carried on radio stations in case of attack, offering instructions to the public. And hidden in a vault were tape-recorded addresses by President Eisenhower and two prominent broadcasters.[11]

"It was thought by the Eisenhower administration that two voices were well known and were trusted, and it was pretty tough to imitate us," explained Godfrey in 1981. "One was Edward R. Murrow who had become much beloved during World War II for his broadcasting from London.... And the other was Godfrey. And it was a great honor for me to be considered on the same level with Ed."[12]

On the broadcasts, the two would announce that the country had come under nuclear attack, but assuring everyone that the government continued to function. In addition to the tapes, Godfrey and Murrow, along with other prominent newsmen who were all under an oath of secrecy, were somehow to make their way to the president's cave and go on radio or television with him.[13]

With the cave only 12 miles south of the Godfrey farm in Virginia, the government had also designated his estate as the location where the vice president, then Richard Nixon, was to stay. "Fortunately," Godfrey concluded, the attack "never came to pass; we never had to do it, because we got SAC [the Strategic Air Command] built up to its proper strength pretty fast and were able to deter [Russia, which] couldn't countenance an atomic attack any better than we could. They knew what would happen: the holocaust would get them as well as us."[14]

His audiences were well acquainted with Godfrey's intense interest in SAC, national defense and air power. Early on, it had become a regular part of his on-air conversations with listeners and viewers. In his 1955 memoir in the *Saturday Evening Post* he told his readers, "I expect to continue in broadcasting for a while longer because I have a job to do. I've been working on it for some years, but it is still far from finished. The job is simply this: I want to help inform the people of this country about America's desperate need for air power—now! I believe that because of our failure to understand properly the modern meaning of the term 'adequate air power' we are gradually reaching a dangerous and untenable situation."[15]

His "mission" could be traced back to the summer of 1951 when he attended a banquet at which a high-ranking Naval officer ranted on and on about the "dangerous propaganda being foisted upon the American public by the U.S. Air Force," about the ridiculousness of the B-36, and about the fact that the Strategic

Air Command (SAC) under General Curtis LeMay was a waste of time, money, and manpower. The officer was enraged, and Godfrey wondered why the high brass—supposedly unified—were at each other's throats. He decided to find out and mentioned the matter to his friend General Hoyt Vandenberg, then head of the Air Force, who arranged for Godfrey to meet with General Curtis LeMay on his next visit to Washington.

After a brilliant World War II career in which he had helped improve the accuracy of bombing raids on Germany and led the low-altitude nighttime incendiary raids on Tokyo and other Japanese cities, Curtis LeMay had become the head of SAC in 1948. LeMay was a doer, who saw things as black or white and had little patience for diplomacy or red tape. LeMay's mission with SAC was to develop a bomber attack fleet and establish American air superiority to such a degree it would be the major deterrent to Soviet aggression. LeMay quickly sold Godfrey on the value of the B-36, which the Navy officer had criticized, explaining how it was the first weapon in American military history that could strike an overseas enemy without help from the Navy.

The two quickly became friends, and over the next few years, Godfrey flew virtually every type of Air Force bomber. LeMay showed him bases throughout the U.S., then personally took him on a tour of sites around the world. Over time, LeMay convinced him that all of the bombers, including the B-36, were becoming obsolete and a major investment by the United States was needed in a new bomber, the fast, long-range, nuclear bomber, the B-52.

"The Eisenhower administration, for whom I had been very enthusiastic, would have nothing to do with it," Godfrey explained to readers of the concluding article of his 1955 *Saturday Evening Post*

memoir. He had tried to sell his good friend Charles E. Wilson (the former head of General Motors who now was secretary of defense) on the idea, but Wilson was opposed. Obsessed with the notion that the B-52 was the answer to our overall defenses, Godfrey took time in his *Saturday Evening Post* series to explain the need in detail to his readers: "The next major war, if we have one, will open with a battle of long-range bombers, and we must be able to get the upper hand in this battle. ... At the rate [B-52's] are being produced it will be twenty-four years before we have the number required to provide the minimum protection this country must have."[16]

Frustrated, he sought out his long-time friend Bernard Baruch for advice. "And he said to me when you want to get something done and the present administration won't have anything to do with it and you believe in it, what you do is go to the opposition." In this case, the opposition was headed by then minority leader of the Senate Lyndon B. Johnson. Through mutual friends, Godfrey got himself an invitation to the Johnson ranch in Texas and in the late summer of 1955 he and several colleagues, including old friend "Scoop" Russell from his Washington NBC days, spent four days in Texas with the Johnson family, touring the ranch, the town, meeting all the locals, and bird hunting.

Godfrey and the new majority leader hit it off well, particularly when Godfrey insisted that he would get runway lights installed at Johnson's small airport, saying, "I can't go for this business of you being brought in here without lights on that runway. We have to protect our [majority] leaders." Finally, on Sunday morning, with Godfrey scheduled to leave Sunday night, Johnson said, "Well now, Arthur, you didn't come down here just to shoot doves with me; what's on your mind?" "And I told him the story of the B-52s as I knew it.... And I told him about LeMay's theories and so forth. And he listened, never spoke a word until I had finished, and said, 'I know you well enough to know that you wouldn't come down here if you didn't believe that,'" and that he would send someone up to New York to see Godfrey. It turned out to be the president of a major corporation, and Godfrey arranged for the emissary to meet General LeMay for a briefing. On his return to Washington, the man wrote a comprehensive report that led to a Senate investigation of strategic air power, and that led to the Senate's passing a bill, a Presidential veto, and a Senate override. "It was finally passed and they got a billion dollars to build the B-52s. And I was very proud of that one."[17]

They later worked together on a pay increase for servicemen. "They were losing...the cream of the military brains, the young men of the service...to industry because of the absurdly low pay." There was a bill before Congress and Godfrey "had [the minority leader] and Lady Bird and...General LeMay and his wife...at the farm and we spent the whole weekend together." Johnson told Arthur and the General that the bill would never get out of committee and that if it did come to a vote, it would be thrown out, and if it was passed it would be vetoed. The problem was not in higher payer for enlisted men, it was the high salaries proposed for the generals. "I said...'Mr. Leader, how are you going to attract men for a lifetime career if at the end of it they're gonna wind up paupers? We have to give them some incentive.'" Johnson didn't think that line of reasoning would change any votes. "So I said, 'Okay...please answer me this. Supposing you're in my position. You're a popular radio and television [personality]. You're live, you're not censored in any way, and you have access to forty million people a week. And you feel as I do about this. What would you do?' He said,

'Constituent mail, Arthur.... You write an intelligent, polite, well-worded letter to your congressman, your senator, and you tell 'em exactly what it is you'd like to see done. And be very polite about it; don't be a wise-guy and don't threaten; and don't send any petitions.'

"I said, 'Mr. Leader, you got a pretty good staff?' He said, 'Why? I said, 'I'm gonna show you mail like you've never seen.'

"So I got on the air and I said that I had talked to the minority leader about this, and...explained what it was he said we should write if we believe it.... In about seven or eight days, Mr. Johnson called me up and said, 'Will you cut it out! [The mail] is up to the ceiling here.' I said, 'Mr. Leader, you said you wanted mail....'" Soon Curtis LeMay was calling Godfrey to tell him the bill had passed the House. "Pretty soon I got a call from Lyndon. He said, 'Well, we got the pay raise for your servicemen, and we got you the billion dollars for the B-52s; now hereafter I want you to stay out of Texas. You cost the taxpayers money!'"[18]

In the years that followed, Godfrey and LBJ kept up a regular series of personal and professional visits. Godfrey would send LBJ copies of his speeches and would come to Texas to speak at Johnson's behest. The Johnsons came to the Virginia farm and the Godfreys to the White House. There were many exchanges of gifts, especially at Christmas time. Their correspondence continued through LBJ's presidency and into the 1970s.

"People are concerned for your health and want you to come home," the announcer pleaded. "*Blip blop bleeeeep*," returned the voice over the CBS radio-television 'simulcast' from 6,000 miles away. "Who wants me to *week wawk* come home *bureek*?" "The people," said the announcer.

The *bleeeeep* was Arthur Godfrey amid the flora and fauna of French Equatorial Africa, where he was stalking wild game and piping an occasional short-wave transmission into 4,000,000 American homes. Before he left the U.S. Godfrey got FCC and French government authority to make his broadcasts, and rival RCA assigned him four of its commercial frequencies. ("A helluva favor," said Godfrey. "Fine thing for good will too.") [19]

So began a *Time* magazine piece on another Godfrey excursion commingling work and play. In early 1957, Godfrey, Jim Shepley, head of Time-Life's Washington bureau, and Dick Boutelle, president of Fairchild Engine and Airplane Corporation, asked LeMay, through his contacts, to arrange for them to go on an African hunt. LeMay arranged "a modest hunt" in the north central part of French Equatorial Africa, now the nation of Chad. The four would be joined by a friend of LeMay's who would be outfitter and guide. But, according to LeMay, thanks to Godfrey the trip quickly grew in scope.

First it was decided that a *Life* photographer should also come along and maybe capture a spread for the magazine. Then Godfrey suggested the photographer shoot film as well and so they added movie cameras. Godfrey then suggested, to save time, why didn't he send his DC-3 in advance to Tripoli; they could fly over on a military jet and then take the DC-3 across the desert to the Lake Chad area. LeMay said if they were going to do that, they better have a single sideband radio on the airplane for emergency purposes. It wasn't installed very long before Godfrey had another idea—to get a generator and take the sideband along on the hunt. So the generator was added.

Godfrey then began thinking about setting up a way for him to pipe radio shows back to the States. With the help of RCA and other communications companies, that too was arranged, making it essential now to add a radio operator and another truck for the generator and more men. Godfrey's next thought: take his Bell

helicopter along to get good pictures and also use it for transportation to difficult places. So the helicopter was shipped over to the Gulf of Guinea in parts. That meant they needed a mechanic. And since Godfrey couldn't fly the helicopter and still find time to hunt and do the radio programs, they would need a pilot from the Bell helicopter people.

"In the end," said LeMay in his biography, *Mission with LeMay*, "it wasn't any modest little five hundred dollar per head hunt.... It was Godfrey's party, pure and simple, and I can't even estimate what it cost. He shipped quantities of his sponsors' products into Fort Archambault via Air France. Fruit juices, Lipton's tea, Lord knows what."[20]

Their camp numbered 75 people. The natives told them that it was the largest hunting expedition that had ever gone into the area. Over 23 days in March they stalked and shot game and spent time with the native tribes.

"He wanted to shoot an elephant.... They're going through the jungle and they had the French hunting guide," Remo Palmier recalls Godfrey telling him. "They finally reached this herd...and the guide tells him which one to shoot, this male elephant. And Arthur gets a bead on him and nails him.... And the cow of that male elephant kept walking closer and closer to Arthur and the guides and the rest of the crew. And so Arthur starts to pick up his gun and the Frenchman said, 'Mr. Godfrey, we don't shoot a cow. It's very humiliating to shoot a cow.' And Arthur says, 'If that thing moves one more foot you're gonna see the most humiliated man in Africa!

"You know, he cried after he shot that [male] elephant; after he thought about what he did, how bad he felt that he killed this wonderful animal. After that, he would never hunt again. He thought it was a terrible thing.'"[21]

LeMay told how they went down to

the villages where they would be entertained by dancers. "When anyone was sick or hurt, they would come up to the camp; thus we all became doctors. I recall Godfrey's dressing…the hand of one of the chiefs' wives where [an infection had developed]…. I think he counted the trip a success. Anyway he did his shows." But the still photographer had not been able to master the movie gear. "We flew and flew in the helicopter, pursuing game, taking pictures of the game. It ended up that the beasts were all out of focus, but there was a beautiful clear view of Arthur Godfrey's big feet."[22]

In the late 1940s, another old broadcaster, Ronald Reagan, was playing out a rather undistinguished career as an actor in Hollywood films. Despite his natural good looks, despite dramatic roles or light comedies, he lacked the ability to move movie audiences. In the late 1940s, though, Reagan's management skills came to the fore. His interests in Hollywood shifted to issues of actor's salaries and working conditions, and he served six terms as president of the Screen Actors' Guild and two terms as chairman of the Motion Picture Industry Council.

Reagan had actually begun in broadcasting as an announcer at WOC in Davenport, Iowa. He loved radio, once regaling an audience of public broadcasters with stories of how he was hired by WOC to announce the University of Iowa football games and how he went on to become a staff announcer there and at WHO, Des Moines. "I'm really one of you," he told the broadcasters.[23]

As his movie career waned, Reagan made an eventful foray into television, becoming host of *General Electric Theater*, a half-hour dramatic series on CBS. The series had premiered in February 1953 in the 9 P.M. Sunday night time slot following Ed Sullivan's *Toast of the Town*. In addition to his hosting chores, Reagan would oc-

casionally star in one of the episodes, and, more significantly, he was the on-air spokesperson for the sponsor, delivering all of the GE commercials. The show ran for over eight years, with Reagan as the very visible and successful host and spokesperson for its entire run through September of 1962.

Later that year, Reagan took on acting and hosting responsibilities for a non-network syndicated anthology series, *Death Valley Days*. A long-time favorite on radio in the thirties and forties, this low-budget anthology series became one of television's first Westerns, churning out episodes for over 22 years. Reagan used the series as a vehicle to solidify his popularity as he sought and then won the race for California governor in 1966.

If it was an eye opener in 1966 to see the former movie star becoming a governor, it was startling when he not only won the Republican nomination for president in 1980, but went on to become president later that year. Reagan had become the first broadcaster ever to go down that path successfully.

But not the first to consider it. With Arthur Godfrey's formidable influence on the American public in the 1950s, the subject of government service or the seeking of political office had come up more than once. And why not? He was the most recognized and most believable man in the country, on the air and off the air as well. His knowledge and advocacy of national issues, particularly air power and national defense, and his constant discussion of them on his programs, gave him a strong philosophical base to work from. And good old American patriotism was a basic part of the Godfrey persona. By the mid–1950s, with his broadcasting career bogging down, government and politics might be just the direction for him— though it would be ten years before Reagan's California election, and public recognition that such transformations were not only possible, but also logical.

His first thoughts were about the Navy. With long-time friend Charles E. Wilson installed as Eisenhower's secretary of defense in 1952, Godfrey certainly had the ultimate friend in high places. Many Cabinet officers and other Washington officials had visited his Virginia farm. According to Steve Allen, "When the American Legion bestowed its highest civilian award upon Godfrey more Pentagon brass appeared than was seen at any similar Capitol event of the year."[24] The subject of secretary of the Navy often came up. But it is hard to conceive that in 1952, though Godfrey might have been flattered by such suggestions of government service, he would have taken it; he was having too much fun on radio and television and with his other interests. And by 1955, now under the influence of Curtis LeMay, Godfrey had forsaken the Navy for the Air Force.

Later, talk shifted to thoughts of elective office, the most obvious targets being those of U.S. senator or governor of Virginia. After 28 years of broadcasting, that kind of a change probably had considerable appeal for Godfrey. His impact on America could move to another level.

It's unclear at what levels these discussions were held or who initiated what, but off the air Godfrey was always in the company of men like LeMay, Baruch, and military officers, as well as Washington and Virginia politicians. He was constantly being asked to speak before veterans' groups and all kinds of national associations, hip-hopping across the country. There were many dinner parties in New York and at the farm in Virginia. He knew so much on so many subjects and articulated it so well that if the subject of public office had not come up frequently, it would have been surprising.

But by March 1958, even these possibilities were dismissed. In a long feature article in *TV Guide*, Godfrey explained why: "For a man to run for public office, he must declare himself a Democrat or Republican. The moment he does that he alienates everybody in the opposing party and his sphere of influence immediately narrows down to his own constituents."

He basically said he was too old, that the way Congress seniority worked, he wouldn't even be able to lead a committee like Military Affairs until he was in his seventies. He preferred to work with government from the outside in, "briefing senators and congressmen about air power as I know it." Possibly, Godfrey had been disappointed by a lack of support from old friends. In an obvious swipe at Charlie Wilson in the *TV Guide* article, he called "the business of bringing in auto and soap manufacturers to run the government" foolishness, since they couldn't possibly understand the "intricacies" involved.[25]

He might have made an interesting public figure, but unlike Reagan, Godfrey had few managerial skills to bring to a governorship, nor much of the necessary patience or interest in the compromise and horse-trading he would have needed to become an effective member of Congress. So it was back to broadcasting.

As the 1950s advanced, his adventures outside of broadcasting, and his incessant talk about high-level friends and trips and activities far beyond the reach of the average American, began to further distance him from listeners and viewers. "One hot day," remembers Remo Palmier, "at the end of the morning show, he said, 'Well, it's a hot day. I think I'll go over to the Island and go out alone on my sailboat. You get out too!'" "Yeh," murmured Remo to a band member, "Get out on your fire escape!" Later, Godfrey became very conscious of language. "He started saying 'tewnah' when doing his tuna fish commercials. One woman wrote in, 'You moron! There's only one way to say tuna. T-U-N-A. Tuna. Stop your la dee da pronunciation!'"[26]

During the 1956-57 season, *Arthur Godfrey's Talent Scouts*, under the leadership of Jan Davis, had shown signs of new life, jumping back to 12th place in the Nielsen's after two lackluster seasons. When the show's longtime producer, Jack Carney, died suddenly of a heart attack in 1955, Godfrey had named his longtime vocalist, Janette Davis, as the new producer. Davis had always been a good judge of talent and Godfrey had often relied on her opinion when considering additions to the weekday morning cast. Adapting to new musical trends, the show began booking young country-western and rock and roll performers along with the more mainstream singers and musicians. The most notable winner during the 1956-57 season was a young country-pop singer named Patsy Cline. Cline was a big hit on the subsequent morning shows and though talks to have her on continually with Godfrey did not pan out, she went on to tremendous national popularity until her untimely death six years later.

The daily weekday morning shows on television and radio had settled in again with a new mix of Little Godfreys (Carmel Quinn, Pat Boone, the McGuire Sisters, Tony Marvin, and Janette Davis) and special guests like Lucille Ball.

Sometime over the summer over 1956, Godfrey and CBS had second thoughts about giving up the Wednesday night shows and when September of that year rolled around, the show was back. Significantly, there was a new title: *The Arthur Godfrey Show*. Frank Parker was gone, but the rest of the morning cast members would appear off and on throughout the season. Godfrey liked the new flexibility. "We no longer put anybody under con-

tract," he explained to *TV Guide*.[27] He was free to do what he wanted, like showing the film of his African safari or doing shows on air power. But it was to no avail. *Disneyland* and *Father Knows Best* were eating away at his remaining audience. For the second April in a row, CBS announced that the show would be discontinued after the June 1957 broadcast. This time they stuck to their decision.

By the fall of 1958, CBS was coming heavily under the influence of James Aubrey. Aubrey had joined CBS radio in 1948, advanced to programming, and by 1956 had moved to ABC-TV where he developed many of the action-oriented shows that had made the third network so successful in recent years. In 1958, he was rehired by CBS's Frank Stanton and soon became president of the CBS-Television Network. Aubrey moved CBS away from its focus on big stars and pleasing William Paley. He was obsessed with ratings and building audiences first, quality of programming second. "His formula for success was simple," wrote Sally Bedell Smith in her Paley biography, "'broads, bosoms, and fun, as a colleague put it in a memo leaked to a congressional committee. He jettisoned all live drama and moved entirely to filmed weekly series in two categories: inane comedy and fast-action adventure."[28] In the years that followed he doubled profits for CBS-Television, but in the process gave pink slips to everyone from Jackie Gleason to Jack Benny to Lucille Ball. He and his staff would have had little patience with Godfrey's Wednesday show.

But *Arthur Godfrey's Talent Scouts'* demise was not due to Aubrey as much as to the adult Western craze. A new Western, *Tales of the Wells Fargo*, had premiered opposite it on NBC and had become a runaway hit. When the 1957-58 season ended, *Scouts* ended its long tenure on Monday nights.

There would be one opportunity given to Godfrey, however. At the behest of Frank Stanton and Bill Paley, Oscar Katz, who had been head of daytime programming at CBS, was assigned the task of reviving the television career of Arthur Godfrey. "I had a sit-down with Godfrey," Katz told author William Henry III, "at which I summarized his problems. After years of being a sort of Peck's bad boy ... [he] had become such a strong ego that the other performers on his show were frightened into being monosyllabic. And he had turned into a complete bore with only three topics of conversation: his own airplane; General Curtis LeMay and the United States Air Force; and Godfrey's farm and pet horse, Goldie. I told him what he needed to do was invite in performers who felt themselves equals and would stand up to him and have free-form conversations that would let the public in effect discover the charms of Godfrey all over."[29] The new show would be a talk show with Godfrey as host. Guest stars would include singer Roberta Sherwood, comic Sam Levinson and others in a roundtable setting. The only survivors from the original Godfrey group were Tony Marvin, who was on board each week as announcer, and Carmel Quinn, who made an occasional appearance as a roundtable guest.

The series started off with great promise when comedian Jackie Gleason, whose weekly CBS variety shows had also disappeared, joined Godfrey for several discussions. The Gleason-Godfrey conversations had been the brainchild of Katz and they proved to be a great success. Gleason rivaled Godfrey in his knowledge and interest in events outside of show business, and both reveled in the opportunity for unscripted, free-flow conversations. They talked about everything from atomic energy to youth gangs, and received much favorable press attention. But subsequent guests and talk weren't nearly as compelling, and by the following March it was clear that the audiences in general weren't buying Godfrey's new format. That month, CBS announced that the series would end after only one season in favor of yet another television assignment for Godfrey.

Impressed with his interviewing skills and still wanting to revive his career, CBS agreed that Godfrey should take over the reigns of host Ed Murrow on the perennial celebrity interview show *Person to Person*. Murrow had asked for a year's leave of absence, and the choice of Godfrey seemed to be not only a comfortable one but an enlightened one. The *Person to Person* format (live) and its commitment to interviewing two outstanding personalities each week (the list had included Fidel Castro, Margaret Mead, John Steinbeck, John Kennedy, inventors, scientists, musicians, actors, and actresses)[30] offered Godfrey, with his endless curiosity about the world and what made it tick, a chance to sink his teeth into something substantive each week. It could well have opened the door to a whole new career for Godfrey. But it was never to happen.

25

Cancer: Grace and Courage

IT WAS IN HAWAII IN THE SPRING of 1959 when Godfrey first noticed the pain. He was doing a telecast. It wasn't severe or steady, but it made him uneasy. He thought it was his heart. So, he reasoned, "Okay, let's see if that's what it is," dove into the Waikiki surf, swam out and told himself, "If it's a coronary, okay, let it come now."[1]

But the coronary didn't come. Godfrey changed his self-diagnosis to gas pressure. Back home, a week later, his local physician disagreed. His diagnosis was based on X-rays that showed a black mass near the left breastbone. "It was the kind of verdict nobody wants."[2] The X-rays showed a chest tumor, with a 98 percent chance that it was malignant. Surgery was necessary—immediately.

It is difficult to imagine the impact of the diagnosis on Godfrey. On the one hand, he was a veteran of many operations and hospitals. Beginning with the 27 fractures incurred during the

automobile accident in 1931 and the painful limp, back pain, and inability to unlock his legs that was its legacy, through the numerous horse falls, an appendectomy, and the successful hip operation in 1953, he had looked on operations and the like as small payment for the joy that flying, riding, and traveling afforded him. Indeed, it had become his trademark that when he went to the hospital, microphones and television cameras went with him.

He understood pain. "When you've been through as much physical pain as I had after my smash-up, you stop being afraid of being hurt." In 1944, during an appendectomy, he recalled the doctor inspecting the stitches on the day after the operation, probing around the scarcely-healed scar. "It felt exactly as if he was rubbing a lighted cigarette over my skin.... He thought I'd yell, but all I said was, 'You open that thing up again and I'll knock your block off.' When you've had a lot of

176

pain, you learn how to control it with your mind."[3]

And he understood surgery. While hospitalized for his appendix operation, Godfrey's unrelenting curiosity took him into the medical arena. "I'd spent so much time in hospitals by then…I wanted to *see* an operation. I begged until my doctor said okay. He picked out the most gruesome operation he could think of for me to watch—one for a rectal cancer—and put me in the observation room. Pretty soon I was complaining because I was too far away, so they dressed me up in a white nightshirt and a mask and let me stand beside the table. They were all hoping I'd pass out but I didn't."[4]

On the other hand, this time it was very likely cancer. He was 56 years old now, and the odds were clearly against him. The recovery rate from malignant chest tumors of this type in 1959—survival for five years—was, *Newsweek* reported, less than five percent.

"It didn't look too good. And I was mad, because there was so much I wanted to do yet. And I didn't want to go. Fear? No. Ah, I decided a long time ago there's no use to fearing that because eventually we all go…. No, it just never occurred to me."[5]

Yet his public persona would not allow him to hide all of this from his audiences, which, though on the wane, still comprised millions of Americans who watched or listened to his weekday morning and Tuesday night broadcasts. He had always been straight with them and had always been there to reassure them—about America's greatness, about the safety of their soldier sons, about the quality of the products he chose to promote. This was no time to hide his head. And so he set about to tell them and the media what lay ahead, that he would be going in for an exploratory operation.

On his last television appearance from his farm, reported *Time*, in an article entitled "Grace and Courage," Arthur carried on with the "same folksy jokes, the same rasp-voiced sentimentality about things, places and people." As he finished the show, he announced that he was to undergo surgery. "This Irish ruin has got some ivy growing in his chest." He thanked his fans for their prayers and good wishes. "Keep your fingers crossed," he told his audience. "I think I'll be back with you again one day…. If we have some of the wondrous luck which has shadowed me all of my life, this thing may be benign."[6]

The press was already on the case. According to *Time*, "Black lugubrious headlines and sob-sister stories followed Godfrey through every trying hour of every trying day."[7] America's father figure had been stricken. "As never before," mused *Newsweek*, "the minds and emotions of the American people are caught up in the tragedy of cancer."[8]

He entered Columbia Presbyterian Medical Center in New York on April 26 and the vigil began. Mary Godfrey spent the night before surgery at the hospital. On April 30, Godfrey underwent surgery. What the team of three surgeons led by Dr. Robert Wylie and three nurses found when they opened him up surprised even them. Not only was there cancer of the upper lobe of his left lung, but it was not confined to his lung. It had wrapped itself around his aorta, the main artery to the heart. For the next four hours they worked to remove part of the lung and all of the tumor. It was a delicate operation.

Godfrey's personal doctor told him later that Wylie "would have been perfectly within his rights to have declared the situation too dangerous." But Godfrey had given him carte blanche and so they proceeded. Or as Godfrey later liked to put it, "[Wylie] said to the other doctors, 'I understand this old bastard has a lot of guts. Well so have I.'"[9]

Within hours, newspaper headlines were blasting out the news: "GODFREY HAS KING CANCER," "GODFREY TO BE TOLD."

At noon on May 15, two weeks after his surgery, the press gathered in the doctors' waiting room of the Harkness Pavilion, a private section of New York's Columbia-Presbyterian Medical Center, to cover Arthur Godfrey's departure from the hospital. He arrived with his aides, dressed in an open neck, green-flowered shirt and a green-speckled sports jacket, but looking quite tired. It was an emotional moment. Sitting in a chair, he smiled at the news cameras and then the questions began. How did he feel?

"'If you remember when I came in [to the hospital], I said that physically I felt better than I had in years...I looked better than I had in years, but I told you that deep down inside was this—" He pointed a finger to his chest and momentarily broke down. His voice already shaky, quivered and stopped. Tears ran down his cheeks.

"OK," said his press agent. "That's all." "No, wait a minute," Godfrey said, recovering his composure. "I've got to tell them this." He lowered his head for a moment and then began to talk. He said he hoped the press "will take to the people the message from me which may be of help to others." He had been frightened before the operation and had realized that his fears arose from not knowing what lay ahead of him.

"I don't know how much any of you know what they did to me. That thing—that damnable thing—was not only in the lung, it was wrapped around the aorta, that's the main blood vessel to the heart.

"The surgeon would have been perfectly within his rights in sewing me up and saying, 'I can't do a thing.'" Dabbing his eyes with a handkerchief, he went on. Because of his [the surgeon's] courage and his competence, "I got a break—

he got it out, under circumstances so trying that one slip one way or the other and I wouldn't be here talking to you. I do not know why I got that break but I tell you this: I'm grateful for it and I will do my damnedest to deserve it."

His voice broke, aides rushed to his side and helped him to his waiting limousine.[10]

It is difficult today to re-create the mood of America in 1959 when it came to cancer. Advances since then in detection and treatment have greatly reduced the gravity of a diagnosis of the disease. In 1959 cancer was not only feared, it was not discussed openly. The word itself carried with it a death sentence and it was not unusual for family members and a victim of cancer never to utter the word between them.

On radio and television today, there is hardly a subject that is not discussed openly. But reflective of the society then, broadcasting never mentioned the word or discussed the subject of cancer any more than it was discussed in social gatherings or public forums.

For a public figure to be so forthcoming about his diagnosis, his prognosis, and his surgery was startling. Except in this case it was Arthur Godfrey, and rather than a surprise, his candor was remarkably consistent with the way he always conducted himself on the air and off. He was an open book. And because he was, he helped topple the wall of silence that had existed when it came to public discussion of cancer.

In its cover story that week, *Newsweek* reported that in the three weeks since his initial announcement that he would be going in for exploratory surgery, Godfrey had received 130,000 pieces of mail. "At the rate of 6,588 messages a day, it has poured into his office...keeping six girls working full time opening it. Even those who had disliked the star, and there were many, were writing in," said the magazine.

"There are typed letters from business-men, get-well cards from housewives, religious medals from nuns, paintings from teachers, mass cards from widows, photographs from old folk, postcards from vacationers, crayoned drawings from children. Quacks send blood tonics; cancer victims proffer understanding and the hope of recovery.... A small boy and girl sent a picture showing themselves kneeling, hands pressed together in prayer, before Godfrey's framed picture. In Shohola, Pa., 32 rural grade-school children wrote that they were praying for him....

"There were some authentic tear jerkers. 'Dear Arthur, My 9-year-old daughter Patty wanted to write to you personally, but I was afraid you wouldn't understand a word she wrote because it would be in Braille. She's blind.... She says don't be afraid. Trust in God.' 'I didn't realize we were such a God-fearing nation,' commented a researcher in Godfrey's office. 'I haven't picked up one piece of mail that hasn't mentioned prayer or the Lord.' ... Even those who had disliked the star, and there were many, were writing in. 'Dear Arthur, In the past I have never liked you very much. I always considered you too big for your britches. However, I am sure that at this moment you have lost all of your enemies and people who dislike you. In my business [as a doctor] I frequently run into many serious cases, but I have never had a patient express himself as clearly as you did. I honestly pray that your operation is successful and hope to hear you from your home soon. I know now that you consider yourself just another fish in the big pond. I guess we are all the same regardless of education, brilliance, or fame. At any rate you have another friend rooting in your corner for what little that is worth.'"[11]

Newsweek was clearly overwhelmed by what they called the Godfrey Phenomenon. "Why are people writing this way?

They have, of course, lived with him for almost 30 years...but his television ratings have slipped...his total air time...is now half as much as it used to be. Moreover, Godfrey's reputation has been deeply nicked.... The public—so thought the industry—was beginning to sour on the flamboyant redhead. If the letters were an index, this made little difference now.... To those close to Godfrey, the deluge of emotional mail is not surprising.... A business associate theorized: 'He never does a program in the proper sense of the word. He's really writing a goofy novel about a guy called Arthur Godfrey, and each show is another page in that novel. The illness is the climax. How will our hero get out of this situation?' ....He seems more accessible than other celebrities.... Didn't he come up the hard way, too? Admiring him for this very American career, fans don't envy Godfrey's wealth. More important still, his success hasn't spared him from human troubles."[12]

Godfrey spent several weeks in his Manhattan apartment at Gracie Place, returning regularly to the hospital for X-ray treatments. Then he went to the farm to recuperate. His morning shows had been split up, the radio portion handled, as usual, by Robert Q. Lewis. The morning television portion was assigned to soft-spoken humorist Sam Levenson, a frequent guest and sub. A situation-comedy series titled, ironically, *Peck's Bad Boy*, which was to replace his Tuesday night show in June, began five weeks sooner.

By July, it was clear that Godfrey was recovering well enough to plan ahead for his return to the air. The first hour-long television special of the four he had agreed to do for the following season was scheduled for Wednesday evening, September 16. He was soon immersed in it.

On August 2, still recuperating, he traveled back to Hawaii. The plan was to tape portions of the show he would use on his return to the air in September. Ten pounds lighter than he had been the previous March, greeted by a horde of friends and a mound of leis, he looked the picture of health as he arrived at the airport. As soon as a reporter asked about his surgery, he stopped to explain, praising the medical team. "My doctors say I'm in better shape now than before the operation…. I can't tell you how much it meant having so many people pray for me. I'll try to deserve it."[13]

He explained the plans for the television special in detail. "Next year when I come back I hope to have a television tape truck. Then I'll go to places like Molokai and Kauai, and show the folks on the Mainland some of the real beauty spots of Hawaii."[14]

He had other things to do in Hawaii as well, including taking a morning of intensive training in a new Convair jet in preparation for buying one for himself. As the *Honolulu Star Bulletin* reported, he "took off, landed, took off again, stalled, feathered an engine, hooded the cockpit, and flew on instruments—the same training given commercial pilots." He crossed over a Navy submarine doing surface maneuvers. "Hey, let's go get him," he joked to his co-pilot, adding, "I love to fly."[15]

And when he wasn't flying or taping or "recuperating" in some other active way, he was talking to the press about his growing concerns about what had happened to Waikiki Beach since statehood. "It's Coney Island with palm trees," he groused.

Other portions of the show were taped in New York and at the farm.

The Arthur Godfrey Special, in black and white, ran opposite *This Is Your Life* on NBC and a boxing match on ABC. It opened without credits on a darkened close-up of Godfrey in profile. As he slowly turned to the camera, the lights went up. He was wearing a black tie and a tux and he had a broad smile on his familiar face. He

looked exceedingly trim, healthy, and dapper.

"Hi. Yes, the good Lord was willin' and I'm back again. And, as usual, speechless, as you always are. You can think of a million things to say before you get there, and then—You know when you're lookin' for a greeting card in the store and find one that says what you want to say much better than you know how? Well, Gordon Jenkins has written a song which serves me very well right now. It's called, 'This Is All I Ask.'"

The music began and as he sang the prologue, the camera pulled back to show Godfrey seated:

> As I approach the prime of my life
> I find I have the time of my life
> Learning to enjoy at my leisure
> All the simple pleasures
> And so I happily concede
> This is all I ask,
> This is all I need.[16]

Then he gave a perfect rendition of the refrain, asking that beautiful girls walk slower, sunsets be longer, children stop to play with him, rainbows bring him color and if they do, "I will stay younger than spring." It was an auspicious beginning.

On the empty stage, with no audience, Godfrey continued to talk, softly, slowly, and directly to the camera:

"Well, lots of other things I want to say too tonight. I want to thank you for your good wishes and your prayers. Your kind intercession, I'm *sure*, had a great deal to do with the fact that the good Lord *was* willing. And you know, I've had more good fortune through my life than any six men are entitled to. This old Irish ruin has been pulled apart and sewn up together so many times, I wonder that there's anything left!"

This was his chance to help the audience understand more about this disease that everyone else was afraid to speak about. And he seized it. In a preview of what he would espouse day after day on his television and radio programs and interviews from that day on, he explained, "You see, your prayers were answered by the fact that the cancer was discovered *in time*, which is very important. And it was removed by the most competent and courageous surgical team that anyone could hope to have. I got a break—a real break—an additional one. I don't know why. But I'll sure try to deserve it."

And in typical Godfrey fashion, even at a time when the logical thing would have been to cut away for a commercial, he personally introduced the list of sponsors for the show—Hoover, Sara Lee, and Benrus.

Now he was rolling and inching his viewers on to the content of the show. And it was typical Godfrey. Only Arthur Godfrey, on an occasion like this, would take time to explain a new technology just now sweeping the industry: "You understand, don't you, that this show is on videotape—electronic videotape, that's the technical term. And by its use, we are able to travel anywhere in the world…. For example, go through this door (he pulls open the handle) and through the magic of videotape (we see him on the opposite side in an outdoor setting) here we are at Beacon Hill, our farm in Virginia." It was probably a better demonstration of videotape than the makers had ever dreamed up on their own. There was Godfrey, in his front yard, and the camera began panning the lush surroundings and the mountains in the distance. Fearful of new technology? Hardly. Godfrey was excited. "See, I don't need to worry about sets anymore. The whole world's our set. And that's the way it's going to be for me from now on," said the man who had always done his shows live in the past.

Back in the studio, he used the new technology to introduce members of his band who appeared on the set shot by shot, joining in on a jazz arrangement. He introduced Gene Traxler on bass, Joe Marshall on drums, Ludwig von Flato on piano, Johnny Mince on clarinet, and Remo Palmier on guitar—all of whom had been with him for many years—and Chris Griffin on trumpet, Honey Cutchill on trombone, and orchestra leader Dick Hyman. He picked up his guitar and joined them for a jumping version of "It's Wonderful."

For viewers of the day, it was more than wonderful. It was amazing. As if he had never been operated on for cancer just four months before.

The scene shifted to Hawaii, and there was Godfrey in a large canoe rolling along on the heavy surf with the Honolulu skyline in the background. Set to music, there were shots of surfers, then Godfrey rowing, stopping, standing up in the boat looking pudgy but healthy as a horse, diving off the boat into the water and emerging—through tape—in his pool, back in Virginia.

The Godfrey touch continued. From the pool, he extolled the virtues of his Benrus watch, which was waterproof. It was curiously riveting. He hadn't lost his ability to keep us watching every move he made.

He spent the next 45 minutes introducing young singers, driving a miniature car "that gets 100 miles on a gallon of gas," showing off his horses and his cattle, riding a quarterhorse and explaining how he keeps a steer or cow in line, pushing Sara Lee cake, going back to Hawaii to sing one of his standard numbers, "I Want to Get Back to My Little Grass Shack," with a group of hula dancers, going back to his farm to feed a new addition—a three-year-old elephant from Pakistan, and hawking Hoover vacuum cleaners. He finished by announcing that he would be back on his morning radio shows beginning Monday, September 28 for an hour each weekday. And he closed with a note of advice:

"Meanwhile, if you're over 35.... Take a tip from me and see your doctor at least twice a year. Remember the surgeon is helpless if you wait too long. I'm gonna keep after you about that.... God helps only those who help *themselves*."

Over closing credits and lush music, he and Mary were seen riding on horseback across the hills of the farm. It was quintessential Godfrey. He was back from another adventure. And you couldn't help but marvel at the man.[17]

26

Not in the Cards

IN GODFREY'S OFFICE, HANGING ON the wall, was a framed quote from the legendary baseball pitcher Satchell Page. Page, whose age was always in dispute but who was thought by most to be considerably older than he said he was, had once advised, "Never look back. They might be gainin' on you." Godfrey had lived that quote every day.

Now, though, for one of the few times in his life, he showed signs of slowing down for at least a bit of introspection. The surgery had sobered him. "I thought," he later admitted, "as everyone else, that I wouldn't be around very long."[1]

But that wasn't going to stop him, any more than the doctor's prognosis back in 1931 that he might never walk again. "Why do you subject yourself to the strain of show business? Why not retire?" asked *TV Guide* at the time of his fall return to the air. "I just don't think I'd be happy if I had to stop working…. Any close brush (of which I have had a few) makes one

realize more vividly that our individual terms of office on this planet are far too short to afford any waste of time or waste of opportunity." For one thing, he was heavily involved and committed to a number of charities. "As secretary of the Damon Runyon [Cancer] Fund, I will continue to work for contributions for cancer research." Then there was the issue of private pilots and keeping the skies open "for the little feller…. Also the air power story needs retelling every now and then, so I will most likely be heard still 'yakking too much about aviation.'" And, in a reference to the Cold War and his constant fear of complacency, "I would like to see more of us placing honor and love of country above peace and the desire for so-called security."

His personal goals were clear: "Long life is a privilege…. I believe we make a mockery of it if we fail to do three things: strive for personal excellence, strive to leave the world a little better for our passage, and try to learn to live without fear."[2]

For now, his radio shows would give him that opportunity. Sitting at the mike and having the opportunity to share his ideas and concerns and interests and knowledge with the hundreds of thousands of people—many of whom had contacted him in the past few months—was what fueled him. Just as it had been for 30 years, broadcasting—communicating over the airwaves—was his elixir.

He was glad to be free of his weekly television chores for now, though he still had three more taped television specials to deliver for the 1959-60 season. Plans to have him host Ed Murrow's *Person to Person* that season had been scrapped back in May as soon as the cancer appeared. Though Godfrey's future career might have benefited greatly from that opportunity, CBS was not about to make that kind of commitment to a lung cancer survivor; it was too tentative. The assignment was handed over to CBS newsman Charles Collingsworth.

Godfrey was embarking on a new adventure now, the length of which was uncertain.

The specials, though far from memorable television, did allow him to travel extensively and mix his avocations with his vocation. The early May 1960 show, for example, featured segments from a New York studio, a Boston horse show, his farm in Virginia, the island of Jamaica, and the stage of the Broadway show, *Take Me Along*, with lead Jackie Gleason taking time out to appear with Godfrey. The producers allotted plenty of time for Godfrey to mix in his usual talk and songs. Fully sponsored, the shows were a comfortable vehicle for him.

CBS could afford to give him these outings. With James Aubrey now in command, Paley's organization reinforced its position as the dominant television network with 15 of the Top-25 shows. Godfrey's specials were a nice but relatively minor addition to an already star-studded CBS lineup that included Red Skelton, Danny Thomas, Perry Mason, *Father Knows Best*, *Gunsmoke*, and *Have Gun Will Travel*. At most, it was a little frosting on the cake.

But it wasn't in Godfrey's makeup to just glide through the season. During his recuperation, he had embraced the prospects of videotape and editing. One of his great joys was to share his travel experiences with his viewers. Someday it would be possible to broadcast live from Hawaii or Africa. For now, videotape would do just fine. It looked as good as live television, so much better than the film he had always had to shoot on earlier trips, which came across to viewers as home movies. Now he could intersperse live and tape seamlessly, or, even better, tape his shows completely on the road and then edit them afterwards, freeing him up from the merciless clock that had controlled his work ever since the early 1940s, when he was running up and down the stairs at the old CBS building between live radio shows.

All of that made sense. What didn't was the idea that he could perfect his own performance. He was taken by film star Fred Astaire's seemingly flawless television dance presentations and would try to model his own after him: "If it is no good, tape it again and yet again until it is ready."[3] But others did not agree.

As Remo Palmier saw it, "He hired dance instructors and different people to perfect what he was doing. And in a way he was refining himself into nothing. What people loved about the show was him getting up there, trying to dance and messing it up. It wasn't amusing anymore. He was competing now with the professionals and in that aspect he wasn't a professional."[4]

Referring to a top hat and tails routine with eight female dancers on one of his specials, *Variety* commented: "He's just not the man for a big production number and seems out of place doing same."[5]

There would be more television specials scheduled the following season. But, to their credit, CBS executives also had another idea, one that would return Godfrey to weekly television.

The vehicle would be a new version of an old series called *Candid Camera*, which was begun back in radio as *Candid Microphone* by an ambitious writer and stunt man named Allen Funt. Funt, a rather nondescript individual with an awkward on-air presence, had nonetheless come up with a clever idea: to plant hidden microphones (and later cameras) and observe people and their reactions to unusual situations. Famous sequences included a talking mailbox and another with a woman asking for help since her car wouldn't start (the willing helper finding that there was no motor or anything under the hood). Its first television season was on ABC in 1948, and for the next 13 years it appeared on and off network television and local New York City stations.

Interested in reviving the series, CBS thought that Godfrey could help with the show's one weak point: the dull host Alan Funt. Godfrey would serve as Master of Ceremonies and interview Funt at the start of each excerpt. According to Godfrey, "Funt came to my house and cried like a baby. 'Make something of me on the air,' he pleaded. And I did it."[6] This version of *Candid Camera* quickly became one of the most popular programs on television, but it was folly to think that two egos like Godfrey's and Funt's could work together indefinitely.

By December, rumors were circulating that the two had had a falling out; that Godfrey wanted a bigger part in the show, and Funt was worried that that would take the emphasis off the candid film portions. Neither spoke about a rift in public but there were clearly strains behind the scenes. A typical altercation, according to Godfrey, took place during a rehearsal. Godfrey, who one would imagine had been giving Funt advice all year on how to improve his pallid performances, said, "Here's a joke for you, Allen," and Funt suddenly exploded, saying, "I'm sick of this! Who the hell are you to tell me what to do?" Godfrey's ego and short temper were not about to take that kind of treatment. He walked off the set.[7]

By the end of February, he had announced that he would not be back the following season. In a public statement from CBS he said, "Don't get me wrong... overall I've enjoyed doing the show. I was delighted when asked by the network and the sponsors [Funt isn't mentioned] to take the job and it has been fun for the most part. I want to be free to do my own shows and am looking at several formats that have been proposed. I wish...Allen Funt and associates the best of luck."[8] Funt's public statements were more catty and sarcastic. Godfrey, he said, "didn't intend to unseat anybody on *Candid Camera*," adding coyly, "He didn't even realize that I had a seat."[9]

In any event, it was Godfrey's last regular appearance on prime-time television. Except for a few scattered specials over the next ten years, it was also the end of Godfrey's television work for the network.[10]

Years later he would say that it was Mike Dann, president of CBS Programming, who kept him off because he had walked away from the *Candid Camera* show. The truth was, *Candid Camera* was a rarity; CBS saw no other place for him on television except doing specials. The institution itself was changing dramatically. When William Paley brought in James Aubrey to head up the television network, it was the final sign that CBS had become big business first and a broadcasting institution second. It was Aubrey who brought on *The Beverly Hillbillies* and *Green Acres* and a slew of mindless situation comedies that insured CBS continued success in the ratings as the number one television network. And it was Aubrey who, over time, gave pink slips to Jackie Gleason, Red Skelton, Jack Benny, and even Lucille Ball. The problem for Godfrey at CBS in the 1960s was no different from what it became for his other old cohorts. But he never saw it that way.

And though he stayed on with his radio series and worked out of his offices there for eleven more years, he found himself completely cut off from both Bill Paley and Frank Stanton. In 1975 he told author Robert Metz that his final lunch meeting with Paley took place in 1962. Paley wanted $50,000 for his new foundation and Godfrey reneged, saying he had just given a lot of money to a Virginia Hospital and that Paley would have to wait a few years. That kind of bravado was not what the chairman wanted to hear, and "there has never been a word since, except a card each year that says, 'Merry Christmas, Bill and Babe.'"[11]

The last time he was in Frank Stanton's office was in 1966 when Stanton, who had previously "always closed his office doors and cut off the telephones" when Godfrey had visited, was constantly interrupted while they met. In 1969, when they both received Peabody Awards, Stanton apparently stood with his back to him. "He did write me a note [afterwards] that he would like me to come for cocktails." But Godfrey was not about to let Stanton think that he was at his beck and call, and wrote back saying, "Dear Frank. No, I won't be available Tuesday.... I'll be someplace else. No, I do not care to discuss my plans with you."[12]

Believing that Paley and Stanton still ultimately called the shots on CBS television and clearly had no intention of getting him back on prime time television, he was not about to let them off the hook with acts of friendship. His final interactions with the men at the top were not among Godfrey's finest moments. He still believed that he could come back as a star on television if CBS would only allow it to happen.

27

Radio Days Again

MORE AND MORE, RADIO LOOKED like the right place for him to concentrate, presuming that there was any network radio left for him to be on!

Throughout the 1950s network radio had been in steady decline. Both the audience and the advertising dollars to keep the medium humming decreased dramatically. As soon as the sales of television sets picked up in the early fifties and the television audience became a critical mass, almost all of the advertising dollars from the big consumer goods companies like Proctor and Gamble and the cigarette companies were diverted to television.

At first, the networks—CBS, NBC, Mutual, and ABC—were uncertain as to whether television would actually *replace* network radio; it was possible that the two might coexist. They tried to conduct business as usual, keeping a full complement of news shows, commentaries, soap operas, sports broadcasts, and evening entertainment series. As sponsors departed to chase the audiences, the networks searched for new ones and, where necessary, carried shows on a "sustaining" basis—without commercials—just as they had done in the early days of radio.

To assure that radio continued to get attention and did not just die from neglect, CBS had even split its operations in the two mediums, forming separate television and radio divisions with separate programming and sales forces. For a while it worked.

Many of the early television shows had begun as radio series, and the radio versions of the shows continued. Though Burns and Allen dropped radio in 1950, Jack Benny continued to do radio every week through June of 1958. Groucho Marx kept his *You Bet Your Life* series on radio through 1956. Stars like Bing Crosby bided their time before dipping their toes into television, preferring to continue their weekly radio network programs. Popular radio shows that did not make it on tele-

187

vision, like *Fibber McGee and Molly* and *The Great Gildersleeve*, also stayed around through 1955.

And there were major efforts to develop new product for radio. Many notable new network radio series emerged in the early years of television, including *Dragnet* and *Gunsmoke*, both of which eventually moved on to television but continued on radio well into the fifties.

But the strategy ultimately failed; by 1955, 55.7 percent of all U.S. households had television sets, and the exodus of network radio listeners continued unabated. The ownership of radio sets in homes and cars never declined, but when a television entered the home, it was no contest—time spent listening to radio declined markedly. Large companies and their advertising agencies were mesmerized by television and its ability to show product, whatever it cost (and it did cost considerably more for television ads than radio). The concept of the "marketing mix," where a variety of media such as radio, television, magazines, and newspapers are all used, had not yet fully developed. Simply put, every buck went into television. By the mid-fifties, just about every children's radio program had disappeared from network radio. When *Let's Pretend*, radio's finest children's drama series, ended its run in October 1954 after 25 years on CBS, it was evident that young people's fascination with television was overpowering. By 1960, almost all the morning and afternoon soap operas had disappeared as well. Only the hourly national newscasts kept coming through as they had in the previous decades.

CBS had held out the longest. But by 1960, there was little left of its radio network schedule beyond the news—with one major exception: *Arthur Godfrey Time*. The series remained the CBS Radio anchor, there every weekday morning, fully sponsored, with a steady audience. "Network

radio," noted Fred Friendly in his book *Due to Circumstances Beyond Our Control*, "is, I have always believed, about as secure as Arthur Godfrey's health; CBS, the nearest proximation to a bonafide radio network system may well vanish with his retirement."[1]

Godfrey had stripped the show down and rebuilt it more to his liking. First, except for the band, many of whose members had been with him for close to twenty years, and a singer named Richard Hayes, there were no Little Godfreys anymore, though some of his favorites, such as Carmel Quinn, would be invited back now and again. No more contracts. No more obligations. There was no announcer and so no need for Tony Marvin, his loyal announcer for 15 years. For Marvin, the change (which he never considered a firing) allowed him to return to his earlier career as a news announcer and he joined the Mutual Broadcasting Company, earning key assignments such as appearing on the dais during the inaugural of John F. Kennedy in January of 1961.

Second, just as Godfrey had done with television, he now embraced taping and editing for his radio programs. And with many more shows being done on the road, he gave up having a studio audience.

It sounded different. The band would strike up the theme, and Godfrey, without any introduction, would just begin talking, sometimes in the middle of a conversation with someone in the studio that day. It was, strangely enough, a return to the sound of the very first morning network radio shows in 1945. More talk, more performance, less of a "show." But every bit as engaging.

His listening audiences were smaller and the demographics had changed. Many women were now entering the work force and weren't available at nine or ten in the morning. And television was stealing away many who were. On the other hand,

Godfrey gained a whole new audience now; the increasing number of business men, salesmen, truckers and other trades-men who traveled the burgeoning high-way system and tuned to the radio. It was an unlikely mix, older housewives and salesmen, but a mixed audience had never affected Godfrey's popularity before and it didn't seem to now.

The list of sponsors was long and loyal, with many still waiting in the wings. Each day, Godfrey would recant the virtues of the products in his own words—still the only one on network radio or television doing that. Ovaltine, Cuticura Soap, Con-tac, the *Saturday Evening Post*, the *National Observer*, Breast o' Chicken Tuna—as always, some days these sponsors got their plugs, some days they didn't. Some-times it was a long plug, sometimes a short one. That much had not changed.

It became much more of a music show. "Godfrey really liked music," recalled en-tertainer Max Morath, one of the irregu-lars, following his first appearance on the show in 1965. "He had a great feeling for musicians. He was very supportive of singers. And one of the things he would miss about current day radio is that care and feeding of musicians and music and putting out the best stuff you can get. He'd have young people on lots of the time. He was a better musician and a better con-noisseur [of music] than a lot of people give him credit for."[2]

Max Morath led the effort to bring rag-time, America's first popular music, back to popularity in the 1960s and 1970s. He had two breakthrough series in the early days of public television on which he sang long-forgotten and overlooked songs, ac-companying himself on the piano. He and his music are still in great demand today.

I loved performing with the [Godfrey] band. God, these ten or twelve people were the *last* of the [network radio] staff musicians. These were fabulous musicians—Hank Jones, Cy Mann and Remo and Andy Fitzgerald on clar-inet and Gene Traxler on the bass and his son John on the drums, Al Cusack, Harold J. Lieberman, cornetist.

People are stuck with that image of God-frey and that ukulele.... He had made for him this custom guitar. It had just four strings—like a banjo! And it had a beautiful tone. So here's Godfrey before these tapings and Remo, who had one of the best chord senses that I've ever seen, instructing Arthur [on] how to play the right four notes of an extended modern jazz chord that might have seven notes in it! And Arthur would work and work and work to get these musically sophisticated sounds. He didn't just sit there and strum away.

God knows he provided a lot of other people in the business, particularly musicians and singers, with a lot of opportunities and credit.... Another thing that has to be said over and over to his credit: he was one of the first people in that position of power in the business to go out of his way to bring black musicians, both soloists and sidemen, into his work.

He didn't know much about it [ragtime music]. But he was so knowledgeable about putting things into context that he would ask the right questions. He wouldn't ask questions like "How'd you get interested in ragtime?" His line of thought was much more interesting than that.

I developed a good bit of interplay with him conversationally. His interests were very wide. He was very well read. And highly informed. And he had a lot of inside information. He was wired into a lot of things that were happening in Washington, happening in the military, happening around the country. He traveled all the time. He was always out doing something somewhere.

Once he was talking about something con-troversial at the time and I contradicted him and we had a bit of an argument...not a heated argument. And I said after we stopped taping, "I didn't mean to involve you in contradicting you." He said, "Don't ever refrain from doing that. I want you to do that. It was fine. I love it. Don't ever think you can't say anything you want to."[3]

Morath, who was heard on *Arthur God-frey Time* off and on over the next eight years, was invited to join in whenever he was in the city.

Richard Hayes became a favorite of Godfrey's and a regular on the shows. A pop singer in the Fifties, Hayes had a quick mind and a great wit. "Richard had a wonderful wry sense of humor," recalls Morath. And if things were bogged down he was the guy with the right line, without being smart-assed. He was a foil, but a nice straight man."[4]

The new format allowed Godfrey to invite whomever he wanted on to the show and have them back only if he wanted to.

Singer Carol Sloane remembers being invited to appear on his show by Dave Garroway, who was filling in for him. When Godfrey returned from vacation, he called her back and she wound up becoming one of the "irregulars." She would perform and never knew when she left the studio whether she'd be called back again or not. This went on over several years of appearances. Singers June Valli and Ethel Ennis could also be heard frequently over the years. Jazz pianist Errol Garner was also a semiregular.

Duke Ellington made an appearance. So did singers like Joe Williams, Margaret Whiting, Pearl Bailey, Mel Torme, the Clancy brothers and Tommy Makem, Sergio Franci, and Robert Merrill. Comedians and entertainers including Art Carney, Bob Hope Phyllis Diller, Nipsey Russell, Jackie Vernon, Jonathan Winters, Carol Channing, Victor Borge and Sammy Davis, Jr., all took part in the Arthur Godfrey morning shows in the sixties.

Leading actors of the day appeared as well, including Peter Ustinov, Audrey Hepburn, and Jimmy Stewart. When Godfrey went off for two weeks in the summer of 1963, a singer-pianist-entertainer named Merv Griffin filled in for him and then went on to have his own syndicated talk and variety show on national television for many years.

Godfrey frequently took the show to Miami Beach, and when he did he'd invite a highly popular young radio talk show interviewer from the area, Larry King, to come on.

"I first met Arthur when he came down to Miami in the sixties," King told readers in his book *Tell It to the King*. He had heard me broadcast a few times and he put me on his radio show. Then I cohosted with him for a week, which meant that he let me interview people. Godfrey was never afraid to let me do anything, he let me emcee his birthday party. He was forever boosting me to the public to the people in the industry, and for that I have always been grateful to him."

King learned a lot from Godfrey as they did shows together. He taught him timing and to take risks and to be yourself on the air. "Without question, the single most potent influence on my style of broadcasting was Arthur Godfrey."[5]

"In 1970," recalls Pat Boone, "I was in New York making a movie and one morning Arthur did me the incredible honor of having me come in and host the show. And having watched him so much I thought, 'I can do this.' But when that light came up and I had to ad lib and read mail and do the stuff he did for an hour I sweat blood....And now we didn't even have the audience. It was just the musicians who we had who were on. And I came to [an] even greater appreciation for Arthur who could make *any* hour seem substantive, enjoyable, personal, and seem so effortless."[6]

His Hollywood guests were sometimes a problem for Godfrey. He knew a lot about a lot of things but he rarely moved in Hollywood circles. And, as Remo Palmier, pointed out, "he never went to movies. So when you spoke about these different big actors, he had no idea what their importance was. He was very naïve about these people's standing in their professions. He'd have people coming on, like for instance [film star] Gregory Peck. He didn't even know the name. I came up to rehearse with him once and he said, 'Everybody's making this fuss about Gregory Peck. Do I know him, Remo?' [One time] Rex Harrison was going to be on the show. And he came to the studio and was waiting around. Nobody comes over to Rex Harrison and says, 'Well, Arthur'll be here in ten minutes or whatever.' And he just kept him standing there. And [Rex] just did an about face and walked out. If Arthur knew who he was he would have come down. After he saw Marlon Brando for the first time in a movie called *Sayonara*, he told his audience, 'That guy's a comer. He shows promise.' Brando was already a tremendous star!"[7]

Everywhere he went, Godfrey took the radio show with him. It would be years before communication satellites would be launched and allow for live television broadcasts from abroad. But on the radio end, technology had already progressed to the point where he could instantly send a broadcast from abroad back to New York, and he was quick to take advantage of that.

On a trip to Korea in April 1960, he stopped long enough in Tokyo to do several shows. Joining him for one was CBS comedian and entertainer Jack Benny, who was in Japan arranging for two of his future television shows to be taped from there. The conversation was sent live at 1 P.M. in the afternoon, Tokyo time, to New York, where it was 11 P.M., and the band and the studio engineers were on hand to receive it and interact with the two stars. It would be taped there and played the next morning on the air. Benny was in top form—completely relaxed in Godfrey's company—and he

didn't need much coaxing to start talking about how delighted he was that Tokyo cab drivers didn't accept tips and how worried he was about his wife Mary, who was out spending too much money shopping. Godfrey and the band back home made the perfect audience, especially for Benny's remarks about his violin playing. Godfrey proved again to be a superb interviewer, asking just the right questions to keep Benny going and laughing heartily at Benny's remarks. Arthur was curious about how Jack produced *his* television shows, and Benny explained that he was using film, tape, and doing live shows, always with a live audience. They talked about vaudeville and burlesque, the band and Johnny Nash did a number, Arthur did a live commercial for the *Saturday Evening Post*, and the half-hour was gone in a flash.

At moments like this—and there were many of them—there was little doubt that Arthur Godfrey was back in top form in a medium (radio) and a format that fit him like a glove. And that he could interview as well or better than anyone in the business.

By October 17, 1961, he was off on the road again, taking a two-week "barnstorming" trip across the country to, as he put it, "sell our wares" and find out what the tastes of the public were. "The time has come in the profession of radio broadcasting," he told a press conference in Little Rock, Arkansas, "when people no longer tune in simply because there's a spot on the radio dial. The housewife doesn't just reach for a brand because it's on the grocery shelf. You have to sell 'em, you have to move people to want that spot on the dial or that brand on the grocery shelf." And from Godfrey's point of view, "there's no better way than the old politician's way of pressing the flesh." In characteristic fashion, he added, "It's easy to be influenced by Madison Avenue and advertisers who don't always know what the people want, and I want to find out from the people."[8]

The one-day visits, sponsored in each city by the CBS affiliate there, featured a press conference, luncheon speeches by Godfrey at chambers of commerce, and an evening performance in a large auditorium featuring a troupe of 19, including a number of relatively obscure singers and Dick Hyman's orchestra. The shows were taped for later airing as part of his morning shows. The cast and the musical instruments traveled in Godfrey's Convair with him at the controls. There were three advance men who went to each city in another of his smaller planes. Godfrey traveled from New Orleans to Little Rock, then on to Oklahoma, Texas, Iowa, and other points in mid-country.

He was correct in recognizing the need to sell his radio show. He needed to insure his sponsors that the audience was still with him. Competition had increased even on the radio dial. Not only had the number of AM stations grown, but in every city, FM now offered another whole set of choices for listeners. Disc jockeys and local talk shows were the vogue. Without a television presence, he needed to promote his network radio show just to remind people he was still on the air!

But whether he really found out anything useful about people's tastes in music or what they wanted to hear, and whether he was influenced by any of it, is questionable.

At his Little Rock press conference, he spent much time talking about his views on national affairs, and less time looking for feedback. The prospect of nuclear attack didn't mean "we should give up in despair and not even try." He was a firm believer in fallout shelters, with two or three on his farm, ready with water and food. "It's not a question of panic. It's just facing reality." Of course young people

dislike military life. That's because Americans just don't like regimentation. No, Americans were still patriotic, but "we're getting so sophisticated...that we feel self-conscious about expressing [it]." A combination of the manned bomber and the missile was "essential to this country's security."

There were the inevitable questions about his health. "It's great," he noted, then went on to implore people to go to the doctor when the don't feel well. "If I had waited another 30 days, my case would have been hopeless. Now I go every six months for a check up."[9]

Several years later there was an unprecedented 30th Anniversary celebration. For thirty years, Arthur Godfrey had been on radio for CBS, first in Washington, then in New York, and then across America on the full network. The dates: January 20–24, 1964. The place: New York. The location: CBS network studio at 49 East 52nd Street. Each day that week a cross-section of America's leading entertainers, journalists, musicians, and politicians of the time gathered together on his morning radio to celebrate with Godfrey. The shows were repeated on the CBS Radio Network each evening as well. It was undoubtedly one of the biggest gatherings of celebrities morning radio had ever offered up.

"Gee, and they said it couldn't be done. They said it couldn't last," Godfrey began on the Monday morning show. "CBS has been very nice to me. Which is of course not to say that we haven't had our arguments, you know. Our arguments never seem to change their opinion of me though. That's the nice part about it. They have always said, 'Arthur, we don't care if we have a thousand arguments with you—as long as we don't lose one.'" And with the laughter from the assembled studio guests, the show was off and running and on to the introductions of Monday's studio guests, including musician and composer Meredith Willson and his wife Rini, humorist Pat Buttram, actress and playwright June Havoc, two former Little Godfreys: Haleloke and Carmel Quinn, legendary journalist Edward R. Murrow and SAC founder and Chairman of the Joint Chiefs of Staff, General Curtis LeMay (both by telephone), mainstay Richard Hayes, and several young talents Godfrey was showcasing on his show at that time.

Each day, guests gathered an hour before, in person or by phone line, so that by the time they hit the airwaves they were already in high gear. There was no script. Just Godfrey to hold things together. The camaraderie was exhilarating. To the listener, it was like falling upon a private party at a club, where celebrities you had only known in their formal roles till now, were relaxing off the set, off the air, and just being themselves. They seemed a family, connected by show business, well aware of each other's accomplishments, planning future meetings with each other, and at home with Godfrey. During the shows he'd ask about their families—how were Abigail Van Buren's children, Rosemary Clooney's husband. He expressed awe to "finally be working together" with film legend Joan Crawford. "Give my love to Gracie," he told George Burns.

Monday's discussion ran from kudos from those who had seen June Havoc's new play to a discussion of bathtubs and bathing customs prompted by Godfrey's commercial spot for a bath oil, to his trip up that morning from Florida with Haleloke, wife Mary, and his manager Leo DeOrsey with stops in Philadelphia and Washington.

There were songs by Godfrey, Haleloke, Carmel Quinn, and others including a salute to Meredith Willson. The three-minute taped phone conversation with Ed

Murrow was a memorable one. Murrow, now with the USIA, had just recently had lung cancer surgery, and in that short span they reminisced about WJSV days in Washington, talked about Murrow's recuperation, if the USIA job had proved satisfying to Murrow, and when Arthur was going to see Ed. "Soon," said Murrow, "as soon as you light somewhere." "God bless you," Godfrey ended. And then the group chatted about the great Ed Murrow. In and out of all of this Godfrey delivered seven commercials.

On Tuesday, there was comedian Jackie Gleason (who complained about the lack of something real to drink), singer Rosemary Clooney, legendary actress Joan Crawford, CBS newsman and commentator Lowell Thomas, Richard M. Nixon, and in Los Angeles, entertainers George Burns and Art Linkletter, and long-time announcer Harry Von Zell. There were telegrams from President Lyndon B. Johnson and Former President Dwight D. Eisenhower.

On Wednesday, old stand-in Peter Lind Hayes, his wife Mary Healy, and comedian Jack Carter were all in the studios. Singer Steve Lawrence and director Abe Burrows joined in from Philadelphia, and in Los Angeles was alumnus Pat Boone, along with columnist Abigail Van Buren.

Thursday's cast included columnist Jimmy Cannon, Garry Moore, singers Marguerite Piazza and June Valli, and, from Los Angeles, Danny Kaye and Peggy Lee. Lee, a songwriter as well as a star vocalist, and Kaye, a great wit, began humming and talking in the background while Godfrey did a commercial for a baked bean company, and when he finished, they came on with their own unsolicited original jingle for the product. As the show went on, they added original jingles for each of the products from D-Caf Coffee and Robert Burns cigars to Aunt Jane's

Pickles and Ovaltine, with everyone joining in. Hilarity reigned. At one point, Godfrey had Garry Moore presented one of the commercials and he ad-libbed his way through it just as Arthur would have. Many offered their own endorsements for the products. It was a sponsor's dream come true.

The orchestra in New York joined June Valli from Detroit in a song, and "This is radio, folks!" offered Arthur. When the Mayor of Detroit, Jerome P. Cavanaugh, congratulated Godfrey and reminded him that he started his career there as a cemetery lot salesman, it set off sixty seconds of one liners from just about everyone in the group, each better than the next.

Friday brought film star Robert Cummings and Lawrence Welk from Los Angeles, performer Robert Preston, comedian Nipsy Russell and Jonathan Winters, and jazz pianist Erroll Garner and Sammy Davis, Jr. in New York.[10]

For any lesser entertainer, moderating this diverse, uncommon and often unruly group would have been close to impossible. But Godfrey was definitely up to it, deftly leading the often-raucous conversation from one subject to another, joining in the general mayhem with laughter and singing, and seamlessly weaving at least six commercial messages into the fifty minutes available. It was a tour de force and great fun. Late night talk shows paled in comparison.

The affection for Godfrey was genuine. No one had to be there. "Congratulations, Arthur," said just about everyone. "We hope you have thirty more." "You've outlived all your enemies," said one. And so it seemed. Five years after his cancer surgery, ten years after the firing of his lead singer had cost him much of his audience's adulation, four years since the new CBS leadership had all but banished him from television, Arthur Godfrey was still

at the table, still a welcome guest for millions of Americans including its leaders and entertainers. And still held in high esteem.

That summer, Godfrey took to the stage for the first time since his ill-fated 1945 debut in the Broadway review, *Three to Make Ready*. The role: stage manager in Thornton Wilder's Pulitzer Prize play, *Our Town*. Premiering at the Bucks County Playhouse, the show's reviews were highly positive. "It is a part almost tailored for the star," wrote Daniel Webster of the *Philadelphia Inquirer*. "Godfrey assumed a command of the part able to stand on any stage." The *Philadelphia Bulletin* critic, Ernest Schier, wrote, "He brings an unmistakable touch of Virginia ham…but on the whole, his pleasantly rumbling voice and homey style are assets that will grow in importance as he gains experience with the play and the role."[11] The two-week engagement set a new house box-office record for the 25-year-old summer theater.

The following April, Arthur premiered on Broadway for a limited run opposite actress Maureen O'Sullivan as co-star of the long-running hit, *Never Too Late*. "He was wonderful. He was very good," remembered Carmel Quinn. "He never wanted a lot of publicity. Let me get on with what I want to do. Let me go for a good long walk. Let me be with my horses and planes. It's an impossibility but he managed it: to have a brilliant career and a great time in his ordinary life. I went to his last night in that play and I thought, 'It'll be jammed…the dressing room… closing night.' So Bill and I went around and there he was in his dressing room packing his bag by himself…. But you thought, 'Good, this is the way he does it…. He did some things all by himself.' And Lord, when he was riding the horses in Madison Square Garden. I went back to see him after that show. He was there washing down Goldie himself. And you know he had people to do that. But that's the way he was."[12]

Thanks to his agent Joe Higgins, who booked all his personal appearances, he found other roles to his liking, like the musical *Take Me Along*, and over the following summers he would fit in a month for rehearsals and performances. In 1968, he played Captain Andy in *Show Boat* for one week in St. Louis and another in Kansas City. He certainly wasn't doing it for the money, though he was still a good draw. He had all the money he'd ever need. What he loved was the travel and the spotlight—and the challenge. It was keeping him young.

In 1966 he played opposite Doris Day in a feature film. He played her father and the skipper of *The Glass Bottom Boat*. Then there were the horse shows that he starred in for years. In 1964, he and his palomino Goldie traveled to the 9th Annual National All Breed Horse Show, the third largest horse show in the country, at the Ohio State Fairgrounds Coliseum in Columbus, Ohio. Close to 25,000 horse fanciers, a record for the equine classic, packed the coliseum to see their dressage exhibitions. Four years later, in 1968, he and Goldie were still at it, appearing in three weekend stints in Youngstown, Ohio, at the Indianapolis Horse Show, and the Michigan State Fair in Detroit. Then that fall they were starred for two days at the Jacksonville Florida Horse Show.[13]

The next month he was on the road for three weeks to Miami Beach and the Bahamas, originating his morning shows from hotels there.

The rest of the time he shuttled between New York and Beacon Hill. His energy level was enormous. On October 8, 1964, Arthur Godfrey Field was dedicated in Loudon County, Virginia. Located two miles south of Leesburg and ten miles west of Dulles Airport, the new airfield contained 3500 feet of runway, a far cry from the old "cow pasture" landing strip that Godfrey often referred to on his broadcasts. He had given land to the project and was the principal guest that day, and he was praised for his giving. "The people…of Leesburg…know him for his benefactions and bestowals and his ever-ready willingness to give his time and talent to worthwhile community endeavors." They referred to the Godfrey wing of the Loudon City Hospital, his participation and sponsorship of rodeos, and the Hereford cattle shows at Beacon Hill Farm.[14] By 1994, thirty years later, Arthur Godfrey Field was home to 50 hangars and 165 airplanes.

There were more trips—to Iceland, Europe, and Africa, and then an unprecedented one in 1966, when Godfrey fulfilled a lifelong dream by flying a Rockwell "Jet Commander" business aircraft around the globe. Along with Dick Merrill (Eastern Airline's most celebrated captain), TWA captain Fred Austin, and Karl Keller (a Rockwell Standard Corporation test pilot), the 23,333-mile flight, which included 20 refueling stops, was made in 55 hours and 30 minutes of flight time, setting 21 world flight records for speed and distance.

Planned as a dramatic demonstration of the business jet's capabilities, particularly its safety and reliability, the flight began at 9:09 A.M. EDT on June 7, 1966 in New York after the four co-captains outlined their plans at a press conference. The flight itinerary took them across the Atlantic to Europe, India, the tropics, Japan, then north, closer to the Arctic, and finally into the United States. The crew touched down 20 times for refueling at airports including Madrid, Athens, Teheran, Bombay, Manila, Tokyo, Anchorage, Seattle, Los Angeles and Oklahoma City.

At the U.S. Air Force base at Shemya, in the Aleutians, Godfrey, seemingly tireless, entertained the troops during a stayover. Less than seventy-five hours later, the flight ended at La Guardia airport in New York at 11:18 P.M. on June 7, 1996.

Thanks to Godfrey's promotion of the event on his radio shows, before, during, and after, attention was brought not only to Rockwell and its new plane, but to the relatively new option of business jet travel in general. And more than a few eyebrows were raised regarding 62-year-old Godfrey's participation in the short, grueling exercise. *Popular Science* magazine devoted three pages to an exclusive interview with him and a big photo spread. When asked how he had personally prepared for the flight, Godfrey replied, "I studied. Hard, too." Did they sleep? "We didn't actually. We catnapped when we weren't on duty." Were there problems? Yes, losing radar during a thunderstorm on their way into Madrid. Godfrey was handling the radio and navigating and arranged for special help from Madrid Approach Control to get them around the storms and allow Keller to land smoothly and easily in a pouring rainstorm. They had radio trouble several times. And because they had had to purchase a different kind of kerosene fuel at Chitose, in northern Japan, the fuel metering system was thrown off, and when they landed in the Aleutians they found they had had only 15 minutes of fuel left, instead of the 45 minutes they had thought.

Of course the flight wouldn't have been complete without an update for his listeners. Godfrey managed to tape several while on route, and radioed them on to New York for broadcast.

When old friend General Emmett "Rosy" O'Donnell (USAF, Ret.), president of U.S.O. Inc, invited him to spend a month visiting American troops in Viet-

nam, Guam, and the Philippines, Godfrey jumped at the chance. It was August 1966, and the conflict in the far-flung Asian country had expanded into a full-fledged war, with thousands of U.S. troops deployed to the area. The United Service Organization (U.S.O.) had already had shows touring the Far East starring comedians Bob Hope, Danny Kaye, singer Perry Como, sportscasters Frank Gifford and Red Barber, and showman Georgie Jessel. Many were veterans of U.S.O. tours from the Korean War and World War II eras. Hope had been conducting Christmas shows at bases around the world throughout the 1950s and 1960s, and the television shows that were culled from his trips had become an annual viewing event each January after he was back home.

Like his predecessors, Godfrey was to visit the front line and servicemen at Army, Navy, Marine, and Air Force installations in all three areas. Similarly to Hope, he planned to send back material for his radio audiences in the States. He carried a portable tape recorder during his month-long visit, and his interviews were rushed back to the U.S. via jet planes for airing on his morning shows. Unlike the others, as a Colonel in the U.S. Air Force Reserve (retired), Godfrey was flown on special aircraft and was privy to behind-the-scenes military planning wherever he went.

If he was going abroad, he wanted to speak the language, so, as he had done many times before, he readied himself with a course in Vietnamese at the Berlitz School of Languages. "It's a fascinating tongue they have there. Just by changing an inflection, you can turn perfectly innocent words into the exact opposite," he remarked at the time. [16]

As the trip unfolded, he made frequent reports on *Arthur Godfrey Time*. Most of his interviews were with servicemen in the battle zone and in Guam and the Philippines.

Knowing Godfrey, he would have loved to be able to present his interviews on television as well. Considering his interviewing skills and his own background in the military, they might have made a valuable contribution considering how divisive the war had already become back home. It also might have been a bridge for him to some of the younger generation as well. But that was not to be, and the only ones who heard his interviews were the shrinking number of his older radio listeners at home, or salesmen and commuters in their cars.

Godfrey was also on the road with nightclub and other stage appearances. In 1966, he took to the road for three weeks, headlining shows in Reno, Orlando, and West Palm Beach. As always, he took his radio audiences along. Included was a week-long supper-club revue with vocalist Kaye Stevens (two shows a night) at the Nugget Club in Reno, a weekend of dressage exhibitions for the Sunland Hospital Fund at the Orange Blossom Horse show in Orlando, and the week-long show at the Music carnival at West Palm Beach, where he teamed up with former cast-member Carmel Quinn. He also appeared in Las Vegas and Lake Tahoe. "He sang and danced, " recalled Peter Lassally, who produced the Godfrey radio shows at the time. Peter was also President of Arthur Godfrey Productions which oversaw the road trips, and remembers those years as busy ones for Godfrey: "We flew in all sorts of planes. We'd make two or three cross-country trips a year to California. We'd land and he'd see a plane sitting out and say, 'Oh, I'd like to fly that. So up we'd go and my heart would be in my mouth. It was terrible!"[17]

It was a jolly good time for Godfrey in the 1960s. He had his travels, his friendships, the opportunity to explore stage and film work, and always the ability to link it back to his daily radio shows. Radio was his one true anchor.

28

Ecology, a New Passion

"I GUESS NO ONE REALLY APPRECI-
ates it.... Unless you've been to the moon
like a handful of astronauts and you can
look...up and see that beautiful planet
...and...see that it's only so big. Just so
big—and that's all."[1]

By the late 1960s Godfrey's morning
soliloquies on the radio were bound to include words like these. The public was always aware of his love of the land and his
passion for being out on the water sailing
or in the air flying. Now, however, it was
no longer just chitchat for Godfrey and his
guests; there was urgency in his voice.

"As a pilot, as a sailor, as a farmer, as a
hunter and fisherman—nay, as just a lover
of the outdoors!" he wrote in *Esquire* magazine in November 1969. "I have been very
conscious of the deterioration of our environment for many years; ever since the end
of World War II, in fact. I worried about
it and talked about it with my friends and
on my daily nationwide broadcasts.[2]

With the publication of these words,

Godfrey began a dogged campaign—on
radio, television, whatever medium he
could gain access to—to change America's
thinking about the world around it. He
had been observing and reading and
studying for years; now he would have an
increasingly visible presence as a leader in
the anti-pollution and population control
movements; movements that were just beginning to register with the American
public.

"The late Rachel Carson's book, *The
Silent Spring*, electrified the country a few
years ago but still there was no accurate
documentation. I personally had noted the
pollution of the Hackensack, Passaic,
Delaware and Potomac Rivers, where I
had once fished and crabbed to my heart's
content. I had observed that, whereas for-
merly it had been an easy matter for a pilot
to find the nearest city merely by heading
for the closest [smoke], this was no longer
the case along the eastern seaboard. The
entire area has become a solid mass of fog

and smoke and gook." Godfrey had also noted the scarcity of eagles, hawks, crows and owls. "All these things told me something was very wrong, but I didn't know what to do about it."[3]

And in the same way he had always tried to bring his arguments to a familiar level for middle America, he personalized it, confessing his past sins. "I, too, pumped raw sewage into the waters I cruised in my boat and, once out of sight of land, I dumped the garbage overboard, as is the custom. I smoked cigarettes and flipped the butts into the nearest gutter.... When the pack was empty, I dropped that in the street, too. In the fall, I raked the leaves off my lawn and burned them in huge bonfires. Like most of my fellows I was a thoughtless, careless citizen of the world traveling everywhere and leaving an unbroken trail of trash to mark my progress."[4]

He talked about resigning from the Larchmont Yacht Club on Long Island and shipping his sail boat to Florida in the early Sixties because of the pollution in the water; then giving it away to the University of Miami because he found Biscayne Bay going the same way.

He talked about his farm in Virginia and how surprised he was to find that there were high levels of arsenic from chemical fertilizers in his stream, enough to kill many of his cows for years until it was discovered.

The conversion came in 1966. A book called *Moment in the Sun* was published by Robert and Leona Rienows, and Godfrey thought it the first book to address the issues in common man's language, with facts that had been gathered and documented over thirty years. He talked about the book and quoted the book—daily—on his radio broadcasts, bought hundreds of copies for friends and associates and "almost anyone who even looked slightly interested." Other books came along: Wesley Marx's *The Frail Ocean*, Dr. Paul Erlich's *The Population Bomb*, and *Science and Survival* by Barry Commoner. He read and studied. He attended seminars and symposia. He met and talked with leading conservationists and biologists and even a few full-fledged ecologists—"a rare species, indeed." He interviewed them extensively on his radio shows.

And as always, Godfrey would make it simple. "The thing people don't understand," he mused on a December 1971 radio show, "is that we got only one quarter of [the planet] upon which you and I can live. That is, two-thirds of that one quarter. One quarter is land but one third of that one quarter is either covered with ice or is pure desert and we can live in neither place. So, we have two-thirds of one-quarter of the earth." Later in the same show, after singing a song on universal brotherhood, he repeated one of the lines: "In peace and harmony.... Yes, why *can't* we...on this very small...fragile...finite... planet. *Why* can't we? (*pause*) We better had. 'Cause we don't have too much longer to fool around."[5] "Arthur would say that if we didn't clean up our rivers and streams someday we'd be buying our water at the supermarket," recalls Carmel Quinn. "How right he was."[6]

Armed with statistics and his extraordinary ability to communicate, he made powerful speeches throughout the late Sixties and early Seventies. In an address to the national PTA convention in the early summer of 1970, he laid out what he had honed into a compelling case. The problem was over-population. Human beings had always polluted, but until recently our land, sea, and air had always had the ability to absorb the pollutants and overcome them. But now, with people living longer, with advances in agriculture, with livable land area running out, and the population out of control, the planet was in a state of crisis. "At our present rate of population increase, there will be 300 million Americans 30 years from now (with seven *billion* on the entire planet). We have less than 450 million acres of arable, usable soil upon which to raise food and we're losing about a million acres of that per year to highways, airports, and urban sprawl."[7]

He said that while older people often expressed incredulity or suggested that "I should take a long overdue vacation," young people in school or college understood the problems. "Looking about, they see the obvious deterioration of the environment…they know from hearsay that it wasn't always like this" and they know "they didn't cause it. We did…. The 'priceless heritage' of which we seldom miss an opportunity to remind them turns out to be garbage—our garbage…. The better informed among them know that our progress down the road to eventual oblivion is accelerating exponentially. Hence, they are tortured by endless frustrations because the 'establishment' is maddeningly dragging its feet."[8]

He pointed to some progress that was taking place—a request by President Nixon for $4 billion for water pollution control. But these efforts, he felt, were overwhelmed by Federal highway construction projects and the subsequent pollution that would result from the cars that would travel these new roads. There were no controls over oil company spills in the ocean. The Government had its priorities mixed up. They were not the answer.

Nor was technology. "The technology of which we now so proudly boast cannot manufacture one square millimeter of soil, one drop of water or one breath of air."[9]

It was up to individuals to take responsibility. In all his writings and speeches and radio talks and television talks, he would hark back to the Bible.

"In Genesis 1:28, God said: 'Be fruitful and multiply and replenish the earth and subdue it.' The Judeo-Christian world heard every word except one. 'Subdue it' came loud and clear, and so did 'multiply.' But practically nobody heard the word 're-plenish.'"[10]

What could people do about the problem? First, learn the facts. Read the books he had mentioned. Encourage others to do the same. "Make sure your candidate knows at least as much as you do. Raise hell with him if he cops out. Make every effort not to pollute or litter." Recycle. Don't waste. And remember: "Nothing will work unless we cut the population down…. Man is now an endangered species and nobody can save him but himself."[11]

On his frequent trips to Hawaii, Godfrey became increasingly vocal about his concerns about the Islands. He urged officials there to put a cap on tourism. "More people are coming here all the time," he warned. "Let's hold tourism and put up no more tourist rooms or accommodations until we can handle what we have. Fifty million gallons of raw sewerage are dumped per day at Sand Island—3500 feet offshore…. This kind of stupid pollution still exists." He put his faith in young people and correctly predicted that "as soon as the Vietnam War is settled, youth will all go toward this survival of [the] environment kick." He offered solutions including fish farming as a way of raising food without violating the ecological balance. He urged the creation of a "Secretary of Environment" position in the Federal government and a Federal Board to look at ecological consequences "before, not after the construction of a road, airport and those bloody dams." "Guided by ecologists, we can stop this rape."[12]

Radio was fine, but what he never stopped seeking was a chance to get back on television, not just to entertain, but to bring these messages home to the medium that Americans turned to the most. "We've got to find some way to educate people on the deterioration of the environment," he would say. After years of effort, he got the opportunity. In 1969, he entered into a contract for a series of six television specials on ecological matters. Sponsored by Colgate, the shows would be produced over the next several years and sold to whichever networks were interested. Entitled *Arthur Godfrey's America*, the series began with a program entitled "The Ocean Frontier," taped in Hawaii at the Oceanic Institute and Sea Life Park.

The show was considerably ahead of its time—long before any cable nature channels, years before public television's science series like *NOVA* and *Nature* appeared. Jacques Cousteau had only just begun his specials on oceanography, and early *National Geographic* specials were basically travelogues. These were entertainment shows, with few if any messages about environmental concerns. That would not come till years later.

The premiere show ran on his old network, CBS, and focused on experiments with porpoise intelligence at the Institute and a sub-sea research team near the island. It was well received. Godfrey, said *Variety*, gave the show "a stamp of authenticity that might not have rung true in more detached hands. The underwater photography of the flora and fauna of the deep was superlative, and Godfrey's narration was informed and sensitive."[13]

A year later, a second *Arthur Godfrey's America* special followed, this time on preserving the Everglades, and was carried on ABC-TV. With this program, Godfrey was in very familiar territory. "For years, he had been warning that efforts to dam up the Everglades would ruin the ecology of the whole state," recalled Lenore Meyer, wife of Miami Beach public relations man, Hank Meyer.[14] The special had splendid

views of the Park, Cypress Gardens, and other areas within "the river of grass." There was a clear recounting of the animal and bird species endangered there. But the production itself spent an inordinate amount of time with Godfrey on camera interviewing people of a similar mind. It became a talkfest and more than likely lost a good deal of its audience along the way. After that, the networks declined any further specials from the syndicated group. As happens often with television productions, the idea is only part of a successful program; execution is key, and on that count the producers had failed.

Godfrey was miffed. But he was not to be dissuaded. The lack of network interest in television shows on the subject only spurred him on to more speaking and writing on the subject.

Ironically, he did find a place on television to make his ecology case in an unexpected and highly visible way. An agreement to do a series of celebrity endorsement spots for a new Colgate product opened the door for him to do some extraordinary lobbying.

"All the commercials that Arthur had ever done were for products that sponsored his shows. And he improvised as he went along," explained agent Peter Kelley.

Kelley, whose responsibility it was to get commercial work for clients, was introduced to Godfrey by Joe Higgins, a fellow employee at Ashley Famous Agency, who handled Arthur's personal appearances. "I asked Joe one time, 'You suppose Arthur would do a regular commercial?' He said, 'I don't know, let's go ask him.' So we went over and Arthur says, 'No! I'm not going to do any commercials or anything that's not on my show.' 'Not ever?' I asked. He says, 'Not ever.' And I said, 'Not for any amount of money?' 'Look,' he said, 'if you find a blue chip company with a good product that's willing to pay me 250 thousand dollars, I'll consider it.'" Kelley went out and found Axion. Axion was a new Colgate laundry pre-soak product that had just been test-marketed successfully against a similar Proctor and Gamble product named Biz. A meeting with the Colgate people was set up. "And Arthur, very environmentally concerned about things said, 'Well, I want to know what's it made out of.' 'Enzymes' he was told. 'Enzymes are a very environmentally neutral product that eats up the organic materials and that's why it's a pre-soak and it's revolutionary.' And Arthur said, 'Well, it won't mess up rivers and streams, will it?' 'No, no, no, not at all. It's only a pre-soak.' So he said he'd check it out. He called a lot of his friends like Barry Commoner and told them what it was and they said 'Okay.'"[15]

Godfrey did a test spot (though it was rough going getting him to read other people's copy and confine it to exactly 60 seconds). And when it was played in a test market, "they couldn't believe the scores. It blew it off the scale. People went out [and bought it so fast] they could not keep it on the shelves. So they paid [Arthur] the $250,000 and they went on with it for several years. To this day, I think it's the only product that Colgate ever had that [outsold] Proctor and Gamble so decisively."[16]

But a few months later, according to Kelley, when Godfrey was on the set doing another Axion spot, he asked if they couldn't specifically say, Axion doesn't louse up the rivers and streams, that it's environmentally safe. After all, the Colgate people had initially told him it was biodegradable. "One of the Colgate lawyers that had been sitting back there [on the set] said, 'Oh, I'm sorry, Mr. Godfrey. You can't say that because one of the main ingredients in Axion is phosphates.'"

Godfrey knew a lot about chemicals and water. He knew that the element phosphorus was essential to life in animals and plants; that phosphorus-bearing minerals promoted the growth of plants in water; that when enough phosphates got into streams they stimulated the growth of algae; and that algae crowded out other life and depleted oxygen supplies. But he had no idea that Axion contained phosphates as an additive. "Arthur blew up, blew sky high. I got a call from the ad agency. They said, 'Please come over here. He's getting ready to leave, walk off the set, and God knows what he's going to say or do.' So I went over and he was raging, talking about how dishonest they were in not telling him about this stuff and he was going to blow the whistle on them. And I asked him to hold off for a while. And he said his integrity was at stake and he couldn't continue doing commercials for them. So there was a period...when we tried to negotiate with Colgate."

"About six months later, a CBS reporter got to Godfrey and asked him, 'Is it environmentally safe?' and Arthur says, 'No, it's not.' And the reporter asked, 'Are you still doing commercials for Colgate?' And Arthur answered, 'I don't plan to unless they change things.'

"Like so many other things it got misinterpreted where Godfrey blows the whistle on Colgate when actually it was the media that came to him and asked him a question, and he always told the truth!"[17] Indeed, publications like *Business Week* reported that Godfrey accused Colgate of "tricking" him into doing commercials for Axion.

The resolution was two new ads in which Godfrey was allowed to say that clean water and fresh air were endangered by nitrates, phosphates, human waste and farm fertilizers, and that even household products contributed to the problem, including Axion. Then he added that he was proud to say that the makers of Axion were well aware of the problem and were trying to fix it. Proper sewage treatment was the real answer and it was "comforting" that the Federal government was starting to take some action in that area. Meantime, he said, Axion was a great product and one day it would be even better and viewers should stick with it.

It was an unprecedented event, one that has rarely occurred in the world of advertising before or since—a spokesperson talking about defects in the product he was pitching. But Colgate had little choice.

"A lot of guys got fired at Colgate and the ad agency," concluded Kelley. Godfrey had his integrity back. And as a result, phosphates were soon banned in many parts of the country.

Whether with Axion or in his public speaking or his writing, it was clear that when it came to ecology, Godfrey knew what he was talking about. "I did and daily do my homework—reading, writing and asking questions when I'm in doubt, visiting threatened sites of remaining wilderness. I had long been a member of the Izaak Walton League and Ducks Unlimited, but now I joined more of these organizations in my zeal to lend a hand in the great work they are all doing."[18]

Prince Bernhard of the Netherlands, President of the World Wildlife Fund, appointed him one of his international trustees. He was named to the board of the U.S. Appeal of the World Wildlife Fund. The news had spread in the publicity-starved environmental community that finally a major public figure had taken up their cause, and Godfrey was in constant demand. In 1968, at a luncheon at the Sky Club in New York, he and Charles Lindbergh delivered short talks and raised $375,000 for the Nature Conservancy. Lindbergh had become a partner, leaving his self-imposed exile from public view to devote, as Godfrey carefully phrased it, "his remaining days to the cause of conservation." He was clearly talking about himself as well.

Lindbergh and Godfrey still had major currency with the American public, they received wide coverage of their conservation activities, wrote articles, and, in Godfrey's case, appeared on television's leading talk shows of the day. Soon the National Wildlife Federation published the results of a poll showing an overwhelming majority of Americans so concerned they were even willing to pay extra tax dollars to address the problem.

By 1971, Godfrey could feel the tide turning. Invited to speak at a one-day conference of New York State conservation commissions, he noted, "When I first started barking about population explosions, urban sprawl, smog, sewage and garbage disposal several years ago, many listeners actually became so incensed that they wrote vicious letters urging the networks to throw me off the air. 'How dare you speak of birth control! Conception is an act of God!' 'Pipe down about pollution of the rivers. If your filthy mind wasn't always in the sewer, you'd never notice it. What do you propose: a return to the backyard privy? Stick to your ukulele and your tea-bags!'"

"They kept at it too, up until about a year and half ago when suddenly 'conservation' became the 'in' thing."[19]

He lauded a group of twenty Protestant theologians who had convened a three-day symposium in California to consider the religious dimensions of the ecological issue and determined that "theology, like Western philosophy, has gone too far in making man the center of attention."

Looking back, he was only one of many who made a difference in the areas of ecology, the environment, and conservation. Measuring his actual contributions is impossible. Yet, for many Americans, it was Arthur Godfrey who introduced them to the topics and the urgency. "I mean you couldn't smoke around him," explained

Peter Kelley. He wouldn't want to be in a room where there was cigarette smoke. He was way ahead of his time on many, many things, particularly environmental things, health things.[19]

Actually, it had been a jolt to watch this man, whose humor and adventures had made him so popular and familiar, turn so serious. And he was criticized for it. "He regretted [that] on his television and radio shows he was a little preachy at times," recalled Kelley. "But he [saw them as] a platform." He saw the potential to use these media to inform and educate people. "He was very strong in his beliefs, very strong."[21]

In 1971, the Federal Communications Commission issued one of the most sweeping rulings ever to be applied to commercial broadcasting: it banned the advertising of cigarettes. Cigarette advertising had been a mainstay of radio and television from the earliest days of the medium. The giant tobacco companies— R. J. Reynolds, Liggett and Myers, American Tobacco, Philip Morris, and P. Lorillard and Co. had been among the first sponsors. Through the years, the names of their products were etched in the titles of the shows: The *Lucky Strike Hit Parade, The Chesterfield Show, The Philip Morris Theatre, The Camel News Caravan.* William Paley himself had used his family's cigar company dollars to buy CBS.

Cigarette ads were often among the most effective campaigns and slogans having been developed by some of the greatest minds in American advertising. "Reach for a Lucky Instead of a Sweet," "Not a Cough in a Carload," "Lucky Strike Green Goes to War" became part of the American lexicon in the Thirties and early Forties. Cigarettes often had their own theme songs, like Chesterfield's "Smoke Rings," and when television arrived, it added a whole new dimension as announcers like Dennis James demonstrated the product

with prolonged inhaling of smoke. There were the marching Lucky Strike cigarettes that formed the titles of programs and the Old Gold Dancing Pack and Matches, which featured giant packages worn as head-to-waist costumes by female dancers with shapely legs.

It seemed as if everybody smoked, particularly actors, sports stars, and doctors ("More Doctors Smoke Camels Than Any Other Cigarette!"). If there was a concern about the effects of cigarettes on people, it wasn't on the mind of the majority of Americans up to and including the early 1950s. Arthur Godfrey was no exception.

Not only did he smoke Chesterfields on the air, he was often introduced by announcer Tony Marvin as "Arthur, Buy 'Em by the Carton, Godfrey." He was the ultimate endorser. He believed in his products and his audiences believed in him. The sales of Chesterfield skyrocketed after the brand became a sponsor on Godfrey's first network radio shows after World War II.

Actually, Chesterfield also had two other major entertainers of the time under contract. They sponsored singer Perry Como's radio shows and early fifteen-minute television series on CBS as well. And Bing Crosby, one of radio's biggest stars, rounded out the trio. Full color advertisements with all three entertainers smiling back at the reader ("ABC— Always Buy Chesterfields") appeared regularly in the leading magazines of the day.

In April of 1950, Chesterfield brought their three famous pitchmen to Chicago for the annual convention of the National Association of Tobacco Distributors. In addition to personal appearances, Como and Godfrey would join Crosby, who had yet to make the leap into television, on his still highly popular radio show, *The Bing Crosby Chesterfield Show.* It was the first time the three had ever appeared together on the same stage and the audience loved it. There was a good deal of kidding about Godfrey and all his sponsors and his endless number of weekly shows, along with some good barbershop quartet singing by the three. But the real star of the show was Chesterfield cigarettes. There were the commercials, of course. In addition, just about every second joke referred to smoking. The skit of the night was called "Mr. and Mrs. Chesterfield and their son Ash Tray."

In 1988, several years after his death, he became a featured player in one of the early suits brought against a tobacco company by an individual seeking damages for misleading advertising. Godfrey's statements from television and radio shows were played for the jury and one of them was particularly damning. It was delivered on September 24, 1952 on the Wednesday night show. He held up a newspaper ad for Chesterfields. "You hear stuff all the time about 'cigarettes are harmful to you,' this and that and the other thing.... If you smoke it will make you feel better, really...." He read the ad copy: 'Nose, throat, and accessory organs not adversely affected by smoking Chesterfield. This is the first such report ever published about any cigarette.' A group of smokers from various walks of life were recruited to smoke only Chesterfields for six months and then were given extensive medical examinations. 'Now here's the important thing,' and he went on to read how the medical specialist had found no ill affects. 'Now that ought to make you feel better if

you've had any worries at all about it. I never did and I smoke two or three packs of these things every day. I feel pretty good. I never did believe they did you any harm and now we've got the proof.'"[21]

"Arthur Godfrey was incredibly trusted," noted Richard A. Daynard, Professor of Law at Northeastern University in Boston, who heads up the Tobacco Control Resource Center there. Based partly on this testimony, the plaintiff was awarded damages.[22]

Less than a year later, when Godfrey emerged from hip surgery and discovered that cigarette smoking now made him nauseous, he gave up cigarettes—and Chesterfield's sponsorship as well. But at the time he, like most Americans, saw no connection between smoking and lung cancer.

It was only his personal ordeal with the disease in 1959 that gave Godfrey firsthand experience with the connection. He was devastated, knowing he had influenced the purchases by millions of people who now might be as vulnerable as he was to the effects of tobacco. And in later years he would often speak of smoking as a dirty habit and encourage anyone he met who did to stop, though there was no effective way to correct the damage he had done. All he could take for comfort was the fact that, at the time, he was relying on the information available. If he had known the consequences of smoking, as he later did in the Axion debacle, he surely would have dropped Chesterfield long before he had.

29

The Last Network Radio Show

IT WAS A COLD BLUSTERY THURS-
day morning, the kind one still expects in
New York City in April. The sun seemed
permanently caught behind the fast-moving clouds and the idea that spring had
officially arrived over a month before provided little comfort. The streets of mid-
Manhattan were clogged with the usual
mid-week mid-morning traffic. It was
April 27, 1972.

At 10 A.M., Neil Sullivan pulled the
Bentley up next to the Old CBS Radio
Building on East 49th Street, and out
stepped Arthur Godfrey, a bit shorter and
stockier now, but still with his auburn hair,
still looking like Godfrey. He waved Neil
off and entered the building just below a
sign that read CBS RECORDS.

Godfrey had been on the air continually
for 43 years, first on local radio in Baltimore and Washington D.C. and New York
City, then on network radio and television
and back to network radio again. That
deep, full voice with the heavy nasal twang

was listened to by more people each day
during the 1940s and 1950s than anyone up
to that time. In all, he had done over
11,000 morning radio shows, from *The
Breakfast Club* to *The Sun Dial Show* to
Arthur Godfrey Time, most of them for
CBS.

Arthur Godfrey had been coming to
this CBS Radio Network studio for
twenty-seven years to host his daily network radio program. Today, he was arriving to tape his last three shows. Indeed,
when the final show aired on the network
the following Sunday it would not only be
his last broadcast, it would also be the last
commercial network radio broadcast of a
continuing entertainment series.

It was a long and tumultuous journey
from the halcyon days when each of four
radio networks provided some fourteen
hours a day of news, music, comedy,
drama, soap operas, children's shows, quiz
programs, and talk shows. Few who had
been there when network radio began were

still working at it when it ended in 1972. Arthur Godfrey was the last of his kind.

Network radio, which once had been the most popular form of entertainment in the nation, had shrunk to hourly newscasts, having been completely obliterated by television. CBS had tried to keep the medium alive for network programming, running series such as *Suspense* and *Yours Truly, Johnny Dollar* into the 1960s, but every vestige of the network's rich history of radio entertainment programming—from Crosby and Benny and Burns & Allen to the *Lux Radio Theater* and Orson Welles' *Mercury Theater on the Air;* from *Our Gal Sunday* and *Ma Perkins* to the rest of the soap operas—all of it was gone, save *Arthur Godfrey Time.* He had outlasted them all.

American radio had changed drastically in order to survive. Now the medium had become so format driven, so concerned about audience flow, and so ratings conscious, that Godfrey's daily broadcasts had become white elephants and an anathema to the managers and owners of the CBS affiliate stations. Besides, new local formats of music or news didn't adapt well to interruptions from the network.

Typical of the new breed was WCBS in New York, flagship station for the network. It had been Chairman Bill Paley's idea to turn the station into an all-news operation and in 1967 it took up the format twenty-three–and–one–half hours a day. The other half-hour was reluctantly saved for *Arthur Godfrey Time.* The same was true at CBS stations across the country. The show was like a family heirloom; no CBS station manager wanted to be in the position of kicking it off the schedule. (In fact, they were required to carry it as part of their affiliate agreement.) But the truth was that its audience numbers, compared to the rest of the day's programs, were abysmal.

This didn't mean that the show was car-ried locally at the same time it was offered by the network. Its presence, depending on the city, varied from early morning to evening, making it increasingly unsaleable to national sponsors. "He said he was very hurt and angry to find out that stations were carrying him at two-thirty in the morning because they were under contract to carry him," remembers Max Morath. "He may have inflated it, but I'm sure I remember his saying that when he went off the air after whatever donnybrook he had with CBS—that he was still billing $12 million a year. Because there were *always* commercials on that show."[1]

In truth, it was Godfrey who ultimately pulled the plug on the show. The announcement was made towards the end of the year in 1971. The last show would be broadcast on April 30, 1972.

As always, he went first to his office on the top floor. As always, Remo, his guitar player, was waiting and they rehearsed the musical numbers. And as always, he stayed in his office and didn't descend to Studio 22 on the basement floor until just before airtime. By then, the performers and musicians had rehearsed their planned numbers and the director had gone over the proposed script with the engineers.

Indeed, little if anything was different about his arrival today from his arrivals throughout his 27 years of daily radio broadcasts. The band, the crew, and the staff were waiting for him. The show was unscripted in 1945, and it was unscripted today. No one really knew what would happen once the red light went on, the orchestra struck up the theme song, and Godfrey began to speak. This feeling of spontaneity, the Godfrey hallmark, the characteristic that had made him an original and had never been duplicated, was still in the air on this, his last production day.

But everything else had changed. Long gone were the adoring studio audiences that sat in rapped devotion. Gone too were the young male and female vocalists who had performed at his whim. Gone were the guests that included movie stars and nightclub acts, US Navy admirals and foreign dignitaries.

And gone was the listening audience. From some forty million listeners a day, these last programs were purportedly reaching no more than a million people a day, most of them aging listeners who had grown up with him or travelers on the road.

Most strikingly, no members of the press were present. Even as history, the broadcast was not news. If anything, by now, most Americans who knew who he was were not even aware that he was still on the air. Here was a sharp contrast to that morning in 1953 when he had fired Julius La Rosa and the entire American media machine, from newspapers to magazines to radio and television newscasts, had made the event into one of the most important national news stories of the decade. A sharp contrast, too, to that other morning in 1953 when he underwent hip surgery and press from around the world fretted and waited at the hospital gates. And a sharp contrast to that morning in 1959 when hordes of reporters traveled to New York to report every hour on his condition following cancer surgery.

The musicians in the studio and the engineers in the control room this gray Thursday in 1972 were all old friends of Godfrey and he knew them and their families well. On many occasions he had flown them to his Virginia farm, to Florida, or to Hawaii for weekends or vacations. He had given many of them jobs when they were down and had championed their careers.

If *Arthur Godfrey Time* had been casual and unrehearsed and a marvelous example of conversation and the power of the spoken word in its prime, the final shows seemed to be even more so.

An advertising executive in Ohio, Ann Stahl, had suggested that the series end by devoting a day's broadcast to each of the 27 years in reverse order. Arthur liked the idea and so, beginning on April 3, the countdown began with reminiscenses about 1971; the following day, 1970 was reviewed, and so on. Each day, there would be items about what had happened in the world that year and Godfrey and Richard Hayes and the band would sing songs of that year. Wilma, in the front office, would provide letters from listeners that had been written to Godfrey in the year at hand. And there was plenty of time left for Godfrey to welcome old friends like Max Morath or Pat Buttram and do the commercials as he had always done them—without a script. The shows were endlessly unpredictable and listening to them almost thirty years later they are surprisingly fresh and engaging.

On a December show, Andy Fitzgerald did such a great job on a clarinet solo that Godfrey spontaneously asked Hal McCusick to come in and do the same song along with Andy. When it was over, Godfrey mused, "These are things I'm gonna miss when this show is over in April. No other place can you do this kind of thing."

On another December show he talked about maybe going off to live on a boat. 'They've wanted my office for ten years." At the end of one show, he gave an environment pep talk, ending with the thought that "there's not much time left. It's a small planet."

Some days, his wheezing was constant. Other days, his voice was so nasal it almost seemed a parody of himself. "Oh me," he sighed.

On the 1956 show, he talked about a new magazine called *Miami Pictorial*. "Look at these color photos," he said, the thick pages rattling. "Have you ever seen such beautiful photography?" You almost could.

On the 1955 show, he dedicated a song from that year, "The Yellow Rose of Texas," to Lady Bird Johnson for all that she had done for the environment; sold Sara Lee pies in the "Bi-lack baw-tummed pan"; talked with his guest, the National Boy of the Year who, when Godfrey asked him if he liked prune juice, said, "I hate it!" leaving Godfrey to mollify the sponsor; spoke the lyrics to "Autumn Leaves" while the band played, and asked Harold Liberman to take a solo in A minor.

On the 1954 show, Godfrey talked the lyrics of "Young at Heart" while Mickey Gravine played a trombone solo. Mickey ended smoothly on an extremely high note and when he finished, the band and the others in the studio burst into applause. "And you gotta *be* young to do that," added Godfrey. "Aw, Mickey that's beautiful! (PAUSE) May you never be called upon for another F for a week!"

On the 1953 show, Godfrey reminisced about it as "the year I got my hip fixed"; sang a duet with Richard, then asked Hank Jones and Sy Mann, "two of the greatest piano players in the world," to do a duet of the same tune; talked with saxophonist Hal McCusick about Hal's photography work for *Time* and *Newsweek*; joined in the laughter as the band accompanied Richard Hayes on a song called "Ebb Tide," replete with seagull cries competing for attention; explained about how many aircraft there were in the U.S. and how most of them were owned by private pilots; and reminisced about Charlie Chaplin's exile that had ended that year and all the criticism he had endured before that. ("Mr. Baruch told me one time… 'You know where they all are, that wrote the nasty things about me? *Dead.*'")

On the 1952 review show, he and Richard sang a duet of "When You and I Were Young Maggie Blues"; he talked about aviation that year, made brief references to Janette Davis ("she was a lot of

fun to work with"), read a letter from the CBS affiliate manager in Minneapolis wishing him well, and then reflected, "I feel much better now really. Because I've been getting so many beautiful letters from people saying how sorry they are to see us go off this show after 27 years." There was another letter from affiliate KMOX in St. Louis, taking pride in the fact that Godfrey enjoyed his largest percentage of audience in that city from the very beginning, and how local personality Bob Hyland had patterned his own long-running morning show around the Arthur Godfrey show. The orchestra and Godfrey teamed up for a great Dixieland version of "Some of these Days." And then he turned to a recent letter which, he said in respectful tones, was a very neat letter from a man who had clearly taken time to sit down and dictate it.

Dear Mr. Godfrey:

After having dialed across you for more than 25 years, my suspicions were confirmed this morning when I heard you put out that adolescent-oriented dribble on ecology. It is the boobs like you who have turned a serious problem into an emotional moneymaking appeal, though largely to the immature. My opinion over the years has been that you are an overemotional, undereducated, overpaid, overopinionated without-a-justifiable-background ass who just happens to have a likable streak that brings him on strong with shallow people.

Although there may be some justification for your wailing about ecology—and you may have some background in this matter, just consider how many times you have spewed your drivel on a lot of unsuspecting old ladies and the immature without the slightest background in the subject. Name almost anything, you'll know all about it from one article or study of the subject for no more than ten minutes. Baloney is baloney no matter how old the waiter who serves it or under what name.

Truly yours,
Edgar W. Reinhardt.
P.S. And I bet you read the funnies every night or you can't sleep. How phony (or funny) can you get?

Godfrey paused, thanked Mr. Reinhardt for the letter and then, with the aid of sound effects, proceeded to flush it down the toilet to the cackles of the band members.

On the next-to-last program, covering the year 1946, he made reference to his Broadway experience in *Three to Make Ready* with Ray Bolger; played the last third of an interview with Bill Rucklehouse, then the Secretary of the Interior and the head of the New York Science Oceanographic Lab, about petroleum and natural gas supplies, and bade farewell to Richard Hayes. When Richard said he would miss the show, Arthur assured him that he (Richard) was "going to do just fine."[2]

There had been three half-hour shows to tape for broadcast that weekend. The first two were accomplished in a two-hour period. Now he was ready to do the final show. Tape rolled and under conductor Jerry Alters, the band began to play his theme song, "Seems Like Old Times." But in his typical unpredictable way, Godfrey interrupted them. "Hold It. Hold it right there. We can't play that song today. Because today we are remembering back to 1945, the first year of this program. And in 1945 we had a different theme song, 'Chasing Shadows.'" And he asked Remo and the others to try reconstructing the song.

In the thirty minutes that followed, he went through all the elements of a typical show: talk with the listener, talk with the band, some ukulele playing with the band, a story or two, and a commercial:

Our sponsor? Remember the old Biblical saying, "the first shall be last?" Lipton Tea. They've been with us right to the very end.

*I know that you know as well as I do the quality of Lipton Tea. All I beg of you is to take advantage of that. When you buy Lipton Tea you're going to pay a premium price for it. It's not the cheapest tea on the market. And when you make it, for heaven's sake, make it in such a manner that you will get the quality for which you paid. All you have to do is use **boiling** hot water, that's all. Use a tea bag if you will. That's great. There's nothin' wrong with that.*

The flow-thru tea bag was designed so that you can get the same steeping qualities to within an inch—a hair of it—as you could if you were using the tea leaves as in the old days. Because this flow-thru tea bag—not that it provides more tea—but it provides more wetting surface.

*But the thing is to get the cup hot. Pour some boilin' water in it. Let it set for a minute. Then dump that out, put the Lipton flow-thru tea bag in the cup and pour **boiling** hot water on it. Let it set there as you watch the color. **You** know, you'll learn how strong you want it. Then take it out and serve it—with cream and sugar, with lemon, with milk, just as I use it. Or just as it is. And you've got the finest cup of tea in the world.*[3]

He lauded the members of the band, the orchestra, particularly Remo Palmier ("My professor, my instructor, my mentor, my good friend") and Gene Traxler ("the one who gives us our structure"), who had been with him from the beginning, and the others, "most of whom have been here 12, 14, 15 years. They're all great musicians with a terrific sense of humor in their music and who each, in his own right, is a virtuoso."

Settling in to a more confidential tone, he talked about his career. "I have always been interested in doing what I thought would appeal to those who listened. It occurred to me that the only way you could achieve any longevity in our business was to grow—to grow in stature, to grow in interest. And so I tried to learn many different things—to learn all about a lot of different things so that I could speak with some sort of authority about them—at least some familiarity with them, and keep my interest going and growing. And therefore perhaps I would intrigue some people to stay with me.

"And I had to fight every inch of the way to maintain a position in this business and to maintain this stardom after I obtained it, that which I had never planned.

"But behind the bland facade of the great corporations there are always some great human beings. And it was a handful of those who saw to it that I got the opportunities to do what I have done. And to list those who helped me along the way would require *fifty* half-hour shows like this."

He did single out Frank Stanton, the retired President of CBS. "It was Frank Stanton who first opened the door for me. And then later on, it was Frank Stanton who, at the suggestion of Art Hayes who was then manager of WCBS, put the people to work to think up an idea for me for a "gimmick" for nighttime radio and they came up with *Talent Scouts*—the late Jack Carney's idea. And then later on we had the Wednesday night show too.

"There are so many people, you see, all of them belonging to this big faceless corporation which you have to buck all the time. But within which are these great human beings....

"Now of course in recent years I haven't seen Paley nor Stanton. I saw Doc Stanton the other day when we both got Peabody awards. We were at the same dais and never spoke, never got a chance to. And it saddened me a little that he's become so involved in the gray, great, huge corporation—conglomerate—that CBS is now.

"In the early days we were very close.

It saddens me a little that as we left we were not together. But that's the way life is, especially in our business. In fact I find it so in all the big corporations and in government the same way. There's a lack of humanness in it—simply because people just get too involved, too busy."

He joined "the boys in the band" for a rousing Dixieland number, then replayed his famous narrative of FDR's funeral procession: "It broke me up because I had known the late President very well. And I decided that day that I must never again try to do that because I am one of those people who cannot be objective. I get deeply personally involved in everything. And I've enjoyed every minute of it with CBS. There have been times of course when there have been arguments and there have been some tough battles. But with the great sales force, with the great esprit de corps that we once had here at CBS. Networks don't have it any more. No big corporation does, I guess. But it was a great joy…. All I can say to you all now is thanks, stay well and happy…and I'll be seeing yuh!"[4]

The familiar strains of "I'll Be Seeing You" came up and were quickly cut off by the network announcer saying, "This is the CBS Radio Network." The tape was stored until Sunday, when at 1:30 P.M. EST it was fed out to the network. When that broadcast ended, each station took back control, identified itself, and went on about its usual business.

Studio 22 was never used for radio again.

30

Crusading

IN THE WORLD OF POPULAR culture, you are either on the list or off it. Thousands of actors, musicians, dancers, singers, artists, broadcasters, writers, directors, producers, and filmmakers populate the world of television, radio, film, theater, and the stage—each seeking a career in one form of show business or another. The American public, in turn, has a remarkable capacity for keeping track of hundreds, if not thousands of these people; aware of their latest film, who they are dating, how they look, sound, and act, thanks in large part to the endless numbers of television gossip shows and magazines. To make the list, you need to reach a critical mass of viewers or listeners. You stay on the list only so long. When your CDs stop selling, your television show is canceled, your age makes you more likely to get motherly roles in the movies, you fall off the list. Then your name, your face, quickly fade from public consciousness. Only your loyal fans continue to remem-ber you, root for you, follow you. The mass audience discards you. And it is as if you have died.

Arthur Godfrey fell off the list, or as the expression goes, "fell off the radar screen" of a majority of the American public in 1959, following his cancer surgery. Television by then had become the center of pop culture and Godfrey was rarely to be seen. The fact that he was present, every weekday, for the next thirteen years on radio was of little significance to most Americans. He had made such an enormous impact on the American psyche in the Forties and Fifties that his name and face continued to be familiar, but most Americans probably didn't know if he were dead or alive. When the radio show ended, like a crowd exiting a theater, Godfrey's last substantial group of followers disappeared.

Now, if Godfrey chose to continue to seek a place in on-air broadcasting, it would truly be an uphill battle. At age 69, any substantial public popularity was a long shot. Few actors or entertainers ever achieve such longevity. Some stars move over to the business side, like Merv Griffin, who transformed himself from a singer to a talk show host and then to an enormously successful producer of television shows. Other stars choose to retire or pursue other interests and put their public lives behind them—completely. When Johnny Carson retired after several decades as the enormously popular host of the *Tonight* show, he disappeared from public view, willingly. But Godfrey was determined to regain a presence, not because he didn't have other interests, not because he needed the money, not even because of ego—though that must have been a factor at some level—but because he believed he had important things to tell the American people, about the environment, about cancer, about flying. Nothing else— public speaking, writing—could take the place of the microphone and camera that reached so many millions of people so quickly and effectively. He believed that even with his wheezing and hacking and aging features, he could get through on these issues to Americans of all ages. And he wasn't about to give up.

The problem in part was that no matter what his causes, even those like ecology that were now being embraced by the mainstream, he was no longer seen as the effective messenger. The social revolution that overtook America in the late Sixties and early Seventies reached down into every home, every family. It began with students and young people, but it wasn't long before parents were also caught up in its impact, and in the end it affected all of us and all of our institutions.

Arthur Godfrey had built his personal career and his private life on the foundation of traditional American values. When those American values were questioned publicly and then privately, and then

jeered at and refuted by large numbers of his countrymen, it appeared to be the final undoing of the Godfrey career. His American Pie approach to life, his gentle humor, his staunch defense of the military, his age, his riches were exactly what the revolution was about.

At first there *was* more radio to do. Working with a private syndicator, Godfrey immediately began a series of five-minute commentaries for radio that were taped and shipped to stations across the country. Designed for daily airing, each show covered a particular topic: sailing, bird life, euthanasia, Ben Franklin, with Godfrey free to observe, lecture, or even preach. It seemed like a fine idea, especially for the dozens of CBS Radio affiliates who now could have him in a package they could deal with, especially within their news and commentary blocks. But the shows didn't catch on and the experiment was soon ended.

In the years that followed, he would frequently sub for some of his good friends who hosted local radio shows like his around the country. In 1975, he returned to WTOP in Washington to co-host a morning television talk show for a day. Typically, he finally decided on doing it only the day before, then arrived expecting breakfast and makeup. But soon, in his usual way, he settled down and got into the show and the non-network low-key manner of the show and cast. "This is fun, this confusion. Just like the good old days. WTOP was always like this." He warned the host not to bring up the Little Godfrey firings or he'd get up and walk right off the show. When the guests appeared, he was the old Godfrey. Talking with a member of the Gray Panthers seniors group, he said, "What burns me is that when you're older, people call you a dirty old man for having the same interests you did 40 years ago. I'm not dirty. I'm sexy." At the end of a segment with an environmentalist, he complained on air about allotting the segment too little time. "It just gets interesting and whoosh...." After the show, he expounded on the subject: "You ought to have a guest on and let him run until the subject's exhausted. You ask the waiting guests to come back another day. They don't mind. This business about a six-minute attention span in the average viewer is just applesauce." He told a reporter who covered the premiere for the *Washington Star*, "Nobody today wants to look at the boards and the lawyers and the sponsors and say 'Phooey to you!'" To which the reporter responded in print, "Not since you, Old Redhead."[1]

With the help of his agent, he continued to get guest slots on television, appearing with Mike Douglas and Merv Griffin on their highly popular talk and variety shows. But though he was warmly welcomed and seemed relaxed with the host, somehow the appearances never captured the man. "For him to really be himself, he had to set his own pace," pointed out Pat Boone. "And Merv, Mike, and others would get into a fast-moving format. And that really wasn't Arthur. And when he would try to conform to their pace and their approach, he didn't seem himself. So when he wasn't himself, he wasn't as interesting. If he wasn't really comfortable, then you weren't as comfortable watching him. It was a difference in style.

"But I felt if he'd been put on in the afternoon, and given time to reestablish his connection with the audience, that he would have been successful all over again, because he was just too magnetic a personality not to succeed. And his mind was too interesting and his sense of humor was too winning for it not to succeed but it would take time.

"Arthur would have been great if someone had revived *Talent Scouts*. If I had been a network executive, especially at CBS, I would have looked for a way to utilize this great resource and this historic character."[2]

Pat Boone's observations proved correct during one appearance Godfrey made on the *Tomorrow* show with Tom Snyder in 1978. He seemed more at home with this late night, laid back conversational format. He was given more time to talk. Responding to questions from Snyder, Godfrey talked about a new pilot for a television series called *Godfrey's World* that he was working on. He talked about continuing to want to help talent get started and, in hindsight, how counter-productive the competitive nature of the *Talent Scout* show had been. "You get some poor guy that worked on a violin for 20 years and then some kid comes in and sings an up-to-the-date song and walks off with the prize." Kiddingly, he said that inflation, not ecology, was now his Number One concern.

There was the usual discussion of his unique approach to doing commercials, the buzzing of the Teterboro airport, La Rosa, and his hip and cancer surgeries. "Everywhere I go, every young man in the press looks in the morgue and finds all these big headlines and brings it up again. Well, as long as they do that we keep Julius La Rosa's name alive and he makes a living, which is fine. Period. Yeh, I'm glad."

He talked about how the surgeon came to him after the cancer surgery and how he felt he had gotten all the cancer out, but just to be sure, was going to "burn" him with cobalt for six weeks. "Which is why I have this chronic bronchitis today, because it injures the bronchial tissue that's left. But I'm so happy to be breathing at all that I don't mind." They talked about the ukulele: "I still play it every day." And Hawaii. Godfrey lamented the degeneration of the Hawaiian language. Did he watch television? "Very little of it. I'm usually reading or studying or writing or something." What he did see often concerned him. "The only thing you can do any more is get more explicit. This show I hope to do will encourage people who have real talent to perform and give them a place to do it." He rambled a bit here and there. But the impression he left was one of vitality and optimism.[3]

Peter Kelley got him a lucrative contract with Chrysler for commercials as well. He worked for Bristol Myers and a direct-response Insurance Company. "He was in his office almost every day and out on the road," recalls Peter Kelley. In the late Seventies, he appeared several times on the popular *Love Boat* series.

"He was always optimistic about the future," recalled Peter Kelley. "He'd say 'once I get back on *live television* with no censors.'" "He couldn't see why he couldn't be Johnny Carson," recalled Max Morath.[4] But by that stage in his life he was not equipped to do the fast interplay show biz style that Carson and his contemporaries were doing.

He tried writing his memoirs. Ralph Schoenstein, a writer and humorist whom Godfrey had met in 1970 and who made a number of appearances on his programs during the last three years of broadcasts, was hired to help him write an autobiography. He found Godfrey unable to expound very much on his life, unable to be introspective. "He'd start recounting things and then hold back. I'd say to him, 'Arthur, the book won't be worth anything unless you tell everything.' I'd say, 'Arthur, you'll have to talk about the women in your life,' and he'd say, 'What's there to say? I screwed them all.' He didn't want to hurt people. He wanted to protect people. Actually he was quite a gentleman." In reality what he wanted the book to be was a propaganda piece. "He wanted to talk about clean earth and the environment. He wanted it to be a public service, rather than an honest confession. It was too hard for him." In

all, Schoenstein and Godfrey produced 80 or 90 pages and the project was dropped.[5]

His aviation life continued unabated. He continued to learn to fly business jets and prop jets and fly around the country in his own Beech Baron D-55. "He flew into Princeton in 1972," recalled Ralph Schoenstein. "Arthur was 69 years old at the time. There was a big crowd. A guy asked me, 'Is he flying alone?' I said 'yes.' He said, 'He shouldn't be doing that at his age!'"[5]

That was not advice Godfrey was going to heed. In July 1974, he flew solo all the way to Point Barrow, Alaska, and then returned—12,000 nautical miles in 62 hours. By that year he had logged over 16,000 hours as a pilot.

When the U.S. Air Force celebrated its 25th anniversary year in 1972, Godfrey was invited to speak. "He didn't want to do it," explained Peter Kelley. "'You know,' he said to me, 'I've never had a promotion from the Air Force.'" Kelley told the heads about this and ultimately Godfrey said he'd go anyway. He was in frail health then. We flew out on an Air Force jet. "I was not at all sure he was going to be able to participate in it and he was essentially the MC of the anniversary event. We went through a rehearsal in the afternoon and I thought, 'He isn't going to make it.' But, in the evening, when he got up and the spotlights hit him, it was almost as if there was a transfusion, an infusion of energy. Twenty-five years evaporated in front of your eyes. He became alive, animated, the old Arthur Godfrey appeared. It was like a resurrection! And no-one would have expected that he was ailing."[6]

At the event, Arthur was promoted to the rank of Brigadier General (USAF Ret.).

Later, on February 6th, 1972, at the DAR Constitution Hall in Washington, the very hall he had refused to appear in twenty-five years before when it would not allow the blacks in his singing group to perform, he hosted and narrated a live concert with the U.S. Air Force Band, The Singing Sergeants, that was also in celebration of the Air Force's 25th anniversary. An LP record was made of the event.

Even without radio or television to boost his efforts, Godfrey continued his involvement with environmental issues. There were meetings and speeches and awards. But there was also disappointment, particularly involving the 1979 sale of Beacon Hill, his 1,970-acre estate near Leesburg.

As early as 1973 there had been signs of discontent with the planners and developers. Though the farm was relatively isolated, Godfrey feared for the county as a whole as the resident population multiplied and the land was subdivided. He feared that the tax rate was driving the farmers from the land. But when the Virginia Highway Commission revealed plans to build a bypass to major highway Route 7 adjacent to the farm, Godfrey joined a coalition to stop the plans. It was too late, and a section of his land through a grove of 150-year-old oak trees was taken for the project.

Calling Loudon "ruined," Godfrey told the *Washington Star* that he was determined to get the American people to take back control of their lives and overcome the bureaucracy which he saw sapping initiative and destroying individuals. He announced a new series of television specials that would address the issues. But the specials were never aired.

The farm was put up for sale in April 1977. Godfrey made it clear he would not sell to anyone who wanted to subdivide it. Two years later it was sold to a Saudi prince for $5 million, with the prince agreeing to the terms. Arthur and Mary kept a non-contiguous 90-acre tract nearby where Mary would move. By the

late 1990s the farm had been sold again, and this time it was subdivided.

Godfrey continued with his equine dressage, training his two palominos, both known as Goldie.

Honors continued to come to him. In 1977, the National Broadcasters Hall of Fame opened in New Jersey and he was among its first inductees. That same year, President Carter signed legislation providing for the first uniform Federal controls on strip mining and Godfrey, who was Honorary Chairman of the committee that spurred the action, was on hand at the White House to receive congratulations. In 1979, *TV Guide* hosted a television special honoring the best of broadcasting including Godfrey, calling his shows "intimate and personal" and recalling that at his peak, he was "the single most important person on television." As part of the show, a young Phil Donahue conducted a brief interview with Godfrey.

Finally, that same year, Godfrey returned to national television, on cable, in a ninety-minute, big-budget show designed to celebrate his 50th year in broadcasting. "Folks want to salute me. I'd rather entertain," is how Arthur began the HBO *Arthur Godfrey Special*. It was a lively, highly visual, upbeat production, undoubtedly his best in twenty years. Godfrey carried the ball throughout and though there was plenty of time for him to talk about his career in each segment, the emphasis was on the visual and the guests and the music. He was joined by comedian and entertainer Steve Allen, country singing legend Eddy Arnold, comedians Art Carney and Jo Ann Worley, and several attractive young singers whom Godfrey took pride in introducing.

There were memorable segments of his Beech Baron taking off with him at the controls, flying in and out of the clouds with spectacular views of the American landscape, all set to music with Godfrey reading the famous James Gillespie McGee poem, "I have slipped the surly bonds of earth...."

Each segment was a mini-program in itself—a documentary, a musical set—and each was paced just right for Godfrey. In return, he was at his best, looking tanned, relaxed, upbeat, and breathing easily.

In one segment, Eddy Arnold told a Reno nightclub audience, "They're honoring a man who was very good to me a good many years ago. When I was just coming along, a very young man selling a lot of records, most of the television shows didn't want me. He put me on. And I'll always remember him and thank him."

In others, Annette Funicello took God-frey on a tour of Disneyland, he remembered Will Rogers, and he and Goldie performed dressage. And in a highly relaxed and entertaining segment, Godfrey and Art Carney teamed up on uke and piano respectively on "Ain't She Nice" and "Candy and Cake." Godfrey talked with Steve Allen and then Allen did his famous "Letters to the Editor" routine. And on and on. With little spared in the way of production values, it was the kind of show one would have expected CBS to have done at some point, but never did. And it left one aware of how different, yet appealing, this kind of television show, rarely seen then or now, revolving around one man's diverse interests in music, history, science, and humor, could be.

31

The Last Television Show

IT WAS ONE OF THOSE NOSTALGIC musical specials that public television always seemed to come up with right in the midst of their on-air membership drives. In the past, there had been three-hour PBS extravaganzas bringing back America's Big Bands of the Thirties and Forties, the top vocalists of the 1940s, and similar fare. All had proven tremendously popular with viewers who had not only watched, but had called their local public television stations in unprecedented numbers with membership contributions.

The technique was simple: target viewers in their fifties and sixties, those who watched public television the most, and those with the most disposable income. Bring back the singers and bandleaders and the music that was popular when these graying Americans were young adults. And build in three or more internal breaks in the specials so that local stations could break away to pitch for contributions.

Six years had passed since *Big Band Bash*, the first such fund-raising special, and now, in 1981, PBS programmers recognized that another generation, those who had been young adults in the early 1950s, had now obtained the desired levels of income and time for watching public television to become prime prospects for giving. And so, once again, the powers that be turned to Jack Sameth, a major producer at WNET-TV in New York, who had created *Big Band Bash*, *GI Jive*, and *The American Pop Singers* for the network and would later produce even more demanding projects like *The Brain* and *The Mind*.

Sameth wanted to chronicle the popular music of the first five years of the 1950s, the years leading up to but not including Rock 'n' Roll. He sought out and signed up the recording stars of the period, including vocalists Rosemary Clooney, Frankie Laine, Patti Page, and Teresa Brewer. He also included a male vocal group that had been extremely popular during the period, the Four Lads. Among the hits of the group had been a nostalgic ballad called "Moments to Remember," and Sameth made that the centerpiece song of the show and part of the show title as well. As he had with his previous specials, he booked the Waldorf–Astoria Hotel for a weekday evening, planning to record all the performances over a four-hour period in front of a live well-heeled audience of people in their forties and fifties who would respond well to the music.

But with this show, now labeled *The Fifties: Moments to Remember*, Sameth wanted to do more than just feature the music that the recording studios had come up with. He wanted to include songs from the musical theater of the period and to look back on the remarkable growth of television as well.

"Nobody was as big as Arthur Godfrey during that period," Sameth surmised. "I began to think what fun it would be to have Godfrey host the program." Sameth knew that Godfrey was getting on in years, but he would inquire anyway. He called Godfrey's office, expecting full well to have a secretary of some level answer the phone. Instead, Arthur answered the phone himself. He was immediately interested in the project and agreed to what was to be a number of meetings with Sameth, most of which took place at Godfrey's hotel room at the Kenilworth Hotel on Miami Beach, and all arranged by Arthur directly. Early on, it was apparent to Sameth that Arthur Godfrey "was totally alone down there. He was all by himself."[1]

From their first meeting, Sameth could see he was failing. "It was obvious that he wasn't the strongest man in the world at the time," recalls Sameth. " So we decided to get what we could from him in a controlled atmosphere." Instead of Godfrey being on stage to introduce each of the performers throughout the taping, Sameth would bring the cameras down to the Kenilworth and simply tape some reminiscences, reduce them to 1½- to 2-minute sound bites, intersperse them with old kinescope excerpts from his shows, and lay them down at the start of each of the show's five segments before going back to the hotel ballroom. But he decided to push Godfrey one step further than the taped recollections: "I asked him to be at the Waldorf and come on stage at the end of the program. We would make it a short number, but I thought it would be a real bonus for those who watched."[2]

Godfrey agreed. And so, a WNET tape crew arrived at the Kenilworth and over a period of four hours, taped the 77-year-old Godfrey reminiscing about his work in radio and television, particularly in the Fifties. Sameth was there to ask leading questions such as, how did he get into the one-to-one method of broadcasting, kidding his sponsors, his role in post–War America, what he thought of today's music, etc.

Sitting by a window overlooking the beach, relaxed, dressed in an open-necked tan shirt and a powder blue blazer, the camera in tight on his face, his eyes as always, looking right through the camera to the viewer at home, Godfrey was in his element.

"'On the Gold Sands of the Old Miami Shore.' We used to use that for a theme song when we were down here doing our shows, the first television shows in the early fifties, out of Miami Beach. Do you remember some of them? Some of the beautiful things that we did down here? And the folks have asked me to talk to you about the Fifties, how it was in those days and how it may have changed, as it certainly has."

He talked about live television. He talked about the need to innovate: "Most everything we did was a first because we had…a lot of shows to do…and it took a lot of ideas. And every week we had to change the locale or do something new."

He talked about returning to television: "I'd love to do it again. I'd love it," he said with a fixed stare into the camera. "Especially if I could do it *live* (PAUSE) and un-cen-sored (PAUSE). Maybe I'll get my chance on—cable," his eyes still riveted on the viewer as if he or she was a cable executive.[3]

He did his best to answer the questions succinctly, but his gift for telling stories could not be quashed. He sounded much the same as ever—direct, slow, articulate. But his emphysema caused him to pause and suck in air regularly. His early comments were succinct, but as the interview wore on, he would occasionally wander far from the questions asked and found it difficult to retrieve names and places and dates. Only fifteen minutes of the all-day taping ever made it to the air, but what did was effective.

The audience at the Waldorf on the night of the taping had been told that Arthur Godfrey's taped reminiscences would be a part of the final program. But what occupied them for most of the evening were dazzling performances by Patti Page, Frankie Laine, Mitch Miller, and the other Fifties singers and performers. They listened, danced occasionally on floor space set aside in the ballroom, sang along, and gave extended applause. Then it was Godfrey's turn.

"After a nice off-stage introduction, we sent him out on to the stage with his ukulele," recalls Sameth. "The audience recognized him on sight and began applauding immediately. Then they stood. Arthur was absolutely stunned. He was overwhelmed that people remembered him and remembered him with such affection. We had to stop the show, have him come off the stage, and re-enter. It was highly emotional for him and for the audience."[4]

In black tux and black bow tie, glasses in one hand, Godfrey stood before an audience who remembered him well. In a deep gravely voice, he sang an upbeat medley of three of the old, dated novelty numbers that he had recorded so successfully in the early Fifties as the big band played behind him. "Candy and Cake" was followed by "Can I Canoe You Up the River?" and the song that was his all-time least favorite, "Too Fat Polka." He smiled throughout, with all of the hand gestures of a professional, giving it his all. But the songs were trivial and they made him seem like a caricature of his old self. By the time he was finished, the audience applause was more courteous than emotional.

Sameth had never been a great fan of Arthur Godfrey. It was recognition of Godfrey's contributions that had guided his desire to have him on the program. "Though in early days, I looked on Godfrey as some kind of an ogre, I have another set of feelings now. I feel sad. Sympathetic. He was such an extraordinary figure in broadcasting," mused Sameth, recalling how that short, fragile individual who "set off enormously strong feelings in people" was, in the end, all alone, making the trip to New York himself for what was to be his final public appearance.[5]

32

King of the Airwaves

IN HIS LAST YEARS, THE MAN WHO had brought in millions of dollars to commercial television wound up watching non-commercial public television almost exclusively. "I love to watch things like the Boston Symphony...the nature studies...the scientific stories which do so much to educate us about things that we just never would hear about otherwise. There are so many things that public television can give us that just wouldn't pay a commercial sponsor to back."

But he had two complaints: "Public television does away with the commercials. And we can see a movie without being interrupted. But that has its disadvantages too. Suppose you have to pee?" And the incessant fund raising: "I think public television should not have to beg for funds. I hate that. They were having a hell of a time here getting their quota in Florida the other day. And I got tired of listening to them begging for five bucks, for ten bucks. And I finally called them

on the phone...and I said, 'This is Arthur Godfrey, and I'm pissed off.' And the woman says, 'What about?' I said, 'You begging there for five bucks. How much do you need? How much are you short?' And she told me. I said, 'You got it. Now shut up and go to bed.'"[1]

He was increasingly puzzled by advertising on television networks and stations. "This business of putting five and six 10-, 15-second slugs, one on top of the other in the middle, who the hell can remember any one of them? How is it possible that those ads can do any good? It would be so much better if we did it the way we used to do it years ago, when we had a 15-minute segment of a show, sponsored [entirely] by one sponsor. People like that. ... And when you got through listening...you knew who [the] sponsor was."

As he watched, he harbored concerns about how gullible the public had become about television personalities, idolizing even news personalities of the day. "I...

shudder sometimes when I think of the adulation of the viewers for those people, who are such obvious phonies. And it worries me that people will have confidence, and can't see through it. It worries me that...those who run the networks, who run the stations, will permit that sort of...shenanigans, because sooner or later the public has got to get hip to it."[2]

Though television still held enormous appeal overall, he felt that it had lost its soul. "I think that the medium has lost a great deal of its power, and...its influence for good, because people have lost confidence in it, just as they have lost confidence in the bureaucrats, and even our elected officials. And it's too bad, because these are things that should be holier than anything we know. That we should be able to depend, in this free country, on, what we hear and what we see on that public screen. We should know when somebody tells us something, that what [is said] is true. I tried to do that my whole career. I hope I succeeded."[3]

Max Morath remembers seeing an article on Godfrey in a New York Sunday newspaper supplement a year before Godfrey died. "I'm sure the press agent planted the article because Arthur was trying to get a television show. The cover picture was Arthur Godfrey looking like death in a Hawaiian shirt and Hawaiian hat playing the ukulele. And I thought, 'Oh Arthur, come on. How did you let yourself get into this.' It made him seem like every old showman who's gone over the hill and nobody gives a damn."[4]

Despite Godfrey's optimism, despite his determination, failing health was winning out. He was having more and more difficulty breathing. His inhaler helped. But according to Peter Kelley, getting started every morning "was murder. I could never get him to work in the morning because it took him two or three hours to cough up all the congestion and every-

thing every day." Despite what he told Tom Snyder on the *Tomorrow* show, he told Peter that the radiation treatments were the cause and that "if he'd known how much that was going to destroy—the tissues and everything—and what kind of problem it was going to be, he wouldn't have had it done."[5]

He had lived most of his last years in Manhattan with a young woman, an athletic dancer and trainer, who ran a gymnastics academy. Max Morath and his wife got to be good friends with her and Morath remembers her as "a lovely, lovely woman."[6] Godfrey had wanted to marry her and in the process asked for and received a divorce from Mary, but the long affair broke up shortly afterwards.

He had turned very bitter about his career and the way his life was ending. There was very little of the old spunk, zest for life, or humor in Godfrey in his final years. "He said to me one day," remembers Carmel Quinn, "'Honey, I hope you'll always have good health. I can't do all the things I used to do. I can't smoke my cigar, I can't have a drink, I can't eat what I want. I can do nothing.' I said, 'What about the ladies?' We always had that joke. He said, 'That's out too.'"[7]

"He had become so embittered by people and audiences," according to Remo Palmier." I remember people coming up to him toward the later part of his life. People...just knew him and they were thrilled that he was in their presence and they wanted to come over and just shake his hand. And he'd recoil from them. I remember this old person came up once and started to talk to him and Arthur pulled back and said, 'What do you want to do, shadow box with me?' And the poor man just wanted to say hello."[8] He had a fixation about not wanting to get old, according to Remo Palmier. " He didn't want to be around old people."[9]

He would complain to anyone who

would listen about how poorly his attorney and financial adviser Leo DeOrsey had ultimately handled his money. "My God, I trusted this guy for years," he told Max Morath, who later observed, "It was one of the areas in his life he probably didn't pay too much attention to, like a lot of people in the business. He had a manager, and managers would say, 'I'm taking care of that.'" [10]

He was very appreciative when old friends and associates remembered him. Max Morath recalls how Bob Hyland, the local CBS radio personality in St. Louis, would call Godfrey on his birthday each year and ask over the air, "Hey, you want to say hell to all our listeners." Just before Godfrey's last birthday in 1982, Ben Lockridge, who had been CBS' Vice President for Radio Sales in the Fifties, sent him his usual gift of a bottle of spirits. A few days later came a hand-written reply: "Ben, you're the only one who remembered."

But he always kept in touch with the people he liked and trusted. Remo Palmier, Peter Kelley, Max Morath, and their wives would get phone calls from him inviting them for dinner at his apartment.

In 1982, alone again, he tried moving to California for his health, and his relationship with Pat and Shirley Boone resumed. They would have him for dinner or he would invite them to visit. "And of course now he was in much worse shape physically. And one day he called from the Bel Air Hotel and he was panting [heavily]. 'I need you to come over and help me move out of the Bel Air to an apartment on Wiltshire. I gotta get out of this place, it's too expensive.' Of course he had sold his farm in Virginia and had several million bucks, but he had this fear he would outlive his resources."

So the Boones rushed over and they found him in terrible condition. "Knowing Shirley was coming, he had shaved. But

he wasn't hooked up to his breathing apparatus and it had taken a lot out of him to shave…. Shirley got him his container of air and said, 'Arthur, may I pray for you, please?' And Arthur looked at her and said, 'Sure…Sure…go ahead.' And so… she put her hands on his chest where he was having the most problem and I put my hand on his back and we just stood there over him, praying earnestly that God would help him, come to his aide, and help him to breathe and have more energy…. And Arthur said, 'Hey, I feel better. Boy somethin' happened here.' And he was really taken aback that, inwardly, he felt somehow something come over him or in him and he felt changed, he felt energized. And the paralysis that kept making it very difficult for him to swallow or breathe or talk relaxed. So then he was much more himself after that."

The Boones got him moved and then Pat got him a Living Bible, a modern translation of the bible, in leather, with his name "Arthur" embossed on the front of it, and took it to him. "And at first he said, 'Nah, if I'm gonna read the Bible I'm gonna read the good old King James.' But somewhere along the line, either when we were at dinner together or talking on the phone, either he or his nurse said he had spent time reading it…. And I hoped it would link to the time when as a boy he thought he might be a priest and maybe tie in with other memories."

"And then I heard that he had moved back to [his apartment in] New York. He hadn't called to say goodbye or anything… And then we heard that he'd died. And we were grieved but so grateful that we had had time during those last three or four years, when we had no ax to grind, no nothing that we wanted from him, only the friendship that we felt he had exhibited toward us. And we were just so grateful for all of that."[11]

Arthur had entered Mt. Sinai Hospital

on March 3, 1983. It was hardly his first hospital stay and it certainly wasn't going to be last if he had anything to do with it. But twelve days later, he was still there, suffering from emphysema and pneumonia. Peter Kelley was with him at the hospital the day before he died. "It was the same thing. *When* is he going to get out of here and go to work. He was always optimistic about the future. Once he got back and could be in *live* television, that's what he wanted with no censors." [12] In a phone conversation from his hospital bed with Phyllis McGuire he told her, "I am *not* going to go!"[13]

But that night, Wednesday, March 17, 1983, Arthur Godfrey died at age 79.

Most of the television obituaries were perfunctory, summing up his accomplishments in three-second flashbacks showing a rather jovial individual playing the ukulele. An exception was raconteur and popular radio personality Jean Shepherd. In a commentary on NPR's *All Things Considered*, Shepherd reminded us that Godfrey was one of the first broadcasters to address each listener individually, to shed the tuxedo and 'ladies and gentlemen' approach and talk to one person at a time. "It's almost impossible now to remember radio before Godfrey," said Shepherd.[14]

Ironically, it was the print media that caught best the image of the man. Newspapers gave front-page notice to his passing with headlines like "'OLD REDHEAD' DIES AT AGE OF 79," "GODFREY MOURNED," and simply, "ARTHUR GODFREY, 79, KING OF THE AIRWAVES." Considering how long he had been away from center stage, the coverage was extraordinary. Articles were long and detailed, many filled with quotations and examples of his selling style on the air. There were photos with almost every report.

The trade paper *Variety* devoted an un-

usual half-page to his obituary, recalling in their headline, "ARTHUR GODFREY DIES IN N.Y.; VAUDEVILLE, RADIO, TV, AND B'WAY PERSONALITY PLAYED 'EM ALL." *Broadcasting* magazine editorialized, "Godfrey is gone, but will not be forgotten. On the totem of broadcasting personalities, he ranks near the top."

Washington Post television critic Tom Shales put it this way: "He as much as anyone helped take the chill off the idea of suddenly having a stranger in the house. The stranger was television. He also extended himself into millions of real families who incorporated him into the daily rituals of domestic American life." And another writer for the *Post*, J. Y. Smith, noted, "Most of all there was the way he seemed to persuade each listener that the whole informal, enchanting, titillating, folksy, and carefully crafted rigmarole was just for the benefit of that one person."[15]

He lived a relatively long life, having skirted death at least twice in earlier years. Had he never been a broadcaster, his other adventures and experiences would have been enough to satisfy a thousand men. But being Godfrey, he had wanted more. And not getting it, he had felt unfulfilled.

The funeral was private and few if any friends or associates attended. In his will, he had donated his eyes to the Eye Bank for Sight Restoration in New York City. And within days, two city residents had undergone cornea transplants.

Considering the huge amount of money he had earned in broadcasting over his long career, Godfrey left a very modest estate of $2.5 million, even in 1983 dollars. Having already provided for Mary Godfrey through the sale of the farm, he left half the estate to his two sons, Michael and Richard, his daughter Patricia, his brother Charlie, his two sisters, Kathy and Dorothy Jean, five grandchildren, and to his employees. He left his boats and planes to his son Michael. The other half of the estate went to five institutions: the International Medical Research Foundation and the Strang Clinic in Manhattan, the New York Ocean Science Laboratory in Montauk, Long Island, the Berks Gymnastic Academy Travel Fund in Reading Pennsylvania, and WNET-TV, the New York City public television station. Included were hundreds of warehoused tapes and kinescopes of his radio and television shows, and sheet music and orchestrations for his broadcasts. The rest of his personal effects were sold at auction in early April, including his Steinway piano—and his ukuleles.

Afterword

FORTY YEARS AFTER HIS LAST television series, twenty-seven years after his last radio shows, sixteen years after his death, Arthur Godfrey's influence can still be seen and felt in the broadcasting, cable, and advertising industries, in other fields, and in the everyday lives of Americans.

No television or radio system in the world speaks so directly or personally to its audiences as does American television and radio. Godfrey pioneered that approach. No system provides as much opportunity for dialogue and discussion as ours, and he led that effort as well. If American businesses often use humor today to sell their products, they do so because Arthur Godfrey showed us how wit and a light touch can sell just as well as dunning. Most of the products he introduced and promoted are still in our stores and still in our homes. And many of the performers we've enjoyed over the years were given their first broadcasting exposure on his shows.

It's true that technology has given us all more choices as to what we watch or listen to at any given time. More television channels, more radio stations, videos, CDs, the Internet, make it impossible for any one individual to amass the concentration of audience that Arthur Godfrey once had.

Yet even if technology *had not* greatly increased the competition, it is doubtful that *any* individual—U.S. President, a broadcaster, a sports hero—will ever again command such attention. With the possible exception of his own hero, FDR, no one in America has ever been such a compelling presence on the air. Call it bravado, courage or folly, the man was willing to literally *live his life* on the air. He was willing to share his adventures, his interests, his knowledge, his passions, his curiosity, his humor, his peeves, his anger, his pettiness. You knew his family, his farm, his friends, what he had for dinner the night before, what ailed him. He was an open book. "People watched because they were interested in his personality," as Andy Rooney put it. "And it did not take great grammar or even always great humor. They were watching this man live."[1]

What performer or entertainer or politician today would ever expose himself or herself that much, every day? And even if the spirit were willing and their attorneys allowed it, who would have enough to say while hardly ever bringing a note or script along with them? Even allowing that, who could then say it in ways that could hold and rivet one's attention? It is frightening but true that in the history of the world, it is usually despots, not entertainers, who hold such power to mesmerize.

Several years back, there was a big stir when it was announced by CBS Radio that Charles Osgood would be delivering his own commercials on his five-minute radio commentaries each day. He would be mixing apples and oranges and would lose his credibility, critics charged. CBS went ahead anyway and Osgood never lost his credibility. Nor has ABC Newsman Paul Harvey, who has been effectively selling products during his news shows his entire career. They and Godfrey remain a rare breed.

Arthur Godfrey's messages for today's broadcasters and advertisers are still worth heeding. First and foremost, personal integrity is what matters. When Godfrey interrupted himself on Washington radio and ended a commercial that sounded suspect, when he dropped Chesterfield cigarettes because he no longer could tolerate them, when he forced the makers of Axion detergent to admit publicly that they were polluting the environment, he was leading by example. He would not represent *anything* or *anyone* he did not personally believe in.

Godfrey also believed that broadcasting should educate as well as entertain. When he discovered he had lung cancer, he used his position to drag the forbidden topic out from the shadows and made it OK to talk about the disease privately and publicly. An entire nation learned from his experience. If there seem to be fewer aspects of our lives that are not discussed publicly today—most to good advantage—that is another of his legacies. But educating must also involve setting time aside regularly to improve public understanding of the world around us, whether the ratings that result are bad or good.

He was also living proof that if a performer wants to last beyond fifteen minutes of fame, or one year or even ten years, he or she has to keep learning, keep experiencing. "If you want to last, you have to grow," he would say. "That little screen is merciless and if you aren't constantly more interesting and intriguing, they—the public—will drop you, ruthlessly."[2] As Peter Kelley put it, "He was the innovator. He was the beginning. Every talk show personality who's on the air right now can thank Arthur Godfrey for their job."[3]

And he left other messages for broadcasters and non-broadcasters alike. First, to keep a sense of humor, assuming you have one. One of the highlights of his daily shows were the critical letters he unabashedly read from his detractors. "Godfrey, you stink!" was more than a funny line, it was a great leveler.

Second, there are no shortcuts to success. It took Godfrey 42 years before he made it on national radio. Growing up in poverty, working long hours by age 10, never finishing high school, he went on to work in a dozen different trades. Yet the reason that he became one of the most effective communicators in American history was because of these early experiences. By the time he arrived on radio, he understood and knew how to talk to people at every level of society.

Third, that if you have a dream, you have to be relentless in pursuing it.

Godfrey's dream was to make it in network radio and, through years of failure and disappointment, he never gave up that dream.

He believed that every individual needs to grasp life, that life is an adventure not to be missed. That if you invest the time, you can master most anything you attempt. He was what we call today a lifelong learner. Through reading and training and often just asking questions, he was *always* learning, be it languages, ecology, or even medicine. During his broadcasts, he kept a dictionary right on his desk.

And you must be willing to take risks. "When I broke into radio," Larry King would later say, "there was a rule hanging up on the wall: 'If in doubt, leave it out.' I always broke that rule. Godfrey taught me that."[4]

There is much we can learn from his mistakes as well. There is an old adage in the entertainment business: "Be nice to people on the way up because you never know whom you might need on the way down." Behind the scenes, Godfrey alienated so many of his co-workers that it literally blocked his path later in his career. "People wanted to get even," is how Frank Stanton put it.[5]

It's impossible to measure his legacy in areas other than broadcasting and advertising, but one could sight his defense of black performers and his opening doors for blacks throughout his career. And if concern with and action on ecological and environmental issues continues to grow in this country and around the world, then his early espousals on radio and television are part of the foundation. His long-running battle with the U.S. Army Corps of Engineers bears fruit today as dams in the Florida Everglades are being eliminated. Causes he espoused like the Nature Conservancy and the World Wildlife Fund are now hugely successful organizations with growing memberships and growing impact.

Because he was so believable, he brought ecology in to the mainstream not so much through his speeches and articles as through his on-air work. To paraphrase Teddy Roosevelt, he often spoke simply and carried a big message.

It would be folly to credit Godfrey for the fall of the Soviet Union. But if it was America's resolve to keep a strong military presence during the 1950s that made for the fall, than his passionate though often preachy sermons on the subject surely contributed.

And as the aviation industry continues to grow and a relatively civil peace prevails among commercial, military, and private plane pilots who often vie for the same air space and field space, it is due in part to years of work by Arthur Godfrey on behalf of all three.

When I began researching this book some ten years ago and began contacting Godfrey's employees, his fellow workers, broadcasters, entertainers, and CBS, I had assumed the worst. I thought Arthur's famous temper, his arrogance, his promiscuity would result in phone calls not being returned or doors being slammed in my face or vitriolic responses during interviews. In most cases, I found just the opposite. I was certainly given lots of fodder about his failings. But more often these same people talked about his generosity, his vision, his honesty, his willingness to fight for what he believed in. And where there was anger, it was often directed at those who had turned on Arthur, who had caused him to stumble, who had spread untrue rumors, who had not been willing to admit that he was, in the words of Peter Kelley, "a very human guy," and that his life was, after all, a series of remarkable adventures.

Arthur J. Singer
Newton MA
September 1999

Chapter Notes

Chapter 1

1. Jean and Kathy Godfrey, *Genius in the Family* (New York: G.P. Putnam's Sons, 1962), p. 256
2. *Ibid.*, p. 214, p. 15.
3. *Ibid.*, p. 131.
4. Arthur Godfrey and Pete Martin, "This Is My Story," *Saturday Evening Post*, part 1, November 5, 1955, p. 118.
5. Jean and Kathy Godfrey, p. 60.
6. *Ibid.*, p. 61.
7. *Ibid.*, p. 64.
8. *Ibid.*, p. 66.
9. *Ibid.*, p. 68.
10. *Ibid.*, pp. 104, 105.
11. *Ibid.*, p. 106.
12. Godfrey and Martin, *Saturday Evening Post*, part 1, p. 116.
13. *Arthur Godfrey and His Gang*, New York: Ideal Publishing Company, 1953, p. 7.
14. "Inside Godfrey," *New York Post*, November 18, 1953.
15. WNET-13 transcript, interview with Arthur Godfrey, Summer 1981, p. 27.
16. Godfrey and Martin, *Saturday Evening Post*, part 1, p. 118.
17. *Ibid.*
18. Jean and Kathy Godfrey, p. 15.
19. Godfrey and Martin, *Saturday Evening Post*, part 1, p 118.

20. "Inside Godfrey."
21. Jean and Kathy Godfrey, p. 16.
22. Lou Lumenick, "A Pioneer TV Scout," *New Jersey Record*, March 17, 1983.
23. Author interview with Michele Maiullo, 1996.
24. Godfrey and Martin, *Saturday Evening Post*, part 1, p. 119.
25. *Ibid.*

Chapter 2

1. Jean and Kathy Godfrey, p. 177
2. Godfrey and Martin, *Saturday Evening Post*, part 1, p. 119.
3. Arthur Godfrey conversation with Peter and Lois Kelley, 1978.
4. Godfrey and Martin, *Saturday Evening Post*, part 1, p. 119.
5. Godfrey-Kelley conversation.
6. Godfrey and Martin, *Saturday Evening Post*, part 1, p. 123.
7. *Ibid.*
8. Godfrey-Kelley conversation.
9. *Ibid.*
10. *Ibid.*
11. Godfrey and Martin, *Saturday Evening Post*, part 1, p. 123.
12. *Ibid.*
13. *Arthur Godfrey and His Gang*, p. 8.

14. Godfrey and Martin, *Saturday Evening Post*, part 1, p. 123.
15. Godfrey and Martin, *Saturday Evening Post*, part 2, p. 20.
16. *Ibid.*
17. WNET transcript, pp. 33, 34.

Chapter 3

1. Godfrey and Martin, *Saturday Evening Post*, part 2, p. 136.
2. *Ibid.*
3. *Ibid.*
4. WNET transcript, pp. 28–29.
5. Godfrey and Martin, *Saturday Evening Post*, part 2, p. 136.
6. *Time*, February 27, 1950, p. 73.
7. Jean and Kathy Godfrey, p. 183
8. Godfrey and Martin, *Saturday Evening Post*, part 2, p. 138.
9. *Time*, p. 74.
10. Jean and Kathy Godfrey, p. 185.
11. Ernest Havemann, "Arthur Godfrey," *Life*, June 7, 1948, pp. 97–98.
12. Arts & Entertainment Network (A&E), interview with Peter Kelley, Summer 1996, pp. 2, 3.
13. Jean and Kathy Godfrey, p. 185.
14. *Ibid.*, p. 286.
15. Godfrey and Martin, *Saturday Evening Post*, part 2, p. 138.
16. Jean and Kathy Godfrey, pp. 213–219.
17. *Ibid.*, pp. 231, 232.

Chapter 4

1. Sydney W. Head, *Broadcasting in America* (Boston: Houghton Mifflin, 1956), p. 108.
2. *Ibid.*
3. Head, p. 110.
4. Head, p. 118.
5. Godfrey and Martin, *Saturday Evening Post*, part 2, p. 138.
6. *The Tomorrow Show*, NBC, December 14, 1978.
7. Godfrey and Martin, *Saturday Evening Post*, part 2, p. 145.
8. *Ibid.*
9. *Arthur Godfrey and His Gang*, p. 8.

Chapter 5

1. *Arthur Godfrey and His Gang*, p. 10.
2. Godfrey and Martin, *Saturday Evening Post*, part 3, November 19, 1955, p. 29.
3. *Ibid.*, p. 143
4. *Ibid.*, p. 146
5. *Ibid.*
6. *Ibid.*, p 30
7. Jean and Kathy Godfrey, p. 245.
8. *New York Post*, November 20, 1953, p. 38.

9. Head, p. 106.
10. Head, p. 121.
11. Lewis J. Paper, *Empire* (St. Martin's, 1987), p. 22.

Chapter 6

1. Harrison Summers, *A Thirty-Year History of Programs Carried on National Radio Networks 1926–1956* (New Hampshire: Ayer), 1986.
2. Godfrey and Martin, *Saturday Evening Post*, part 3, p. 146.
3. Leonard Maltin, *The Great American Broadcast* (New York: Dutton), 1997, p. 129.
4. *Ibid.*, p. 135.
5. *Ibid.*, p. 136.
6. Godfrey and Martin, *Saturday Evening Post*, part 3, p. 146.
7. *Ibid.*
8. *Ibid.*
9. *Ibid.*
10. *Ibid.*, p. 151.
11. *Ibid.*

Chapter 7

1. Godfrey and Martin, *Saturday Evening Post*, part 3, p. 151.
2. *Ibid.*
3. WNET transcript, pp. 4–5.
4. Godfrey and Martin, *Saturday Evening Post*, part 3, p. 152.
5. *Ibid.*
6. *Ibid.*
7. *Ibid.*
8. *Ibid.*
9. Summers, pp. 37–42.
10. Godfrey and Martin, *Saturday Evening Post*, part 4, November 26, 1955, p. 83.
11. *Ibid.*, p. 33.
12. *Ibid.*, p. 73.
13. "Godfrey No Ordinary Tea Salesman," CBS release, October 1955.
14. *Ibid.*
15. *Ibid.*
16. WNET transcript, p. 4.
17. *Ibid.*

Chapter 8

1. Havemann, p. 89.
2. Godfrey and Martin, *Saturday Evening Post*, part 4, p. 73.
3. *Ibid.*
4. *Ibid.*
5. Godfrey and Martin, *Saturday Evening Post*, part 3, p. 146.
6. *Ibid.*
7. WNET transcript.
8. Godfrey and Martin, *Saturday Evening Post*, part 4, p. 83.

9. Stanley Frank, "Tycoons of the Turntable," *Collier's*, March 22, 1949.

10. Godfrey and Martin, *Saturday Evening Post*, part 4, p. 83.

11. *Ibid.*

12. *Ibid.*

13. Godfrey and Martin, *Saturday Evening Post*, part 4, pp. 83, 84.

14. Ray Poindexter, *Golden Throats and Silver Tongues* (Conway, Arkansas: River Road), p. 118.

15. *Ibid.*, p. 85.

Chapter 9

1. Godfrey and Martin, *Saturday Evening Post*, part 5, December 3, 1955, p. 173.

2. *Ibid.*

3. *Ibid.*, p. 174.

4. *Ibid.*

5. *Ibid.*

6. Walter Winchell column, January 26, 1934.

7. Godfrey and Martin, *Saturday Evening Post*, part 5, p. 177.

8. Poindexter, p. 119.

9. *Time*, p. 76.

10. Godfrey and Martin, *Saturday Evening Post*, part 5, p. 175.

Chapter 10

1. "Howa 'ya, Howa 'ya," Raleigh *News and Observer*, January 9, 1987.

2. Godfrey and Martin, *Saturday Evening Post*, part 4, p. 177.

3. *Ibid.*

4. WNET transcript, pp. 6, 7; and *The Fifties: Moments to Remember* (TV special) WNET-13, 1981.

5. WNET transcript, p. 11.

6. WNET transcript, p. 10.

7. Donald Saltz, "Best Salesman Even Traded for Potatoes," *Washington Daily News*, May 1972.

8. WNET transcript, p. 10.

9. Godfrey and Martin, *Saturday Evening Post*, part 5, pp. 177–178.

10. *Ibid.*, p. 178.

11. Granville Klink, "Arthur Godfrey Memoir," unpublished, p. 1, and author interview.

12. A&E interview with Granville Klink.

13. Klink Memoir.

14. *Ibid.*

15. Godfrey and Martin, *Saturday Evening Post*, part 6, December 10, 1955, p. 28.

Chapter 11

1. WNET transcript, p. 37.

2. *Ibid.*, pp. 37, 38.

3. James R. Greenwood, "Aviation's Man Godfrey," *Flying*, October 1958, p. 41.

4. David Lester, "Arthur Godfrey Blasts Off on Air Power," *The American Mercury*, May 1959, p. 97.

5. Greenwood, p. 41.

6. *Ibid.*, p. 74.

7. *Ibid.*, p. 76.

8. WNET transcript, p. 40.

9. *Ibid.*, p. 41.

10. Greenwood, p. 74.

11. Edward Rickenbacker, *Rickenbacker* (Englewood Cliffs, NJ: Prentice-Hall, 1967), p. 197.

12. Jack L. King, *Wings of Man: An Informal Biography of Captain H.T. "Dick" Merrill* (Glendale, CA: Aviation Book Company, 1981), p. vi.

13. Greenwood, p. 76.

Chapter 12

1. Klink memoir.

2. WJSV Sun Dial Broadcast, September 21, 1939.

3. *"Der Fuehrer's* Face" by Oliver Wallace, copyright 1942 by Southern Music Publishing Co., Inc., Copyright Renewed. International Copyright Secured. Used by Permission.

4. WNET transcript, p 24.

5. Godfrey and Martin, *The Saturday Evening Post*, part 8, p. 58.

6. Godfrey and Martin, *The Saturday Evening Post*, part 5, p. 178.

7. *Ibid.*

8. *Ibid.*

9. *Ibid.*

10. Godfrey and Martin, *Saturday Evening Post*, part 6, December 10, 1955, p. 30.

11. *Ibid.*

12. *Ibid.*

13. *New York Times*, March 4, 1944.

Chapter 13

1. Godfrey and Martin, *Saturday Evening Post*, part 6, p. 103.

2. *Ibid.*

3. *Newsweek*, December 8, 1947, p. 49.

4. Godfrey and Martin, *Saturday Evening Post*, part 6, pp. 102–103.

5. Author interview with Remo Palmier.

6. George T. Simon. *The Big Bands* (New York: Collier, 1967), p. 349.

7. Author interview with Remo Palmier.

8. *Ibid.*

9. Poindexter, pp. 215, 216.

10. CBS News broadcast, April 1945.

11. *Arthur Godfrey Time*, final broadcast, April 30, 1972.

12. Author interview with Max Morath, July 1996.

13. Advertisement by WDWS, 1945.
14. Advertisement by WBIG, 1945.
15. Arthur Godfrey scrapbook (press releases complied by Godfrey), 1945.
16. *Arthur Godfrey Time,* January 15, 1946.
17. *Arthur Godfrey Time,* January 14, 1947.
18. *Ibid.*
19. Column by Jack Gaver, United Press, June 19, 1945.
20. *New York World Telegram,* May 16, 1945.
21. Earl Wilson column, September 7, 1945.
22. *Newsweek,* September 3, 1945 p. 76.
23. *Newsweek,* December 8, 1947, p. 49.

Chapter 14

1. A&E, "Arthur Godfrey: Broadcasting's Forgotten Giant," 1966.
2. *New York Times,* July 14, 1946.
3. "Early Bird," *Time,* September 2, 1946.
4. Courtesy of Thomas J. Lipton.
5. *Arthur Godfrey and His Talent Scouts* broadcast, September 26, 1949.
6. Author interview with Ed Bond, March 16, 1996.
7. *Ibid.*
8. Phone interview with Howard Anderson, March 30, 1996.
9. *Arthur Godfrey & His Talent Scouts* broadcast, November 12, 1950.
10. Author Interview with Ed Bond.
11. Phone Interview with Anthony G. Montuori, March 1996.

Chapter 15

1. Aaron Ruvinsky, "Godfrey Lists Farm at $6 Million," *Washington Star,* April 30, 1977.
2. Author interview with Francis Peacock, July 1995.
3. *Arthur Godfrey and His Gang,* pp. 56–61.
4. *Ibid.*
5. Author interview with Granville Klink.
6. *Ibid.*
7. Author interview with Ben Lockridge, July 12, 1989.
8. A&E interview with Peter Kelley, 1996, p. 33.
9. "Man with a Briery Voice," *Newsweek,* December 8, 1947, p. 49.
10. *Arthur Godfrey Time,* January 14, 1947.
11. "Too Fat Polka," words and music by Ross MacLean and Arthur Richardson. Copyright 1947 Shapiro, Bernstein & Co. New York. Copyright renewed. International Copyright Secured. All Rights Reserved. Used by permission.

Chapter 16

1. Tim Brooks and Earle Marsh, *The Complete Directory to Prime Time Network TV Shows* (New York: Ballantine, Fourth ed., 1988), pp. 889, 890.
2. *Arthur Godfrey Time,* November 23, 1948.
3. Godfrey and Martin, *Saturday Evening Post,* part 6, p. 103.
4. *Variety,* December, 1948.
5. CBS press release, September 1949.
6. *Arthur Godfrey's Talent Scouts,* September 26, 1949.

Chapter 17

1. *Variety,* January 19, 1949.
2. *New York Sun,* January 27, 1949.
3. John Crosby, "Arthur Godfrey: Television's Huckleberry Finn," *Television Quarterly,* Fall 1983, p. 10.
4. WNET transcript, p. 3.
5. CBS publicity releases, January 8 and 25, 1952.
6. WNET transcript.
7. Author interview with Hank Meyer, May 1994.
8. *Ibid.*
9. Author interview with Remo Palmier, April 27, 1998.
10. *Arthur Godfrey and His Gang,* p. 42.
11. *New York Times,* January 6, 1952, p. 59.
12. Author interview with Steve Allen, December 5, 1997.
13. Jack O'Brian, *Godfrey the Great* (New York: Cross, 1951), p. 9.

Chapter 18

1. Author interview with Carmel Quinn, summer 1996.
2. *Ibid.*
3. *Ibid.*
4. A&E *Biography* program and A&E interview with Julius La Rosa, p. 22.
5. Author interview with Remo Palmier, April 1998.
6. Author interview with Remo Palmier, March 31, 1995.
7. WNET transcript, p. 46.
8. *Arthur Godfrey and His Gang,* p. 44.
9. Author interview with Pat Boone, January 1998.
10. *Ibid.*
11. Author interview with Dorothea Marvin, May 1998.
12. A&E interview with Julius La Rosa.
13. Author interview with Remo Palmier.
14. *Ibid.*
15. Author interview with Chuck Horner, November 3, 1989.

Chapter 19

1. A&E interview with Larry King, August 1996.

2. WNET transcript, pp. 8–10.
3. A&E interview with Larry King, August 1996.
4. *Ibid.* And Larry King, *Tell It to the King* (New York: G.P. Putnam's Sons, 1988), p. 137
5. Author interview with Carmel Quinn, 1996.
6. Author interview with Remo Palmier, March 31, 1995.
7. *Ibid.*
8. WNET transcript, p. 8.
9. "Oceans of Empathy," *Time*, February 27, 1950, p. 78.
10. Havemann, p. 93.
11. Associated Press biographical sketch, No. 4489, September 1, 1972.
12. "First You Got to Sell Yourself," *Sales Management*, April 3, 1964.
13. Author interview with Dr. Frank Stanton, February 22, 1994.
14. Author interview with Remo Palmier, March 31, 1995.
15. *Ibid.*
16. Phone interview with Steve Allen, December 1, 1997; and Steve Allen, *Hi-Ho Steverino!* (Fort Lee, NJ: Barricade Books, 1992), pp. 49–50; and *Variety*, January 10, 1952.
17. Author interview with Doreen Parton Roberts, April 28, 1998.
18. Author interview with Remo Palmier.
19. A&E interview with Andy Rooney, August 1996.
20. *The Fifties.*
21. King, p. 135.
22. *Sales Management*, April 3, 1964.
23. *Ibid.*
24. *Ibid.*

Chapter 20

1. CBS press release.
2. Robert Metz, *Reflections in a Bloodshot Eye* (Chicago: Playboy Press), 1975, p. 176.
3. John Crosby, p. 10.
4. Author interview with Doreen Partin Roberts, April 1998.
5. *Ibid.*
6. *Ibid.*
7. *Ibid.*
8. Bill Davidson, "Arthur Godfrey and His Fan Mail," *Collier's*, May 2, 1953, p. 11.
9. Author interview with Doreen Roberts.
10. Davidson, p. 11.
11. Davidson, p. 15.
12. *Ibid.*
13. Robert Metz, *Reflections in a Bloodshot Eye* (Chicago: Playboy Press, 1975), p. 182–184.
14. Walter Cronkite, *A Reporter's Life* (New York: A. A. Knopf), 1996, pp. 162–163.
15. *Honolulu Advertiser* and *Honolulu Star-*

Bulletin accounts, July 26–August 1, 1950; and *Paradise of the Pacific*, September 1950, pp. 12–13.
16. Godfrey and Martin, *Saturday Evening Post*, part 8, p. 58.
17. *Ibid.*
18. Godfrey and Martin, *Saturday Evening Post*, part 8, pp. 58, 59.
19. Davidson, p. 12.
20. Margaret L. Coit, *Mr. Baruch* (Boston: Houghton Mifflin), 1957, pp. 655–656.
21. *Ibid.*
22. *Ibid.*
23. *Ibid.*
24. Andy Rooney, "The Godfrey You Don't Know," *Look*, December 22, 1959, p. 91.
25. A&E interview with Remo Palmier.

Chapter 21

1. A&E interview with Granville Klink.
2. A&E interview with Remo Palmier.
3. John Crosby, pp. 11, 12.
4. A&E interview with Granville Klink.
5. Godfrey and Martin, *Saturday Evening Post*, part 7, November 17, 1955, p. 78.
6. *Ibid.*
7. Bill Davidson, p. 13.
8. A&E interview with Andy Rooney.
9. Godfrey and Martin, *Saturday Evening Post*, part 7, p. 78.
10. *Ibid.*
11. *Variety*, May 27, 1953.
12. *Variety*, July 15, 1953.
13. *Variety*, July 1, 1953.
14. A&E interview with Granville Klink.
15. *Variety*, July 29, 1953.
16. CBS press release.
17. *Arthur Godfrey and His Friends*, July 29, 1953.
18. *Broadcasting* magazine, 1953.
19. *Time*, February 27, 1950.
20. A&E interview with Remo Palmier.
21. Rooney, "The Godfrey You Don't Know," *Look*, p. 84.
22. John Crosby, p. 9.
23. Conversation with Gene Rayburn, October 1996.
24. Author interview with Remo Palmier.
25. A&E interview with Remo Palmier.
26. Author interview with Peter Kelley.
27. Author interview with Ralph Schoenstein.
28. Author interview with Peter Lassally, December 1997.
29. A&E interview with Andy Rooney.

Chapter 22

1. Whitney Balliett, "The Man Who Lost His Humility," *New Yorker*, September 28, 1987, p. 57.

2. A&E interview with Julius La Rosa, August 1996.

3. Godfrey and Martin, *Saturday Evening Post*, part 6, p. 104.

4. Balliett, p. 57.

5. A&E interview with Julius La Rosa.

6. Max Wilk, *The Golden Age of Television* (New York: Delacorte Press), p. 152.

7. Author interview with Doreen Partin Roberts.

8. A&E interview with Julius La Rosa.

9. *Ibid.*

10. Godfrey and Martin, *Saturday Evening Post*, part 6, p. 103.

11. *Ibid.*

12. *Ibid.*

13. A&E *Biography* program.

14. Author interview with Carmel Quinn.

15. Godfrey and Martin, *Saturday Evening Post*, part 6, p. 104.

16. Balliett, p. 57.

17. Wilk, p. 154.

18. A&E interview with Julius La Rosa.

19. *Ibid.*

20. Godfrey and Martin, *Saturday Evening Post*, part 6, p. 104.

21. Author interview with Doreen Roberts.

22. A&E interview with Peter Kelley

23. *New York Post.*

24. Godfrey-Kelley conversation.

25. Wilk, p. 155.

26. *Arthur Godfrey Time*, October 19, 1953.

27. A&E *Biography* program.

28. *Arthur Godfrey Time*, October 19, 1953.

29. A&E *Biography* program.

30. A&E *Biography* program.

31. A&E interview with Julius La Rosa.

32. Godfrey and Martin, *Saturday Evening Post*, part 6, p. 105.

33. Godfrey-Kelley conversation.

34. *Ibid.*

35. A&E *Biography* program.

36. Personal interview with Frank Stanton, February 20, 1994.

37. Godfrey and Martin, *Saturday Evening Post*, part 6, p. 106.

38. *Ibid.*

39. A&E *Biography* program and author interview with Peter Kelley.

40. Eleanor Harris, "Julius La Rosa's Life Since Godfrey," *Look*, May 15, 1956, p. 70.

41. Godfrey and Martin, *Saturday Evening Post*, part 6, p. 103.

42. A&E interview with Remo Palmier.

43. *Variety*, October 21, 1953.

44. Max Wilk, pp. 157, 158.

45. A&E interview with Peter Kelley.

46. A&E interview with Julius La Rosa.

47. *New York Post* series, November 1953.

48. Author interview with Peter Kelley.

49. Author interview with Pat Boone.

Chapter 23

1. Text for Godfrey's induction into the Aviation Hall of Fame of New Jersey, 1976.

2. *The Tomorrow Show*, 1978.

3. *TV Guide*, September 17, 1955.

4. Author interview with Hank Meyer, 1995, 1998.

5. Author interview with Peter Kelley.

6. Author conversation with Ralph Schoenstein.

7. Author conversations with the individuals mentioned.

8. Author interview with Peter Kelley.

9. Author conversation with Ruth Ann Perlmutter, 1994.

10. *Variety*, March 8, 1950.

11. Author conversation with Larry King.

12. Author interview with Gail Gans, November 30, 1994.

13. Quoted to author from an ADL report by Gail Gans.

14. Author phone conversation with Arnold Foster, July 31, 1994.

15. Author phone conversation with Herman Klurfield, July 29, 1996.

16. Author interviews with Hank Meyer.

17. Al Morgan, *The Great Man* (New York: E. P. Dutton, 1955).

18. Steve Allen, *The Funny Men* (New York: Simon and Schuster, 1956), pp. 195, 196.

19. "What's Godfrey's Hold on Women," *TV Guide*, June 4–10, 1954.

Chapter 24

1. Associated Press column, April 15, 1955.

2. "The Truth Behind Godfrey's Feud with the Press," *TV Guide*, September 10, 1955.

3. Robert Slater, *This Is CBS* (Englewood Cliffs, NJ: Prentice Hall, 1988), p. 131.

4. "The Truth Behind Godfrey's Feud with the Press," *TV Guide*, September 10, 1955.

5. A&E interview with Peter Kelley, p. 35.

6. CBS press release, October 12, 1956, and other articles.

7. A&E interview with Peter Kelley.

8. Author interview with Carmel Quinn, July 1998.

9. Godfrey, Jean and Kathy, pp. 251–253.

10. Personal interview with Max Morath.

11. Ted Gup, "The Doomsday Blueprints," *Time*, August 10, 1992 , p. 36.

12. WNET transcript, pp. 19–20.

13. Gup, p. 36.

14. WNET transcript, p. 20.

15. Godfrey and Martin, *Saturday Evening Post*, part 8, p. 20.

16. *Ibid.*, p. 59.

17. WNET transcript, pp. 13–16.

18. *Ibid.*, pp. 16–19.

19. "White Hunter," *Time*, April 1, 1957, p. 40.

20. Curtis LeMay and MacKinlay Kantor, *Mission with LeMay* (Garden City, N.Y.: Doubleday, 1965), pp. 489–494.

21. A&E interview with Remo Palmier.

22. *Ibid.*

23. Author attended White House event, circa 1988.

24. Steve Allen, *The Funny Men*, p. 196.

25. Bob Stahl, "Godfrey Deplores a TV Trend," *TV Guide*, March 8–14, 1958.

26. Author Interview with Remo Palmier.

27. *TV Guide*, Jan. 5–11, 1957.

28. Sally Bedell Smith, *In All His Glory* (New York: Touchstone/Simon and Schuster), p. 424.

29. William Henry, III, *The Great One* (New York: Doubleday, 1992), pp. 314–315.

30. Tim Brooks and Earle Marsh, *The Complete Directory to Prime Time Network TV Shows* (New York: Ballantine, 1988), p. 617.

Chapter 25

1. Associate Press Biographical Service Sketch, No. 4489.

2. *Ibid.*

3. "That Man Godfrey," WTOP publicity booklet, circa 1945.

4. *Ibid.*

5. *The Tomorrow Show*, 1978.

6. "Grace and Courage," *Time*, May 11, 1959, p. 74.

7. *Ibid.*

8. "The Godfrey Phenomenon," *Newsweek*, May 25, 1959, p. 65.

9. Two articles in *Today's Health*, November 1959 and January 1972.

10. Various news reports.

11. "The Godfrey Phenomenon," pp. 65–68.

12. *Ibid.*

13. *Honolulu Advertiser*, August 2, 1959.

14. *Ibid.*

15. *Honolulu Star-Bulletin*, August 12, 1959.

16. "This Is All I Ask," words and music by Gordon Jenkins, copyright 1958, 1986 renewed Jenkins Family Partnership (ASCAP). Used by permission. All rights reserved.

17. *The Arthur Godfrey Show*, CBS-TV, September 16, 1959.

Chapter 26

1. WNET transcript, p. 51.

2. *TV Guide*, September 12–18, 1959.

3. *Ibid.*

4. A&E interview with Remo Palmier.

5. *Variety*, May 11, 1960.

6. Metz, p. 188.

7. *Ibid.*

8. CBS news release as quoted in the *Saturday Evening Post*, May 27, 1961, p. 94.

9. Pete Martin, "I Call on the Candid Camera Man," *Saturday Evening Post*, May 27, 1961, p. 94.

10. Metz, p. 188.

11. *Ibid.*

12. Metz, p. 189.

Chapter 27

1. Fred Friendly, *Due to Circumstances Beyond Our Control* (New York: Random House, 1967), p. 206.

2. Author interview with Max Morath, August 1966.

3. *Ibid.*

4. *Ibid.*

5. Larry King, p. 135.

6. Author interview with Pat Boone.

7. Author interview and A&E interview with Remo Palmier, August 1996.

8. *Arkansas Gazette* and *Arkansas Democrat*, October 18, 1961.

9. *Ibid.*

10. *Arthur Godfrey Time*, January 20–24, 1964.

11. CBS press release, September 9, 1964.

12. Author interviews with Carmel Quinn.

13. CBS publicity releases, 1964–1966.

14. Plaque at Godfrey Field, Leesburg, Virginia.

15. Record album jacket, *An American Adventure*, Rockwell-Standard Corporation, 1972.

16. CBS publicity releases, May and July 1966.

17. Author interview with Peter Lassally, December 1997.

Chapter 28

1. *Arthur Godfrey Time*, December 11, 1971.

2. Arthur Godfrey, "The Challenge of the Seventies," *Esquire*, November 1969, p. 28.

3. *Ibid.*, p. 30.

4. *Ibid.*

5. *Arthur Godfrey Time*, December 11, 1971.

6. Author interview with Carmel Quinn, 1996.

7. Address to the National PTA Convention, 1970.

8. *Ibid.*

9. Address to the N.Y. State Conference of Conservation Commissions, July 13, 1971.

10. *Ibid.*

11. *Ibid.*
12. *Honolulu Star-Bulletin* and *Advertiser*, December 14, 1969.
13. *Variety*, May 21, 1970.
14. Personal interview with Frank and Lenore Meyer, February 6, 1998.
15. A&E interview with Peter Kelley.
16. *Ibid.*
17. *Ibid.*
18. Arthur Godfrey, "The Challenge of the Seventies."
19. Address, N.Y. State Conference of Conservation Commissions.
20. A&E Interview with Peter Kelley.
21. *Ibid.*
22. *The Bing Crosby Chesterfield Show*, April 5, 1950.
23. *Arthur Godfrey and His Friends*, September 24, 1952.
24. Author conversation with Professor Richard A. Daynard, July 12, 1996.

Chapter 29

1. Author interview with Max Morath.
2. *Arthur Godfrey Time* broadcasts, 1971–1972.
3. Courtesy Thomas J. Lipton Inc.
4. *Arthur Godfrey Time*, April 30, 1972.

Chapter 30

1. *Washington Star*, April 24, 1975.
2. Author interview with Pat Boone, January 21, 1998.
3. *The Tomorrow Show*, 1978.
4. Author interview with Peter Kelley and Max Morath, September 1996.
5. Author conversation with Ralph Shoenstein, September 1996.
6. *Ibid.*

7. A&E interview and personal interview with Peter Kelley.

Chapter 31

1. Author interview with Jack Sameth circa 1991.
2. Ibid.
3. WNET transcript, pp. 1, 51.
4. Author interview with Jack Sameth.
5. *Ibid.*

Chapter 32

1. WNET transcript, pp. 52–54.
2. *Ibid.*
3. *Ibid.*
4. Author interview with Max Morath.
5. Author interview with Peter Kelley.
6. Author interview with Max Morath.
7. Author interview with Carmel Quinn.
8. A&E interview with Remo Palmier, p. 14.
9. Author interview with Remo Palmier, March 31, 1995.
10. Author interview with Max Morath.
11. Author interview with Pat Boone.
12. Author interview with Peter Kelley, July 1, 1998.
13. A&E *Biography* program, 1996.
14. NPR interview, March 18, 1983.
15. Tom Shales, "Godfrey, Goodbye," *Washington Post*, March 18, 1983.

Afterword

1. A&E *Biography* program, 1996.
2. *New York Times* article, March 17, 1983.
3. A&E *Biography* program, 1996.
4. *Ibid.*
5. Author interview with Frank Stanton.

Selected Bibliography

Allen, Steve. *The Funny Men*. New York: Simon and Schuster, 1956.

_____. *Hi-Ho Steverino*. Fort Lee, N.J.: Barricade, 1992.

Arthur Godfrey and His Gang. New York: Ideal, 1953.

Bowles, Jerry. *A Thousand Sundays*. New York: G. P. Putnam's Sons, 1980.

Brinkley, David. *Washington Goes to War*. New York: Alfred A. Knopf, 1988.

Brooks, Tim, and Earle Marsh. *The Complete Directory to Prime Time Network TV Shows 1946–Present*. New York: Ballantine, 1988.

Coit, Margaret L. *Mr. Baruch*. Boston: Houghton Mifflin, 1957.

Cronkite, Walter. *A Reporter's Life*. New York: Alfred A. Knopf, 1996.

Dunning, John. *The Encyclopedia of Old-Time Radio*. New York: Oxford University Press, 1998.

Friendly, Fred W. *Due to Circumstances Beyond Our Control*. New York: Random House, 1967.

Godfrey, Arthur. "This Is My Story." As told to Pete Martin. *Saturday Evening Post*, eight parts, November 5–December 24, 1955.

Godfrey, Jean, and Kathy Godfrey. *Genius in the Family*. New York: G. P. Putnam's Sons, 1962.

Halberstam, David. *The Fifties*. New York: Fawcett Columbine, 1993.

_____. *The Powers That Be*. New York: Dell, 1979.

Harmon, Jim. *The Great Radio Heroes*. New York: Ace, 1967.

Harrison, Summers. *A Thirty-Year History of Programs Carried on National Radio Networks 1926–1956*. Salem, N.H.: Ayer, 1986.

Hayes, Richard K. *Kate Smith*. Jefferson, N.C.: McFarland, 1995.

Head, Sydney W. *Broadcasting in America*. Boston: Houghton Mifflin, 1956.

Henry, William A., III. *The Great One*. New York: Doubleday, 1992.

Hickerson, Jay. *The New, Revised, Ultimate History of Network Radio Programming*. Hamden, Conn.: Jay Hickerson, 1996.

King, Jack L. *Wings of Man: An Informal Biography of Captain H.T. "Dick" Merrill*. Glendale, Calif.: Aviation Book Company, 1981.

King, Larry. *Tell It to the King*. New York: G. P. Putnam's Sons, 1988.

Kisseloff, Jeff. *The Box*. New York: Viking, 1995.

Klink, Granville. *Arthur Godfrey Memoir*. Unpublished.

LeMay, Curtis E., with MacKinlay Kantor. *Mission with LeMay*. Garden City, N.Y.: Doubleday, 1965.

Lieberman, Philip A. *Radio's Morning Show Personalities*. Jefferson, N.C.: McFarland, 1996.

McCrohan, Donna. *Prime Time, Our Time.* Rocklin, Calif.: Prima, 1990.

Maltin, Leonard. *The Great American Broadcast.* New York: Dutton, 1997.

Metz, Robert. *CBS—Reflections in a Bloodshot Eye.* Chicago: Playboy, 1975.

Morgan, Al. *The Great Man.* New York: Dutton, 1955.

O'Brian, Jack. *Godfrey the Great.* New York: Cross, 1951.

Packard, Vance. *The Hidden Persuaders.* New York: Pocket, 1980.

Paley, William S. *As It Happened.* New York: Doubleday, 1979.

Paper, Lewis J. *Empire.* New York: St. Martin's, 1987.

Penguin Encyclopedia of Popular Music. Ed. Donald Clarke. London: Penguin, 1989.

Poindexter, Ray. *Golden Throats and Silver Tongues.* Conway, Ark.: River Road, 1978.

Rickenbacker, Edward. *Rickenbacker.* Englewood Cliffs, N.J.: Prentice Hall, 1967.

Serling, Robert J. *From the Captain to the Colonel: An Informal History of Eastern Airlines.* New York: Dial, 1980.

Slater, Robert. *This Is CBS.* Englewood Cliffs, N.J.: Prentice Hall, 1988.

Simon, George T. *The Big Bands.* New York: Collier, 1967.

Smith, Sally Bedell. *In All His Glory.* New York: Simon and Schuster, 1990.

Sterling, Christopher H., and John M. Kittross. *Stay Tuned: A Concise History of American Broadcasting.* California: Wadsworth, 1978, 1990.

Summers, Harrison B. *A Thirty-Year History of Programs Carried on National Radio Networks in the United States, 1926–1956.* N.H.: Ayer, 1986.

Taylor, Robert. *Fred Allen—His Life and Wit.* Boston: Little, Brown, 1989.

Variety Television Reviews, 1923–1988. Ed. Howard H. Prouty. New York: Garland, 1989.

Wilk, Max. *The Golden Age of Television.* New York: Delacorte, 1976.

Radio Programs

Arthur Godfrey Time. CBS.
Arthur Godfrey's Talent Scouts. CBS.
The Bing Crosby Show, April 5, 1950.
Sun Dial Show. WJSV/WTOP.

Television Programs

Arthur Godfrey: Broadcasting's Forgotten Giant. Biography series, A&E, 1996.
Arthur Godfrey and His Friends. CBS.
The Arthur Godfrey Show. HBO, 1979.
Arthur Godfrey Time. CBS.
Arthur Godfrey's Talent Scouts. CBS.
The Fifties: Moments to Remember. WNET-13, 1981.
The Tomorrow Show. NBC, December 14, 1978.

Movies

A Face in the Crowd. Directed by Elia Kazan. Warner/Newton Productions, 1957.
The Great Man. Directed by Jose Ferrer. Universal-International, 1956.

Recordings

An Air Force Panorama. U.S. Air Force, 1972.
An American Adventure—The Story of the Record-Setting Around-the-World Flight of Jet Commander. Rockwell-Standard Corporation, 1996.
Arthur Godfrey conversation with Peter and Lois Kelley, 1978 (audiotape)

Transcripts and Special Collections

Arts & Entertainment Networks: Interview Transcripts for *Arthur Godfrey: Broadcasting's Forgotten Giant, Biography,* 1996.
Library of American Broadcasting.
Museum of Television and Radio.
WNET-13: Interview Transcript with Arthur Godfrey for *The Fifties,* 1981.

Index

Page numbers in **bold** indicate photographs.